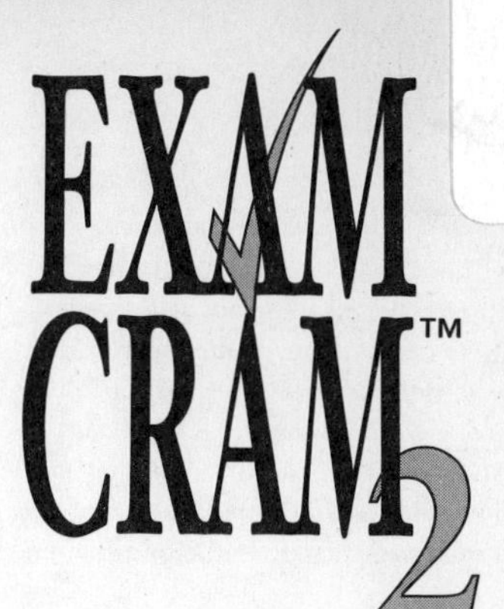

Security+ Exam Cram 2 Lab Manual

Don Poulton

Michael G. Solomon

Security+ Exam Cram 2 Lab Manual

International Standard Book Number: 0-7897-3291-2

Library of Congress Catalog Card Number: 2004108918

Printed in the United States of America

First Printing: October 2004

07 06 05 04 4 3 2 1

Trademarks

Warning and Disclaimer

Bulk Sales

Que Publishing offers excellent discounts on this book when ordered in quantity for bulk purchases or special sales. For more information, please contact

U.S. Corporate and Government Sales

1-800-382-3419

corpsales@pearsontechgroup.com

For sales outside the United States, please contact

International Sales

international@pearsoned.com

Publisher
Paul Boger

Executive Editor
Jeff Riley

Acquisitions Editor
Jeff Riley

Development Editor
Steve Rowe

Managing Editor
Charlotte Clapp

Project Editor
Tonya Simpson

Copy Editor
Kris Simmons

Proofreader
Jessica McCarty

Technical Editor
Clement Du Puis

Publishing Coordinator
Pamalee Nelson

Que Certification • 800 East 96th Street • Indianapolis, Indiana 46240

A Note from Series Editor Ed Tittel

You know better than to trust your certification preparation to just anybody. That's why you, and more than 2 million others, have purchased an Exam Cram book. As Series Editor for the new and improved Exam Cram 2 Series, I have worked with the staff at Que Certification to ensure you won't be disappointed. That's why we've taken the world's best-selling certification product—a two-time finalist for "Best Study Guide" in CertCities' reader polls—and made it even better.

As a two-time finalist for the "Favorite Study Guide Author" award as selected by CertCities readers, I know the value of good books. You'll be impressed with Que Certification's stringent review process, which ensures the books are high quality, relevant, and technically accurate. Rest assured that several industry experts have reviewed this material, helping us deliver an excellent solution to your exam preparation needs.

As a 20-year-plus veteran of the computing industry and the original creator and editor of the Exam Cram Series, I've brought my IT experience to bear on these books. During my tenure at Novell from 1989 to 1994, I worked with and around its excellent education and certification department. At Novell, I witnessed the growth and development of the first really big, successful IT certification program—one that was to shape the industry forever afterward. This experience helped push my writing and teaching activities heavily in the certification direction. Since then, I've worked on nearly 100 certification-related books, and I write about certification topics for numerous Web sites and for *Certification* magazine.

In 1996, while studying for various MCP exams, I became frustrated with the huge, unwieldy study guides that were the only preparation tools available. As an experienced IT professional and former instructor, I wanted "nothing but the facts" necessary to prepare for the exams. From this impetus, Exam Cram emerged: short, focused books that explain exam topics, detail exam skills and activities, and get IT professionals ready to take and pass their exams.

In 1997 when Exam Cram debuted, it quickly became the best-selling computer book series since "*...For Dummies*," and the best-selling certification book series ever. By maintaining an intense focus on subject matter, tracking errata and updates quickly, and following the certification market closely, Exam Cram established the dominant position in cert prep books.

You will not be disappointed in your decision to purchase this book. If you are, please contact me at etittel@jump.net. All suggestions, ideas, input, or constructive criticism are welcome!

Ed Tittel

To my loving wife Terry, who has supported and encouraged me during this project. —Don Poulton

I cannot thank my best friend enough for supporting me through the years in everything I do. She has supported me through the highs and lows for over 20 years. So it is with great pride that I dedicate this work to my best friend and wife, Stacey. —Michael G. Solomon

About the Authors

Don Poulton (A+, MCSA, MCSE, Network+, Security+) has been involved with computers since the days of 80-column punch cards. After a career of more than 20 years in environmental science, Don switched careers and trained as a Windows NT 4.0 MCSE. He has been involved in consulting with a couple of small training providers as a technical writer, during which time he wrote training and exam prep materials for Windows NT 4.0, Windows 2000, and Windows XP. Don has contributed to various certification texts for iLearning/LANWrights, including the *MCSE Windows Server 2003 Active Directory Infrastructure 70-294 Training Guide* and the *70-299 Implementing and Administering Security in a Windows Server 2003 Network Exam Cram 2* books.

In addition, he has worked on programming projects, both in his days as an environmental scientist and more recently with Visual Basic to update an older statistical package used for multivariate analysis of sediment contaminants.

When not working on computers, Don is an avid amateur photographer who has had his photos displayed in international competitions and published in magazines such as *Michigan Natural Resources Magazine* and *National Geographic Traveler*. Don also enjoys traveling and keeping fit. Don lives in Burlington, Ontario, with his wife Terry.

Michael G. Solomon (CISM, CISSP, TICSA) is a full-time security speaker, consultant, and trainer and a former college instructor who specializes in development and assessment security topics. As an IT professional and consultant since 1987, he has worked on projects or trained for more than 60 major companies and organizations, including EarthLink, Nike Corporation, Lucent Technologies, BellSouth, UPS, the U.S. Coast Guard, and Norrell.

From 1998 until 2001, Michael was an instructor in the Kennesaw State University's Computer Science and Information Sciences (CSIS) department, where he taught courses on software project management, C++

programming, computer organization and architecture, and data communications. Michael has an M.S. in mathematics and computer science from Emory University (1998) and a B.S. in computer science from Kennesaw State University (1987). He has also contributed to various security certification books for iLearning/LANWrights, including *TICSA Training Guide* and an accompanying Instructor Resource Kit (Que 2002), *CISSP Study Guide* (Sybex 2003), as well as *Security+ Training Guide* (Que 2003). Michael coauthored *Practicing Information Security* (Jones and Bartlett 2004) and authored and provided the on-camera delivery of LearnKey's CISSP Prep e-Learning course.

Acknowledgments

Many thanks to the guidance and help offered me by Kim Lindros and Dawn Rader at iLearning/LANWrights and the entire team at Que who helped make this project a reality.

—Don Poulton

Thanks to the great folks at iLearning/LANWrights, who made this writing project available to me. Ed Tittel has been gracious in working with me, and Kim Lindros makes the process of writing a piece of cake. You guys are the best!

—Michael G. Solomon

Contents at a Glance

Table of Contents

Chapter 4
Basics of Cryptography 181

Chapter 5
Operational and Organizational Security 219

We Want to Hear from You!

As the reader of this book, *you* are our most important critic and commentator. We value your opinion and want to know what we're doing right, what we could do better, what areas you'd like to see us publish in, and any other words of wisdom you're willing to pass our way.

As an executive editor for Que Publishing, I welcome your comments. You can email or write me directly to let me know what you did or didn't like about this book—as well as what we can do to make our books better.

Please note that I cannot help you with technical problems related to the topic of this book. We do have a User Services group, however, where I will forward specific technical questions related to the book.

When you write, please be sure to include this book's title and author as well as your name, email address, and phone number. I will carefully review your comments and share them with the author and editors who worked on the book.

Email: feedback@quepublishing.com

Mail: Jeff Riley
Executive Editor
Que Publishing
800 East 96th Street
Indianapolis, IN 46240 USA

For more information about this book or another Que Certification title, visit our Web site at www.examcram2.com. Type the ISBN (excluding hyphens) or the title of a book in the Search field to find the page you're looking for.

Introduction to Your Lab Manual

Welcome to the *Security+ Exam Cram 2 Lab Manual*! This book is designed to be a perfect complement to the *Security+ Exam Cram 2* and the *Security+ Practice Questions Exam Cram 2* books. The *Security+ Exam Cram 2 Lab Manual* includes more than 30 labs with nearly 100 exercises that mimic tasks and present real-world scenarios which a network security administrator might face on the job. The exercises were developed based on the Security+ exam objectives.

Written by security instructors, the *Security+ Exam Cram 2 Lab Manual* provides clear step-by-step directions to help the reader through complex exercises and offers ample guidance to prevent potential pitfalls. For topics that don't lend themselves to hands-on exercises, this book includes research-based exercises, such as researching a topic on the Internet and in print media and answering a set of questions based on that research or creating a report or other such document based on that research.

The authors include references to specific chapters and topics in the corresponding *Security+ Exam Cram 2* and *Security+ Training Guide* books; however, this lab manual is a standalone product that you can use effectively both individually and in a class setting. If you feel that you could benefit both from buying this book *and* taking a class, check out the many third-party vendors who offer Security+ training in addition to training offered by CompTIA.

Undoubtedly, experience with the technologies you are going to be tested on is critical. To truly be prepared for your certification exam, we recommend that you read and study, complete a lot of practice questions, and gain solid experience with the technologies you will be tested on. The last point is our intent with this book. We want to offer you plenty of opportunity to jump into the technologies the Security+ exam tests on, complete with ample guidance and feedback to assist you throughout your exercises. So after you finish this lab manual, it is our hope that you will feel more confident and competent with security fundamentals as well as the objectives you must master for the Security+ exam!

Who Is This Book For?

This is always a critical question that readers want to answer before purchasing any book. It can be a frustrating experience to buy a book that doesn't fit your needs, to say the least: We know from experience! With that said, this book is for people studying for the Security+ exam who feel they are at a point in their study that they need to put the concepts and principles of Security+ into action for greater understanding. If you are qualified to be taking the Security+ exam, you are the person right for this book. However, you should use the exercises in this book when you feel you are ready to get hands-on experience. This point, of course, will vary for every reader, but knowing how you learn and what study techniques best breed success for you is the path to passing the Security+ exam.

A word of warning is necessary here: Don't use this book as your sole study vehicle. We know it might sound weird that we are saying our book is not the sole study guide needed for exam success! Make no mistake, we want this book to succeed greatly, but we also know that successful certification students almost always have more than one study source. That is not a sales pitch for Que's other products either! That is tried and true advice that we want you to know because not every book covers items completely or to the degree you might need; having several study aides gives you a greater chance to find the information you need along with different viewpoints and experiences from various authors. That is truly a rich learning environment!

What Makes Up a Que Security+ Lab Manual?

By now, you are probably curious about what makes up a Que Security+ Lab Manual. The following list details for you what a typical chapter contains:

- *Introduction*—Each chapter contains an introduction that gives you the insight on what the chapter covers, why this content is important for the exam, and any other information you might need as you begin to do the exercises.
- *Objectives List*—This is simply a list of the Security+ objectives, quoted from CompTIA, that your particular chapter will be covering.
- *Step-by-Step Lab Procedures*—This is the meat of your lab manual's chapters. Here is where you exercise your skills and develop that all-important set of experiences that will help you on the job *and* on the Security+ exam.

- *What Did I Just Learn?*—This section follows your step-by-step exercises. It is a critical section that sums up and reviews the concepts and skills you should have mastered after completing the exercises. If you don't feel confident that you picked up those skills or understood the concepts provided, try the steps again and consult some of your other study books for review.
- *Need to Know More?*—Every chapter contains a section containing direct pointers to security resources that offer more details on the chapter's subjects. If you find a resource you like in this collection, use it, but don't feel compelled to use all the resources. On the other hand, we recommend only those resources we ourselves use regularly, so none of our recommendations will waste your time or money.
- *Practice Questions*—At the end of each chapter, we provide you with a small amount of practice questions too. There aren't a lot of these, but we want you to use them to make sure that you have an understanding of the concepts and skills central to the chapter you are completing. Again, if you are not comfortable or you are unsure while answering the questions, be sure to visit other study guides to get more information or review.

Other Elements You Will Encounter in Your Chapters

The preceding list gives you the major elements each chapter in your Security+ Lab Manual contains; however, you will see some other elements "floating" around. The following list details these for you:

- *Figures*—Periodically, you are offered a picture or diagram that will help you visualize something while you are doing your exercises.
- *Exam Alerts*—Throughout a chapter, you'll encounter Exam Alerts. The layout and purpose of each is as follows:

Exam alerts are offered to you as an "early warning." If you see something in an exam alert, you should take great care to know the items in it because you can be fairly certain that the topics will be on the Security+ exam.

- *Tips and Notes*—Throughout a chapter, you might also find information highlighted in the special layouts of Tips and Notes. The layout and purpose of each is as follows:

Tips are designed to give you some added piece of information pertaining to a topic being covered, such as an alternative or more efficient way of performing a certain task.

Notes are designed to alert you to a piece of information related to the topic being discussed.

- *Cautions*—The final element you might encounter in a chapter are Cautions, described as follows:

Cautions are alarms to you that something could go really wrong if you aren't careful. Pay close attention to these!

About Security+

The CompTIA Security+ certification tests an individual's basic skills and knowledge of general security concepts, communication security, infrastructure security, cryptography, and operational and organizational security. Candidates are recommended to possess two years of on-the-job networking experience, with knowledge of TCP/IP, an emphasis on security, and Network+ or equivalent knowledge.

System Requirements

The following hardware and software are required to complete the exercises in this lab manual:

- Two computers with a 700MHz (or higher) processor, CD drive, floppy drive, and network interface card; one computer should have two hard disks
- Windows 2000 Professional/Windows XP Professional*
- Windows 2000 Server/Windows Server 2003*
- Internet access

* Differences that exist between operating systems are noted in the exercises. This book focuses on Windows 2000 operating systems.

Users who do not have access to multiple computers will find that virtual computer software such as VMWare Workstation or Microsoft Virtual PC is useful for emulating networks. Time-limited evaluation copies of both of these products are available. For more information, visit http://www.vmware.com/products/desktop/ws_features.html and http://www.microsoft.com/windowsxp/virtualpc/. In fact, it should be noted that the lead author developed most of the exercises in this book using Microsoft Virtual PC to emulate a network of servers and clients on a single computer with 768MB of RAM, a 1.8GHz processor, and Windows XP Professional as the host operating system.

Conclusion

This manual is created as a means for you to gain hands-on experience with the concepts and technologies you are likely to be tested on. Although we can't guarantee you a passing score from using this book, we can offer you plenty of hands-on experience that will be sure to help you on the job and the exam.

Remember, it is best to have several sources of study materials. Que offers, along with this Lab Manual, several products that you can use:

- *Security+ Exam Cram 2* by Kirk Hausmann, Diane Barrett, and Martin Weiss. ISBN: 0-7897-2910-5.
- *Security+ Practice Questions Exam Cram 2* by Hans Sparbel. ISBN: 0-7897-3151-7.
- *Security+ Training Guide* by Todd King. ISBN: 0-7897-2836-2.

In conclusion, study hard; apply your knowledge; practice, practice, practice; and best of luck to you!

General Security Concepts

The Security+ exam, being an entry-level certification in the field of computer and network security, tests you on the general concepts underlying these topics. In this chapter, you perform exercises that acquaint you with topics such as authentication, access control, nonessential services and protocols, attack methods, malicious code, social engineering, and logging. These topics serve as a background upon which we shall build in the later chapters of this laboratory manual.

The following is a list of the exam objectives you will be covering in this chapter:

- 1.1 Recognize and be able to differentiate and explain the following access control models:
  - MAC (Mandatory Access Control)
  - DAC (Discretionary Access Control)
  - RBAC (Role based Access Control)
- 1.2 Recognize and be able to differentiate and explain the following methods of authentication:
  - Kerberos
  - CHAP (Challenge Handshake Authentication Protocol)
  - Certificates
  - Username/Password
  - Tokens
  - Multi-factor

- Mutual
- Biometrics

- 1.3 Identify nonessential services and protocols and know what actions to take to reduce the risks of those services and protocols:
- 1.4 Recognize the following attacks and specify the appropriate actions to take to mitigate vulnerability and risk:
  - DOS/DDOS (Denial of Service/Distributed Denial of Service)
  - Back Door
  - Spoofing
  - Man In the Middle
  - Replay
  - TCP/IP Hijacking
  - Weak Keys
  - Mathematical
  - Social Engineering
  - Birthday
  - Password Guessing
    - Brute Force
    - Dictionary
  - Software Exploitation
- 1.5 Recognize the following types of malicious code and specify the appropriate actions to take to mitigate vulnerability and risk:
  - Viruses
  - Trojan Horses
  - Logic Bombs
  - Worms
- 1.6 Understand the concept of and know how [to] reduce the risks of social engineering:
- 1.7 Understand the concept and significance of auditing, logging, and system scanning:

1.1: Recognizing and Differentiating Access Control Models

At the heart of securing a network is the concept of *access control*: in other words, granting or denying users the access to resources on the network. At the heart of access control is the fact that users are not only identified but also authenticated. All modern operating systems offer the ability to configure one or more types of access control, including the following:

- *Mandatory access control (MAC)*—A strict form of access control mandated by the operating system. A user cannot override this type of control. Originating with the military, MAC is well suited for usage in high-security environments. It includes the concepts of user security clearance and the classification of data according to security labels.
- *Discretionary access control (DAC)*—A form of access control where the owners of data control the level of access granted to users. DAC is well suited for usage in low- to medium-security environments.
- *Rule-based access control (RBAC)*—Sets of rules, for example, those configured on routers and firewalls, that determine the level of access. All users have the same rules applied to them.
- *Role-based access control (also RBAC)*—Also called nondiscretionary access control, RBAC is a form of access control where the level of access granted to a user depends upon the user's job functions or roles. This type of access control is well suited to large organizations in which many users have similar roles and need similar access to resources. Using it in this situation simplifies the administration of access control by enabling you to modify only the role rather than every user's access profile.

Be aware that the acronym RBAC can stand for either rule-based access control or role-based access control. Rule-based access control generally refers to rules that are configured on routers and firewalls, and role-based access control is based on job functions performed by different groups of employees in an organization.

Exercise 1.1.1: Observing MAC

In this exercise, we look at an example of MAC as used by Windows 2000 Professional to help protect the operating system. Windows stores files that are required by the operating system to function properly in the

`Winnt\System32` (or `Windows\System32`) folder. The operating system uses MAC to prevent users from deleting these files because doing so would prevent it from functioning properly and require that the operating system be reinstalled. Perform this exercise at a computer running Windows 2000 Professional. Steps on a computer running Windows XP computer are similar:

1. Log on to the Windows 2000 computer as an administrator or any other user.

MACs affect all users regardless of their administrative rights. You might want to try this exercise more than once as a regular user and then as an administrator to demonstrate this fact.

2. Double-click My Computer, double-click the C: drive, and then double-click the `Winnt` folder.
3. Windows warns you that the `Winnt` folder contains files that keep your system working properly and that there is no need to modify them. Click Show Files to view the contents of this folder.
4. Select the `System32` folder and press the Delete key.
5. Click Yes to confirm that you want to delete this folder.
6. You receive the message shown in Figure 1.1, which informs you that this folder cannot be deleted.

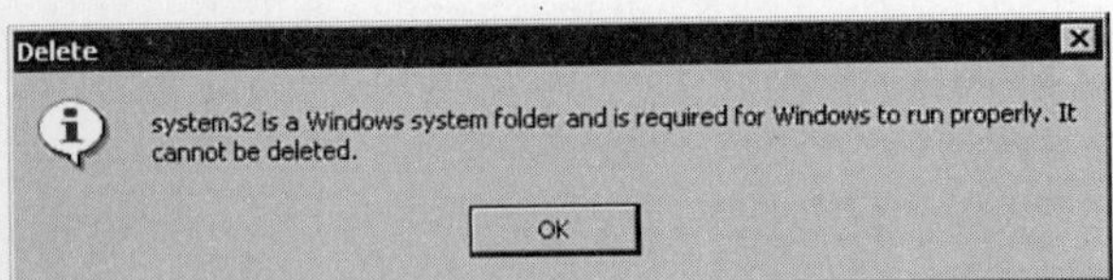

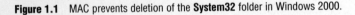

Figure 1.1 MAC prevents deletion of the **System32** folder in Windows 2000.

7. Click OK.
8. Close the `Winnt` folder window.

Exercise 1.1.2: Configuring DAC

In this exercise, we look at DAC as used in Windows 2000 Professional to grant a user access to files on the computer. You configure a discretionary access control list (DACL) with several levels of access and then test them by logging on to the computer as a user.

To perform the following exercises, you need a computer on which you have installed the Microsoft Windows 2000 Professional operating system. The disk on which the operating system is installed must be formatted with the NT File System (NTFS) because only NTFS allows the use of granular file and folder permissions. Disk volumes formatted with the File Allocation Table (FAT) or FAT32 file systems are limited to simple shared folder permissions that are effective only when accessing shared folders across the network. This exercise works in an identical fashion on a computer running Windows 2000 Server without Active Directory installed. You can also do this exercise on a computer running Windows XP Professional or Windows Server 2003, although the steps and the observed DACLs are slightly different. Note that you cannot do this exercise on a computer running Windows 9x/Me or Windows XP Home Edition. Windows 9x/Me does not support the NTFS file system, and Windows XP Home Edition supports only a limited file-sharing model.

Exercise 1.1.2.1: Creating a User

In this procedure, you create a user that you will employ for testing your DACL:

1. Log on to the Windows 2000 computer as an administrator.
2. Right-click My Computer, and choose Manage to open the Computer Management console.
3. In the left pane of the Computer Management console, expand the Local Users and Groups node to reveal the Users and Groups subnodes. (See Figure 1.2.)

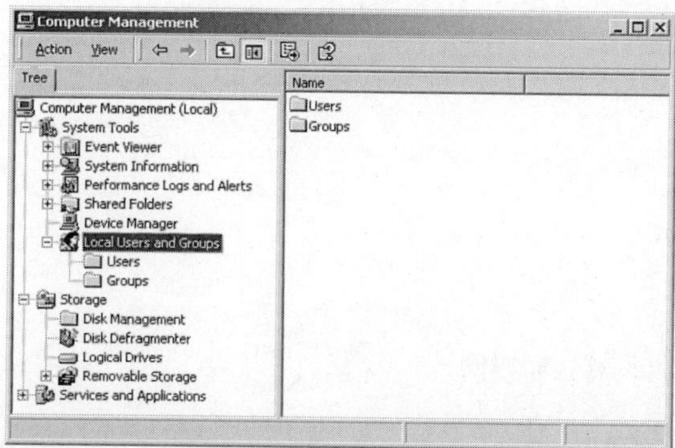

Figure 1.2 You use the Local Users and Groups node of Computer Management in Windows 2000 to manage users and groups on the computer.

4. Right-click Users and choose New User. This opens the New User dialog box.

5. Type **User1** as the username. Leave the Full Name and Description fields blank. In the Password and Confirm Password fields, type **Hello123** as a password for this user (see Figure 1.3). Note that passwords are case-sensitive.

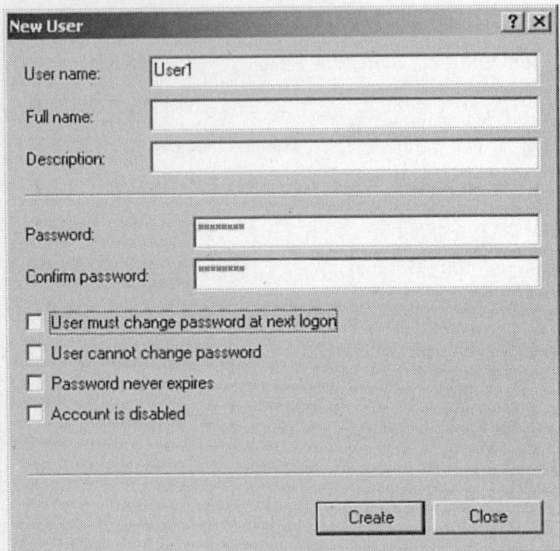

Figure 1.3 Create a local user in Windows 2000.

6. Clear the User Must Change Password at Next Logon check box.

7. Click Create to create the user. Click Close, and then close the Computer Management console.

Exercise 1.1.2.2: Creating a DACL

In this exercise, you create some text files. You examine the default permissions provided by Windows and then configure more restrictive permissions that limit what a user can do with the files:

1. Double-click My Computer, and then double-click the C: drive to open it.

2. Click File, New, Folder. Type **Data** as the name of the folder and press Enter.

3. Double-click the `Data` folder to open it.

4. Click File, New, Text Document. Type **Test1** as the name of the document and press Enter.

This exercise assumes that the default setting of Hide File Extensions for Known File Types in the View tab of the Folder Options dialog box has been selected. If you have deselected this option, you need to include the **.txt** extension when creating all files in this exercise.

5. Repeat Step 4 to create a second text document named `Test2`.
6. Double-click to open each text document (they should open automatically in Notepad) and type something in the body of the document that identifies the document. Save the documents and close Notepad.
7. In the `Data` folder, right-click `Test1` and choose Properties.
8. Select the Security tab. Note the list of permissions, as shown in Figure 1.4. In Windows 2000, the Everyone group is given Full Control permissions, which enables any user on the computer to do anything with the folder and its files that she wants. The selected permissions in the Allow column are shaded because this file inherits these permissions from the folder in which it is contained.

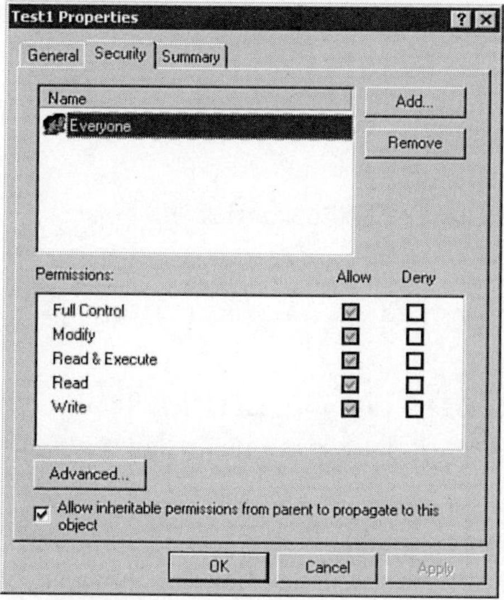

Figure 1.4 A new file in Windows 2000 comes with a default DACL that gives the Everyone group full control over the file.

In Windows NT 4.0 and Windows 2000, the Everyone group is given full control over all new files and folders by default until an administrator changes these permissions. This default obviously doesn't provide any security at all. The defaults in Windows XP and Windows Server 2003 tighten the previously loose default file security.

9. To deny User1 access to this file, click Add. Type `User1` in the dialog box that opens and click OK. This user is added to the DACL with Read & Execute and Read permissions.

10. Select the check box under Read in the Deny column (see Figure 1.5).

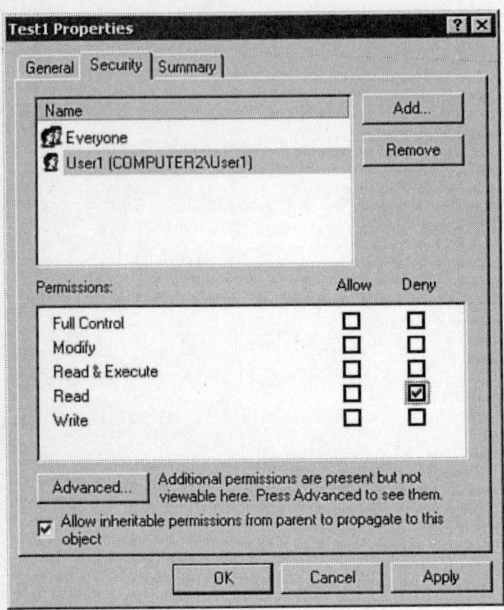

Figure 1.5 Click in the Deny column to deny access to a file.

11. Click OK. You are warned that deny permissions entries take precedence over allow entries. Click Yes to accept this warning.

12. To provide User1 with only read access to the `Test2` file, repeat Steps 7 to 9 with this file.

13. After adding User1 to the DACL, select Everyone and click Remove. You are warned that you must prevent the file from inheriting permissions. Click OK.

14. Clear the check box labeled Allow Inheritable Permissions from Parent to Propagate to This Object. In the Security dialog box that appears, read the information provided (see Figure 1.6) and then click Remove. Click OK to apply the change and close the Test2 Properties dialog box.

15. Log off.

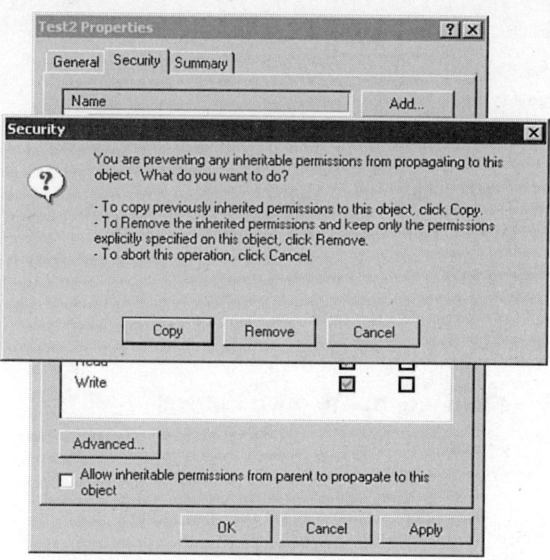

Figure 1.6 You need to remove permissions inherited from the parent folder to remove the default Everyone permission from the file.

Removing access as described in this procedure also removes the ability of an administrator to access the file or folder. You should also give the Administrators group Full Control access except in circumstances where data needs to be secured against everyone except those who actually work with or manage it. For further information, see the Windows 2000 Professional training guide cited in the "Need to Know More?" section.

Configuring Permissions in Windows Server 2003

If you are performing Exercise 1.1.2.2 from a Windows Server 2003 computer, the steps you need to perform are slightly different:

1. Perform Steps 1 to 8 of the same procedure as outlined for Windows 2000. Select the various users and groups displayed and note the results. Administrators and the operating system are given Full Control, but ordinary users are given Read and Read & Execute permissions. This default represents a basic improvement in file security from Windows 2000. However, it is still important to configure appropriate security for a multiuser system.

2. Perform Steps 9 to 11 to deny User1 access to `Test1`.

3. To provide User1 with read-only access to the `Test2` file, access the Security tab of the `Test2` Properties dialog box in the same manner as already done.

4. Click Add, select User1 in the dialog box that opens, click Add, and then click OK. This user is granted Read and Read & Execute permissions on the `Test2` file. Click OK.

Exercise 1.1.2.3: Testing the DACL

In this exercise, you test the DACL you configured in the previous exercise and note that the settings you configured as an administrator limit what the user can do with the test files:

1. Log on as User1 with the password of `Hello123`.
2. In My Computer, navigate to and attempt to open the `Test1` file. You receive an "Access is denied" message because this user was denied the ability to read the file.
3. Open the `Test2` file you created earlier.
4. Add some text to this file, and attempt to save it. You receive a Save As dialog box requesting that you create a new file with a different filename. This occurs because the DACL prevents this user from modifying the file.

In Windows Server 2003, you first receive a message informing you that you cannot create the **C:\Data\Test2.txt** file. Click OK to receive the Save As dialog box described in Step 4.

5. Type **`Test3`** as the filename, and then click Save. The default permission settings allow you to create a new file.
6. Exit Notepad and log off.

You can end up with a type of mandatory access control if you configure permissions in such a manner that only the administrator has a full level of access and no user has any permission higher than Read & Execute.

Exercise 1.1.3: Configuring Rule-Based Access Control

As mentioned previously, one example of rule-based access control is the configuration of policies for access to routers and firewalls. In this exercise, you configure a policy for access to a Windows 2000 Server computer configured as a router. In a business in which no after-hours access is needed, an attempt to access a router outside business hours would represent an intrusion, so you configure your router to allow access only during business hours:

1. Log on to the Windows 2000 Server computer as an administrator.
2. Click Start, Programs, Administrative Tools, Routing and Remote Access.
3. In the left pane of the Routing and Remote Access console, right-click your server and select Configure and Enable Routing and Remote Access. The Routing and Remote Access Server Setup Wizard starts.
4. Click Next, select Network Router, and click Next again.
5. Ensure that TCP/IP appears in the Protocols field of the Routed Protocols page and that the Yes, All of the Available Protocols Are on This List option is selected. Click Next.
6. On the Demand-Dial Connections page, select the No option. Click Next.

In Windows Server 2003, the previous three steps are slightly different. You need to select Custom configuration in Step 4 and LAN routing in Step 5.

7. On the Completing Routing and Remote Access Server Setup Wizard page, click Finish to start the Routing and Remote Access service.
8. Once the service starts, click the plus sign (+) by the server name in the left pane. A series of nodes appears under the server name. Select the Remote Access Policies node.
9. Right-click Remote Access Policies and choose New Remote Access Policy. The Add Remote Access Policy Wizard starts.
10. In the Policy friendly name text box, type `Time Restrictions` as a policy name, and then click Next.
11. On the Conditions page, click Add. The Select Attribute dialog box opens. Note the types of rules (attributes) that you can specify. Select Day-And-Time-Restrictions (see Figure 1.7) and then click Add.
12. In the Time of Day Constraints dialog box, drag to select a time block from Monday to Friday 8 a.m. to 5 p.m. (see Figure 1.8), click the Permitted option, and then click OK. This condition appears in the Add Remote Access Policy dialog box.

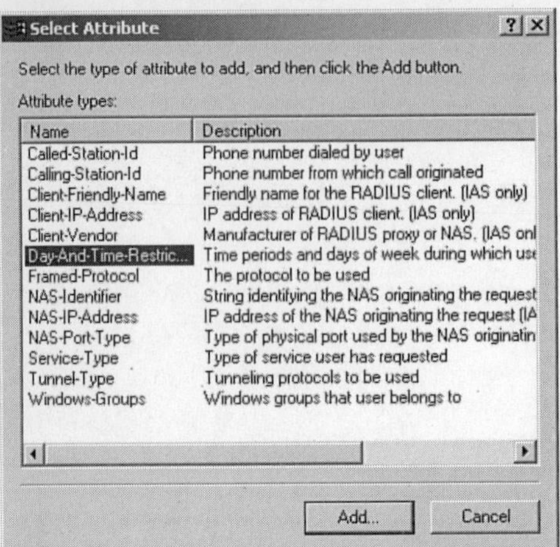

Figure 1.7 Select a rule for accessing a Windows 2000 Server router.

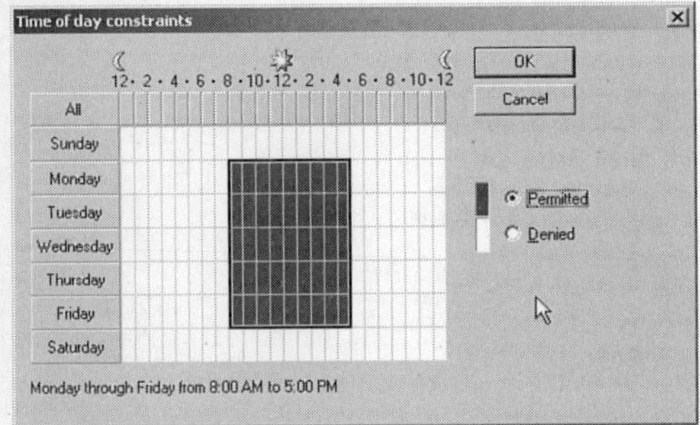

Figure 1.8 You can select the days and times for which users will be granted access.

You can click Add again to add additional conditions users must meet to access your router.

13. Click Next. On the Permissions page, select the Grant Remote Access Permission option, and then click Next again.
14. You can specify a user profile that defines what users are granted access across this router by clicking Edit Profile. Click this button and explore the possible types of conditions that you can configure. Click OK, click Next, and then click Finish to complete defining the remote access policy.
15. Back in the Routing and Remote Access Console, note that the policy you just defined appears in the right pane.

Exercise 1.1.4: Configuring Role-Based Access Control

Let's take a look at some common misconceptions surrounding role-based access control (RBAC). In this exercise, we look at user groups supported in the Windows 2000 Professional operating systems. Remember that RBAC is also known as nondiscretionary access control. The "nondiscretionary" part of the name is significant. It means that a person's job function, or role, determines the types of access that person receives. This role is interpreted by means of a group membership. In other words, each user role is represented by a group to which the appropriate users can belong.

For example, all database administrators could have a specific set of access rules. All database administrators would have the same access and nothing more. They would belong to a group that might be called Deadlines. Similarly, all sales individuals might belong to a group named Sales. Although many operating systems provide user groups and associated group access policies, RBAC is fundamentally different, but the difference is not always clear.

Exercise 1.1.4.1: Creating a Group and Assigning Permissions

In this exercise, you create a group containing the user you created in Exercise 1.1.2 and then assign permissions to the group. Perform this exercise on the same computer used for Exercise 1.1.2:

1. Log on to the Windows 2000 Professional computer as an administrator.
2. Perform Steps 2 and 3 of Exercise 1.1.2.1 to access the Users and Groups subnodes of the Computer Management console shown previously in Figure 1.2.
3. Right-click Groups and choose New Group.
4. Type **Group1** for a group name and then click Add.
5. In the Select Users or Groups dialog box that appears, type **User1** to add this user to the group, and then click OK.
6. This user is added to the group and appears in the Members field, as shown in Figure 1.9. Click Create, and then click Close.
7. Open My Computer, and navigate to the C: volume containing the Data folder you created earlier.

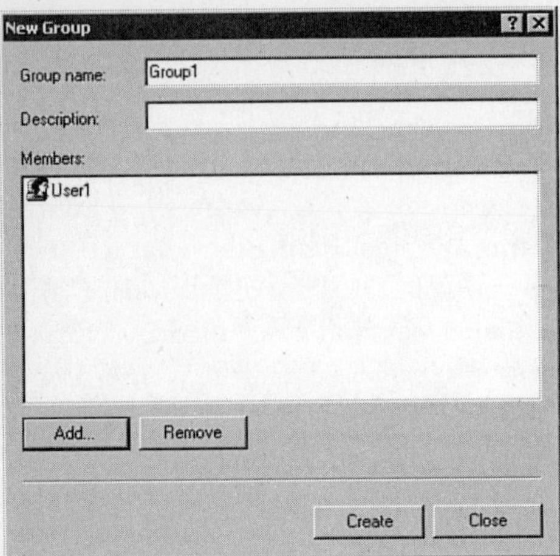

Figure 1.9 Create a group and add a user to it.

8. Right-click this folder and choose Properties.
9. Select the Security tab. Note that the Everyone group has the default Full Control permission on this folder in a Windows 2000 computer similar to that observed in Exercise 1.1.2.2.
10. Click Add and type `Group1` in the dialog box that appears, and then click Apply. This group is added to the DACL with the default permissions of Read & Execute, List Folder Contents, and Read.
11. To demonstrate the use of group permissions, select the Modify permission under the Allow column. This also selects the Write permission, enabling members of this group to write data in the files. Also add Administrator with the Full Control permission selected in the Allow column, and then click OK.

You need to add Administrator to the DACL in the previous step because the administrator was receiving his access by means of the default Everyone group Full Control permission.

12. Follow Steps 13 and 14 of Exercise 1.1.2.2 to remove the Everyone group from this DACL.
13. Open the Data folder, right-click the `Test2` document, and choose Properties. On the Security tab, select the check box labeled Allow Inheritable Permissions from Parent to Propagate to This Object, and

then click OK. This step is required so that the Group1 permission applied to the folder also applies to this file.

14. Close all dialog boxes and log off.

Exercise 1.1.4.2: Testing Group Permissions

Permissions that a member of a group receives are the sum of all permissions that the user has to any given file or folder. In other words, if a user has the Read permission assigned to him individually and the Modify permission assigned to a group to which he belongs, his effective permission is Modify. The exception to this rule is that if the user has an explicitly denied permission to a file or folder, this denial of permission overrides all other allowed permissions and the user has no access to that file or folder. In this exercise, you test these group permissions. Perform this exercise on the same computer used for the previous exercises:

1. Log on to the Windows 2000 Professional computer as User1 with the password of `Hello123`.
2. In My Computer, navigate to and attempt to open the `Test1` file. You receive an "Access is denied" message because the explicit denial of access given to this user overrides the group permission that you configured on this folder.
3. Open the `Test2` file, add some text to this file, and then save the file. You are able to save the modifications to this file because User1 receives the Modify permission from his membership in Group1.
4. Right-click the `Test2` file and choose Properties, and then select the Security tab. You receive a message box informing you that you only have permission to view the current security information. This illustrates the difference between the Modify and Full Control permissions; the user would need the latter permission to change the security information.
5. Click OK and note that all permissions entries are shaded.
6. Close all dialog boxes and log off.

What Did I Just Learn?

Now that you have looked at several types of access control, let's take a moment to review all the critical items you've experienced in this lab:

- MAC is a strict type of access control that is designed, among other things, to protect critical areas of the operating system. Access control decisions in MAC are based on sensitivity labels. Not even an administrator can change items governed by MAC.
- DAC is a type of model where owners of an object decide what level of access will be provided. Although operating systems provide some loose type of access control, the administrator or creator of a file or folder can impose different levels of access as required for security purposes. Relying only on the identity of the user can lead to a weakness that can be exploited, for example, by the planting of a Trojan horse.
- Rule-based access control (RBAC) is a type of model where access to a resource such as a router or firewall is determined by a series of rules configured by an administrator or other responsible individual.
- Role-based access control (also RBAC) is a type of model where access to resources is determined by the role an individual or group of individuals plays in an organization. Roles played by users are commonly interpreted by means of groups to which users are assigned and permissions granted. This type of access control is also called nondiscretionary access control.

1.2: Recognizing and Differentiating Authentication

Before a user can gain access to a resource such as a file or Web page, a user needs to prove that she is who she says she is. This process is *authentication*, which can take many forms, including the following:

- *What the user knows*—A user can type her username and password at a logon dialog box. She cannot log on if she does not have both the username and password. This is currently the most common form of authentication.
- *What the user has*—A user might need to insert a smart card into the smart card reader. She cannot log on unless she is in possession of the card.
- *What the user is*—This is the topic of biometrics and can include such traits as fingerprints, retinal scans, and so on. It is one of the most secure, albeit most expensive forms of authentication.

- *What the user does*—A user could be asked to provide a sample of her voice or handwriting, to be compared with samples included in a database.
- *A combination of more than one of these authentication types*—With multifactor authentication, a user could be requested to supply more than one of these items, such as a smart card (what the user has) and a personal identification number (PIN) (what the user knows).

In the following exercises, you examine the processes behind several forms of authentication.

Exercise 1.2.1: Observing Kerberos Ticket Properties (Optional)

As discussed in *Security+ Exam Cram 2*, Kerberos utilizes a server known as a Key Distribution Center (KDC) to authenticate logons. The KDC creates a ticket known as a ticket-granting ticket (TGT), which the client computer uses to obtain tickets for access to any required resource. In this exercise, you download and use a tool known as `Kerbtray.exe` that provides details of session tickets created on a domain-based Windows computer. To perform this exercise, you need a domain controller running Windows 2000 Server plus a client computer joined to the domain. If you do not have this setup available, you can still access the quoted Web pages and study the details of the available Kerberos tools. You can also refer to the *Exam Cram 2* book for summary information regarding the Kerberos authentication process.

If you want to try this exercise on your company's network, you should always check with the administrator in charge of the network before running tools that interact with domain controllers.

1. Using a Web browser, connect to the Microsoft Kerbtray Web site at http://www.microsoft.com/windows2000/techinfo/reskit/tools/existing/kerbtray-o.asp. Another useful Web site for Kerberos information as it relates to Microsoft operating systems is http://www.microsoft.com/technet/prodtechnol/windows2000serv/maintain/featusability/kerbinop.mspx#XSLTsection124121120120. A useful Web site for overall general Kerberos information is "Kerberos: The Network Authentication Protocol" at http://web.mit.edu/kerberos/www/.
2. Follow the instructions on the Kerbtray Web site to download and install this tool on the client computer.

3. Navigate to the installation location (by default, `C:\Program Files\Resource Kit\Kerbtray.exe`) and double-click the program icon.

4. Observe the details of the Kerberos authentication as shown on the various tabs of the dialog box that opens. (See Figure 1.10.)

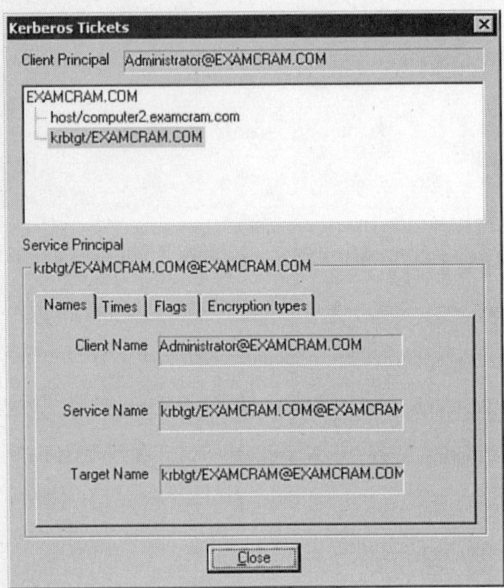

Figure 1.10 The Kerbtray tool provides details of Kerberos tickets on a Windows 2000 or Windows XP domain-based computer.

Exercise 1.2.2: Using Authentication Protocols, Including CHAP

A user accessing a server running Windows 2000 using the Remote Access Service (RAS) can be authenticated by means of several different authentication protocols. These protocols include a basic form of Challenge Handshake Authentication Protocol (CHAP) and two Microsoft-enhanced versions: MS-CHAP and MS-CHAPv2. CHAP is a remote access authentication protocol that uses a three-way handshake process to authenticate the user. When the user connects, the authenticating server sends a challenge message, to which the user returns a one-way hash of the challenge. This hash protects the password in transit across an inherently insecure medium such as the Internet. The authentication server checks the value of this hash against the value it possesses and grants access if the two values match. MS-CHAP stores an encrypted version of the hash for greater security, and MS-CHAPv2 uses a stronger level of encryption. We study the concept of hashing in Chapter 4, "Basics of Cryptography."

You should be aware that the CHAP authentication handshake process can be repeated at any time after the connection has been established.

In this exercise, you configure the use of these authentication protocols on the router you configured in Exercise 1.1.3. Steps on a Windows Server 2003 server are similar:

1. Log on to the computer running Windows 2000 Server as an administrator.
2. Open the Routing and Remote Access Service (RRAS) console. (Click Start, Programs, Administrative Tools, Routing and Remote Access.)
3. Right-click the Time Restrictions policy you created in Exercise 1.1.3 and select Properties.
4. In the Properties dialog box that opens, click Edit Profile.
5. In the Edit Dial-in Profile dialog box, select the Authentication tab.
6. As shown in Figure 1.11, this tab enables you to select from several authentication protocols: Extensible Authentication Protocol (EAP), two versions of MS-CHAP (which are selected by default), CHAP, and the unencrypted authentication protocols Password Authentication Protocol (PAP) and Shiva Password Authentication Protocol (SPAP).
7. Select or deselect authentication protocols as required on your network. If you need to use EAP, click the Extensible Authentication Protocol option. We discuss EAP later in Chapter 2, "Communication Security," in conjunction with smart cards.
8. When you are finished, click OK, click OK again, and then close the RRAS console.

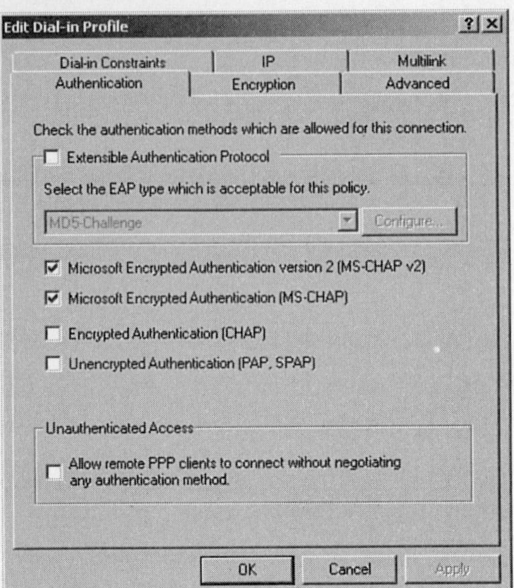

Figure 1.11 The Authentication tab allows you to select from several authentication protocols.

Exercise 1.2.3: Configuring a Local Account Policy

One of the most common forms of authentication is the username/password combination. Windows computers have used this authentication method since the days of Windows NT 3.1 and Windows for Workgroups because of its simplicity and ease of use. However, the common practice of using simple passwords is vulnerable to various forms of attack (down to outright guessing if you use passwords that relate to facts like birthdays, phone numbers, children's names, and so on). In this exercise, you configure a local password policy in Windows 2000 Professional that requires complex passwords that must be changed at regular intervals. You can perform the same exercise on a computer running Windows XP Professional by accessing Local Security Settings in Control Panel, Performance and Maintenance, Administrative Tools:

1. Log on to a computer running Windows 2000 Professional as an administrator.
2. Click Start, Programs, Administrative Tools, Local Security Policy.
3. In the Local Security Settings console, expand the Account Policies node to reveal two subnodes—Password Policy and Account Lockout Policy.

4. Click Password Policy. The right pane displays several policies.
5. Right-click Enforce Password History and choose Security. As shown in Figure 1.12, the default of 0 means that password history is not retained. Type **12** in the text box to remember 12 passwords and then click OK.

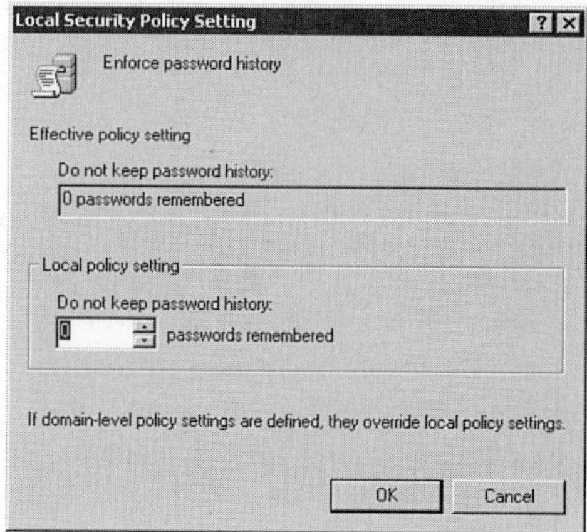

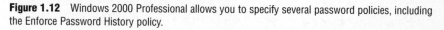

Figure 1.12 Windows 2000 Professional allows you to specify several password policies, including the Enforce Password History policy.

6. Right-click Maximum Password Age and choose Security. The default specifies that the password will expire in 42 days. Type **30** to require users to change their passwords monthly, and then click OK.
7. Right-click Minimum Password Age and choose Security. The default of 0 specifies that a password can be changed immediately. This would allow a user to cycle through a series of passwords until he was able to reuse an old password. Type **7** to require users to use a new password for at least one week, and then click OK.
8. Right-click Minimum Password Length and choose Security. The default of 0 means that a user does not need a password. Type **8** to require a password of at least 8 characters in length, and then click OK.

Eight characters is the desirable minimum length to deter password cracks in a low- to medium-security environment. For high security, you would want an even longer password.

9. Right-click Password Must Meet Complexity Requirements and choose Properties. When enabled, a password must contain characters from at least three of the following four groups: uppercase letters, lowercase letters, numerals, and special characters. Select Enabled and then click OK.

10. Right-click Store Password Using Reversible Encryption and choose Security. When enabled, this policy actually reduces security by allowing a clear-text password to be sent by systems that do not understand basic encryption. Leave this policy disabled and click Cancel.

11. In the left pane of the Local Security Settings console, select Account Lockout Policy to display three additional policies in the right pane.

12. Right-click Account Lockout Threshold and choose Security. The purpose of this policy is to lock an account out if a series of passwords is entered (such as by an intruder attempting to guess a password). The default of 0 means that an account will not be locked out. Type **3** to lock an account out after three incorrect passwords are entered, and then click OK.

13. A Suggested Value Changes dialog box opens suggesting values for the other two policies. The Account Lockout Duration policy represents the length of time before the account is unlocked. The Reset Account Lockout Counter After policy setting specifies the length of time before the number of incorrect passwords is reset to 0. Click OK to set both these values to 30 minutes.

14. To lock an account out indefinitely (until an administrator unlocks it), right-click Account Lockout Duration, choose Security, and type **0** in the text box, and then click OK.

15. To increase the time before the lockout counter is reset, right-click Reset Account Lockout Counter After and choose Security. Type the desired number of minutes (the maximum is 99,999 minutes or about 69 days), and then click OK.

16. Close the Local Security Settings console.

Commercially available tools offer stronger options for enforcing password security and informing users about proper passwords. A good example is available at http://www.anixis.com.

Make sure you understand why you need to enable the various policies that relate to usernames and passwords. For example, why is it important to have a minimum password age? Although authentication methods such as smart cards and biometrics might be more secure than usernames and passwords, the latter is still the most commonly used authentication method because of its low cost and ease of implementation.

Exercise 1.2.4: Exploring Other Important Authentication Methods

The Security+ exam covers several additional authentication methods with which you should be familiar. They include certificates, tokens (including smart cards), multifactor, mutual, and biometrics. Although not yet as popular as traditional username/password authentication, these methods all offer a higher level of security. We provide exercises on the use of certificates in Chapter 4. None of the other methods lend themselves to exercises performed on a simple one- or two-computer setup available to most readers studying for the Security+ exam, so we are presenting an exercise in which you locate information on these authentication methods. You can do this exercise from any computer with an Internet connection:

1. Using a Web browser, go to the RSA Security Web site at http://www.rsasecurity.com/ and search for "SecurID" using the search box in the upper part of the home page.

Those of you who are familiar with another vendor's authentication products might want to compare and contrast features offered by different vendors. If your company utilizes one of these systems, discuss its merits and drawbacks with an individual who is responsible for its administration and maintenance.

2. Select the "RSA SecurID Authentication White Paper: A Better Value for a Better ROI" link. If this link is not available, select any link that describes this authentication solution or a newer product by this vendor.

3. From the information in this paper, find as many reasons as you can why a simple username/password solution is not an adequate security solution for protecting high-value information. You should be able to find information on more than one of the authentication methods discussed in this section.

4. Use this paper to research the topic of multifactor authentication. Note that although two-factor authentication is the most common form of multifactor authentication, it is possible to include additional

factors in an environment where a high level of security is required. What can happen if a user incorrectly enters his PIN several times? When this happens because a legitimate user is having a problem, it can have a negative effect on productivity. What type of authentication does RSA Security advocate as a means of reducing this problem?

5. For an independent account of the SecurID token, go to http://zdnet.com.com/2100-1105-5225434.html?tag=header.newsfeed and note especially Bill Gates's impressions of this tool.

6. Go to http://searchsecurity.techtarget.com/gDefinition/0,,sid14_gci795971,00.html for a good definition of a security token. How is a security token different from a password? What types of hardware devices besides smart cards can be used for a security token?

If the URLs provided in this or other exercises no longer exist, simply use your favorite search engine to locate other sites that contain information pertinent to the topics at hand.

7. Access the Microsoft Developer white paper titled "Mutual Authentication using Kerberos" at http://msdn.microsoft.com/library/default.asp?url=/library/en-us/ad/ad/mutual_authentication_using_kerberos.asp. You should be able to note how Kerberos uses mutual authentication to verify the authenticity of an entity to which a client is connecting. This is in addition to the normal authentication of the client.

8. Access a more detailed introduction to mutual authentication in the paper titled "A Mutual Authenticating Protocol with Key Distribution in a Client/Server Environment" from the Association for Computing Machinery (ACM) at http://www.acm.org/crossroads/xrds2-4/authen.html. This paper explains how mutual authentication can defeat man-in-the-middle attacks. We discuss this type of attack later in this chapter.

9. For information on aspects of biometric authentication, refer to "Bioidentification: Frequently Asked Questions" at http://www.bromba.com/faq/biofaqe.htm#Merkmale. How many different biometric factors can be used? List some of the advantages and disadvantages of each of the more commonly used factors. What problems can occur when employing various biometric factors, and how can they be overcome? What are some of the statistical quantities that define the reliability of various biometric factors? For additional information, refer to the various links included at the end of this reference.

What Did I Just Learn?

Now that you have looked at several authentication methods, let's take a moment to review all the critical items you've experienced in this lab:

- Although usernames and passwords are the most commonly used methods of authentication on computer networks, they are not as secure as other methods such as tokens and biometrics.
- Modern network operating systems such as Windows 2000 Server allow you to create policies that require users to employ strong passwords and that lock accounts out when attempts to guess passwords occur.
- CHAP is a means of authenticating remote access users that employs a hashing function to protect passwords transmitted across an inherently insecure network such as the Internet. Microsoft offers improved versions of this protocol. You have seen how to specify which authentication protocols are permitted at the remote access server.
- You have researched the benefits and drawbacks of more advanced authentication methods, including tokens, smart cards, multifactor authentication, mutual authentication, and biometrics.

1.3: Identifying Nonessential Services and Protocols

When you install an operating system in its default configuration, numerous services and protocols are configured to start automatically whenever the computer is started up. Intruders can exploit many of these services to gain unauthorized access to your computers and networks. In this exercise, you look at the default set of services and see which ones can be disabled on most networks.

Exercise 1.3.1: Identifying and Disabling Services in Windows 2000 Professional

In this exercise, you look at the services that Windows 2000 Professional starts by default and disable unnecessary services. You can also do this exercise from a Windows XP computer; simply click Start, Control Panel, Performance and Maintenance, Administrative Tools, Services in Step 2:

1. Log on to the Windows 2000 Professional computer as an administrator.
2. Click Start, Programs, Administrative Tools, Services. As shown in Figure 1.13, the Services console lists a large number of services that are included in Windows 2000 Professional. Many of these services (labeled Automatic in the Startup Type column) are configured to start automatically when the computer is started up.

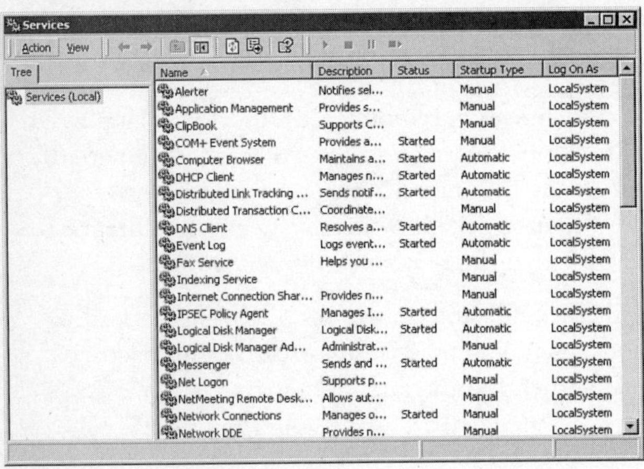

Figure 1.13 The Services console in Windows 2000 Professional displays the available services and the status and startup type of each one.

You can also access Services from the Computer Management console. Right-click My Computer and choose Manage, and then select the Services node under Services and Applications.

3. Scroll down to locate the Messenger service. Spammers sometimes utilize this service to send objectionable messages to many computers at a time. Right-click this service and choose Properties. As shown in Figure 1.14, the Properties dialog box for this service indicates that the service is configured for automatic startup.
4. Select the Dependencies tab. This tab informs you of which services depend on this service (there are none) and which services are dependent on the Messenger service for functioning (the Remote Procedure Call [RPC] and Workstation services).

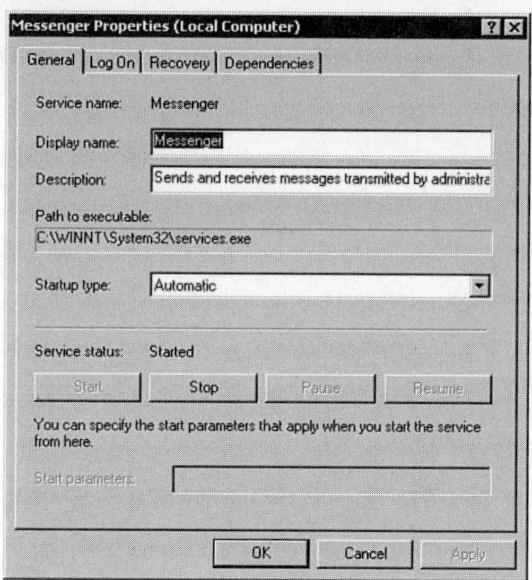

Figure 1.14 The Properties dialog box for the Messenger service displays a description of this service and a startup type of Automatic.

Service dependencies are important because disabling a service might prevent an important service that depends on the disabled service from starting. You should always research service dependencies by checking the Dependencies tab of the service's Properties dialog box before disabling any service.

5. Return to the General tab of this dialog box.
6. Click Stop. A Service Control message box appears briefly as the service is stopped.
7. In the Startup Type drop-down list, select Disabled and click OK. You are returned to the Services console and should note that the Startup Type column indicates that the service is disabled. This prevents the service from starting when you start the computer.

Some administrative tools rely on the Messenger service to notify administrators of problems. You should check on such types of usage before disabling this service on user accounts employed by administrators (including their default nonadministrative user accounts).

8. Disable additional services as needed. The following list indicates services that you should probably disable on client computers. Note that this list is not exhaustive and might differ according to the functionality

of your network. You can note a description of each service in the service's Properties dialog box:

- Alerter (unless administrators use administrative alerts to notify users of intended actions)
- Computer Browser (unless pre–Windows 2000 computers are present on the network)
- Net Meeting Remote Desktop Sharing (unless used, for example, by telecommuting workers)
- Remote Access Auto Connection Manager
- Remote Access Connection Manager
- Server (unless the computer contains shared folders that users must access across the network)
- Telnet
- Universal Plug and Play Device Host

9. When you are finished, close the Services console.

Software that you install on a Windows 2000/XP/Server 2003 computer might install additional services that will appear on the list discussed in this exercise. Do not disable these services unless you are certain you do not need the functions they enable. If in doubt, contact the software manufacturer.

Exercise 1.3.2: Creating a Policy to Disable Services

Group Policy in Windows 2000 Server enables you to configure a policy in a Group Policy object (GPO) that can apply to an entire domain or an organizational unit (OU). It enables you to define the startup type and status of services that will apply to all computers to which the policy is applied. In this exercise, you will configure a services policy. For more information on configuring and editing GPOs, refer to the Active Directory training guide mentioned in the "Need to Know More?" section. Perform this exercise on a computer running Windows 2000 Server:

1. Log on to a domain controller or to a server running the complete set of administrative tools as an administrator.
2. Open the Group Policy console focused on the GPO you want to configure.

3. Navigate to the Computer Configuration\Windows Settings\Security Settings\System Services node. As shown in Figure 1.15, the right pane displays a list of services similar to those you saw in the previous exercise.

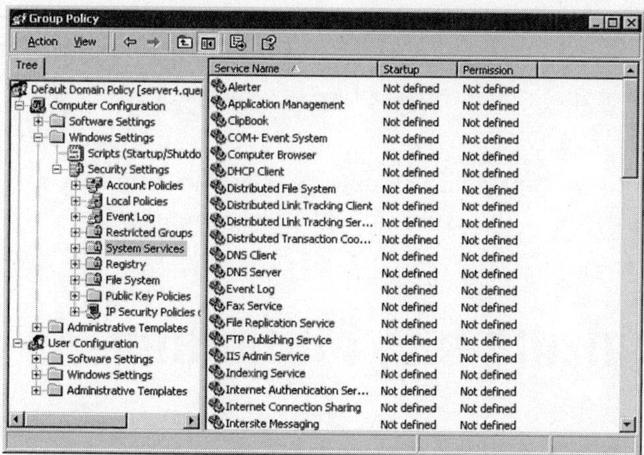

Figure 1.15 The System Services node in the Group Policy console enables you to define service properties for affected computers.

4. To define the startup mode of a service such as the Computer Browser service, right-click it and choose Security.

5. Select Define This Policy Setting. If a Security for Computer Browser dialog box appears, click Cancel. Choose the desired startup mode, as shown in Figure 1.16. Then click OK.

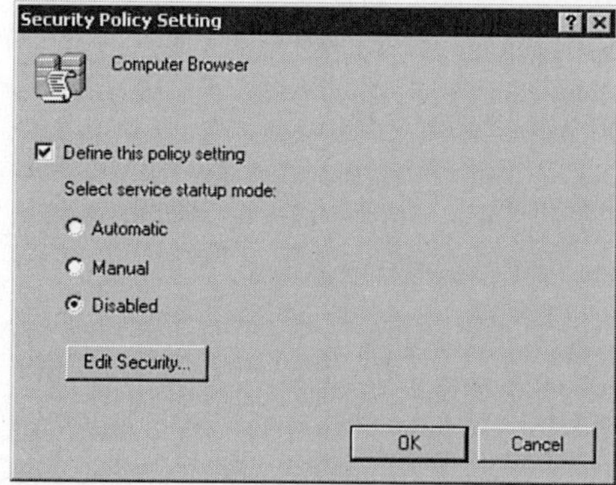

Figure 1.16 Configure a policy to disable a service.

6. Repeat as required for additional services. When finished, exit the Group Policy console.

What Did I Just Learn?

Now that you have looked at several types of access control, let's take a moment to review all the critical items you've experienced in this lab:

- Default installations of operating systems such as Windows include many services that are not required for day-to-day functionality. You should disable many of these services to reduce the means of attack by intruders.
- Group Policy in Windows 2000 and Windows Server 2003 enables you to configure policies that disable services on all affected computers.

1.4: Recognizing and Mitigating Attacks

It has become common these days to hear of new exploits and attacks on computer networks and systems. Recognizing when your network is under attack is vital to your being able to minimize damage and make sure that attackers cannot gain a foothold on your sensitive data and systems. The Security+ exam tests you on the types of attacks that are prevalent these days and how to recognize and combat them.

Exercise 1.4.1: Preventing DoS Attacks

A Denial of Service (DoS) attack is simply the act of overloading a computer with data packets so that it is unable to perform its normal actions. A DoS attack can involve a large number of data packets or simply a single packet that is carefully crafted to orchestrate the attack. Although a DoS attack is generally performed against a server, it is effective against any vulnerable computer. A distributed DoS (DDoS) attack is similar except that it uses a series of computers to attack a victim computer and overload it.

In this exercise, you download and run a utility that performs a DoS attack that relies on NetBIOS functionality and note what happens. You should have two computers running Windows NT 4.0, Windows 2000, or Windows XP to perform this exercise. You then protect the computer by disabling NetBIOS. If you have a single computer only, you can actually crash it by specifying its own name and IP address:

1. Using a Web browser, go to http://www.windowsecurity.com/articles/SMBDie_Crashing_Windows_Servers_with_Ease.html. This article

describes a program called SMBdie, which creates and transmits packets that are designed to attack the Windows Server Message Block (SMB) protocol, which is used on Microsoft computers to facilitate the sharing of resources.

2. After reading about this program, click the indicated link and download the zip file and save it to a floppy disk.
3. Extract the archived files to a folder on the hard disk of a computer from which you want to start a DoS attack.
4. Double-click the executable file to open it. As shown in Figure 1.17, type the IP address and the name of the computer you want to attack.

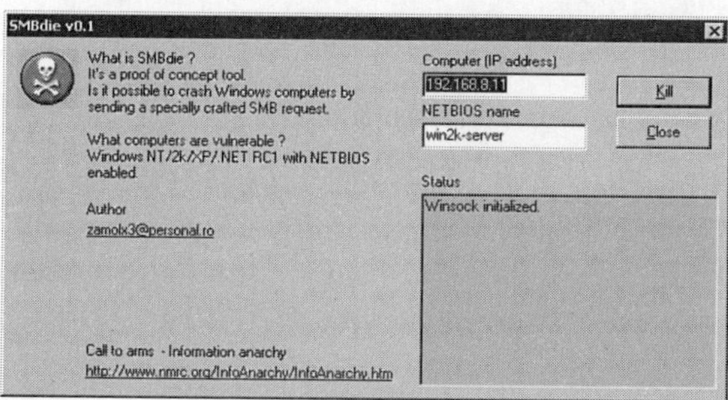

Figure 1.17 SMBdie is a utility that performs a simple but effective DoS attack against any Windows computer.

Make sure that no programs are running on the computer against which you are performing this attack. Save any open files before you proceed any further. Do not perform this exercise on a production network without the approval of an administrator.

5. Click Kill. The computer you specified in the utility immediately crashes, displaying a blue screen of death (BSoD) error, as shown in Figure 1.18.

```
*** STOP: 0x0000001E (0xC0000005,0x804B818B,0x00000001,0x00760065)
KMODE_EXCEPTION_NOT_HANDLED

*** Address 804B818B base at 80400000, DateStamp 384d9b17 - ntoskrnl.exe

Beginning dump of physical memory
Dumping physical memory to disk:  38
```

Figure 1.18 The computer you specified in the SMBdie utility displays the BSoD immediately after you click Kill.

This exercise will not work on a Windows Server 2003 computer. However, you can use a Windows Server 2003 computer to perform the attack against another computer. On a Windows XP computer, the computer will reboot immediately without displaying a BSOD error.

6. Reboot the crashed computer. At the attacking computer, click Close.
7. Log back on to the crashed computer as an administrator.
8. Right-click My Network Places and choose Properties.
9. In the Network and Dial-Up Connections dialog box, right-click Local Area Connection and choose Properties.
10. In the Local Area Connection Properties dialog box, select Internet Protocol (TCP/IP) and click Properties.
11. In the TCP/IP Properties dialog box, click Advanced.
12. In the Advanced TCP/IP Settings dialog box, select the WINS tab and then select the Disable NetBIOS over TCP/IP radio button, as shown in Figure 1.19. Click OK. If you receive a message informing you of an empty primary Windows Internet Naming Service (WINS) address, click Yes to continue.

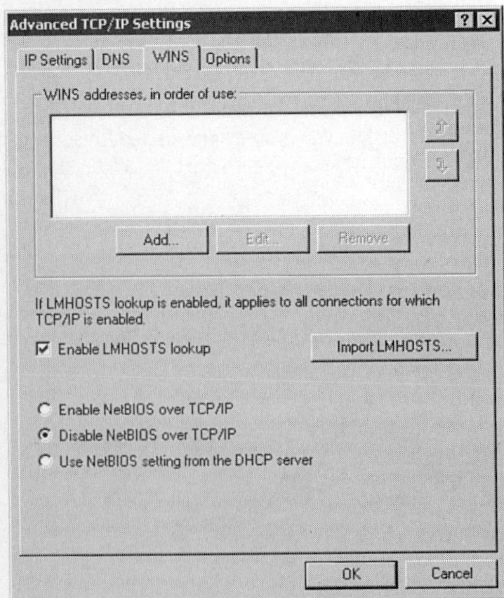

Figure 1.19 Disabling NetBIOS over TCP/IP protects the computer from a NetBIOS-based DoS attack.

13. Click OK to close the TCP/IP Properties dialog box, and then click OK to close the Local Area Connection Properties dialog box.
14. Return to the attacking computer and click Kill again. This time you receive a message informing you that SMBdie was unable to connect to the remote computer.
15. Close SMBdie.

Exercise 1.4.2: Back Door Programs

A *back door program* is any program that allows access to a computer from another computer. Many such programs exist; some such as pcAnywhere or Real Virtual Network Computing (VNC) are benign or even of beneficial use for administrative purposes. Others are dangerous to a lesser or greater extent. We shall look at Back Orifice, a dangerous program, and at Microsoft Terminal Services, a beneficial one.

Exercise 1.4.2.1: Back Orifice

In this exercise, you research the Back Orifice program and some of its capabilities. You then look at some precautions you can take, as well as methods of removal:

1. Using a Web browser, go to http://www.nwinternet.com/~pchelp/bo/bo.html. This page provides comprehensive information about the original Back Orifice program, which runs on Windows 95 and 98 computers. Study this page and the links it contains to find information on what Back Orifice does. How can you detect and remove this program and prevent its installation? Follow some of the links on this page to obtain further information on this back door program.
2. This page contains several links to tools that you can use to detect the presence of Back Orifice on a computer. Follow these links and use these tools to look for Back Orifice on a computer that has been exposed to the Internet for a period of time.
3. For information on the most recent form of Back Orifice, go to http://www.f-secure.com/v-descs/bo2k.shtml. The BO2K version of Back Orifice can be used for remote administration of Windows computers, or it can act as a powerful hacking tool for unauthorized access to computers running Windows NT/2000/XP/Server 2003. Further details and downloads are available from http://www.bo2k.com/.

Exercise 1.4.2.2: Microsoft Terminal Services

Administrators often use one of several legitimate programs as back doors for remote administration of servers from the desktop without the need to physically access the server console. The Terminal Services program provided by Microsoft in its Windows 2000 Server enables two administrators to concurrently connect to a server running the Terminal Services software to perform administrative tasks. You can operate Terminal Services in either of the following two modes:

- *Remote Administration mode*—Enables an administrator to perform nearly all administrative tasks on a server from a computer running a client operating system such as Windows 2000 Professional or Windows XP Professional. It allows for enhanced physical security of the servers.
- *Application Server mode*—Enables remote users to run applications installed on the server from their client computer. The number of concurrent sessions is limited by the number of available licenses as well as the hardware on the server.

In this exercise, you install Terminal Services in remote administration mode and access the server from another computer. You need two computers, one running Windows 2000 Server and the second running Windows 2000 Professional:

You can also use Remote Desktop in Windows XP Professional to access the terminal server. For more information, see the Windows XP Professional training guide in the "Need to Know More?" section.

1. Log on to the Windows 2000 Server computer as an administrator.
2. Click Start, Settings, Control Panel, and double-click Add/Remove Programs.
3. Click Add/Remove Windows Components.
4. Select Terminal Services and then click Next.
5. From the Terminal Services Setup page shown in Figure 1.20, select Remote Administration and then click Next.
6. When requested, insert the Windows 2000 Server CD-ROM and then click OK.
7. Click Finish when the completion page appears, and then close the Windows Components Wizard.

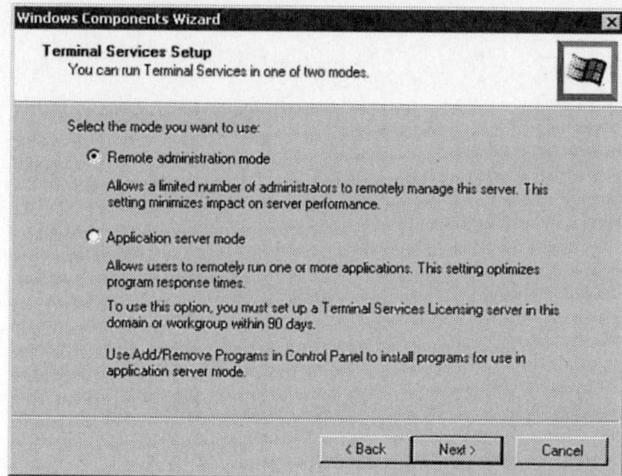

Figure 1.20 Terminal Services in Windows 2000 Server provides two modes of operation.

8. Click Yes to shut down and restart the computer.
9. When the computer restarts, log back on as Administrator.
10. Click Start, Programs, Administrative Tools, Terminal Services Client Creator. This starts the Create Installation Disk(s) program (see Figure 1.21), which is used to create floppy disks for installing the client software on the remote computer.

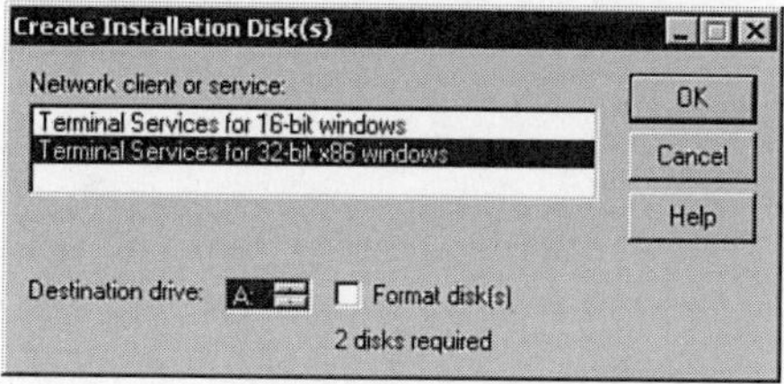

Figure 1.21 The Terminal Services Client Creator program is used to create floppy disks for 16- and 32-bit Windows client computers.

11. Select the Terminal Services for 32-bit x86 Windows option and then click OK.
12. Insert the first floppy disk into your drive and then click OK.
13. A Copying Files dialog box charts the progress of client software creation. When requested, insert the second floppy disk and then click OK.
14. When you are informed that two disks have been created, click OK, close the Terminal Services Client Creator, and then take the disks to the Windows 2000 Professional computer.

15. At the Windows 2000 Professional computer, insert the first floppy disk. Click Start, Run; type `a:setup`; and then press Enter.
16. On the Terminal Services Client Setup page, read the information provided and then click Continue. Follow the instructions provided by the installation program.
17. When requested, insert the second floppy disk and then click OK.
18. Click OK when informed that the setup was completed.
19. To establish a terminal connection, click Start, Programs, Terminal Services Client, Terminal Services Client. The Terminal Services Client dialog box shown in Figure 1.22 provides the available connection information. Type the name or IP address of the server if necessary, and then click Connect.

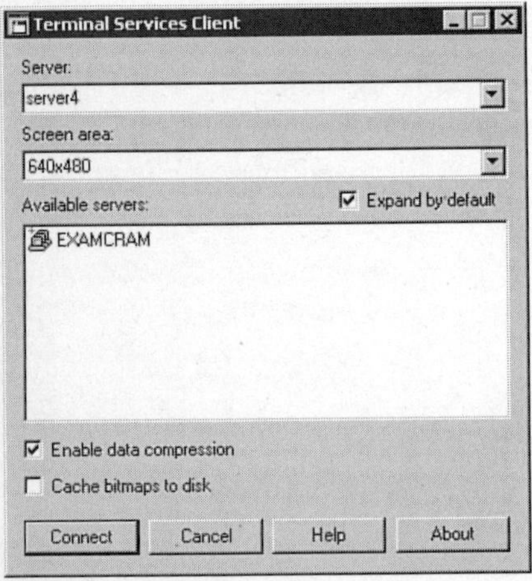

Figure 1.22 The Terminal Services Client dialog box enables the user to establish a connection to the specified server.

20. Terminal Services opens a window to the remote computer. Type the username and password of the administrative account on the server and then click OK.
21. You receive a Terminal Services window from which you can perform server administrative tasks.
22. Perform a server-based task such as creating a new user.
23. When you are finished, log off the terminal server session by clicking Start, Shut Down. In the Shut Down Windows dialog box, select Disconnect and then click OK.

24. Close the Terminal Services Client dialog box.

25. Return to the server and verify completion of the task you just performed from the terminal session.

Exercise 1.4.3: Password Guessing

We have already made reference to how intruders will attempt to guess passwords and the means by which you can require secure passwords on Windows computer networks to reduce the chance of successful guessing of passwords.

In this exercise, you download, install, and test the L0pht Crack password cracker. Perform this exercise on the same computer you used for Exercise 1.1.2.1, in which you created a user:

1. A commercially available password cracker is L0pht Crack (LC45), available from @stake. Using a Web browser, navigate to http://www.atstake.com/products/lc/ and make note of how easily passwords can be cracked. This emphasizes the need for creating strong passwords.

2. Navigate to http://www.atstake.com/products/lc/download.html to download a trial version of the L0pht Crack password cracker.

3. Open the downloaded file and follow the instructions to install L0pht. It installs a shortcut on your computer's Programs menu.

4. Start the program and select Trial. It displays a wizard.

5. Click Next, select the Retrieve from the Local Machine option, and then click Next again.

6. To perform a dictionary attack, select Common Password Audit, and then click Next. The trial version of L0pht Crack will not perform a brute-force attack.

7. Keep the defaults selected on the Pick Reporting Style page, click Next, and then click Finish.

8. After a few seconds, L0pht Crack should display a dialog box containing all users and passwords on the local computer, including User1 with a password of Hello123. Scroll the display to note how fast the passwords were cracked. (See Figure 1.23.) Also select the Report tab to see statistics of the password risk status. For this example, the default administrator using "password" was reported as high risk and the user with Hello123 was reported as medium risk.

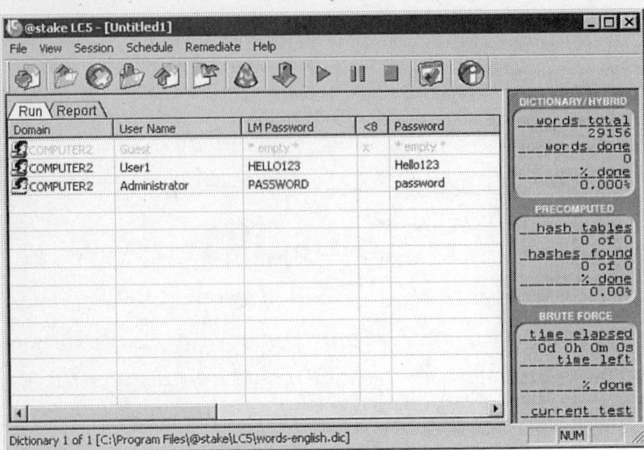

Figure 1.23 L0pht Crack can sniff passwords from user accounts on the local computer or across the network.

9. Use the procedure of Exercise 1.1.2.1 to create a new user, User2, with a password of Qr$12oX#5. Then repeat Steps 4 to 8. This time, the trial version of L0pht Crack is unable to crack this password because the authors of this program have disabled the brute-force method unless you purchase a license to the program.

10. Close the program. If prompted, do not save changes.

Exercise 1.4.4: Other Attack Methods

For the Security+ exam, you need to be able to recognize and distinguish other types of attacks and how to mitigate them. These include spoofing, man-in-the-middle attacks, replay, TCP/IP hijacking, weak keys, mathematical (including birthday), and software exploitation. Recognizing these attacks is important because different attacks require different combat strategies. We discuss social engineering later in this chapter. In this exercise, you research information on these types of attacks:

1. To research spoofing and several other types of attacks, go to the Internet Security Systems Web pages at http://www.iss.net/security_center/advice/Underground/Hacking/Methods/Technical/Spoofing/default.htm. What is a common misconception regarding IP spoofing? What types of intrusions make use of IP spoofing? Follow the links for more information on these intrusions. Some of these overlap on other types of attacks you need to know about for the Security+ exam. Other intrusions include Address Resolution Protocol (ARP) spoofing and Domain Name Service (DNS) spoofing.

2. A form of spoofing that has recently had a large amount of press is that of email spoofing or phishing, in which the attacker sends fraudulent email messages that appear to be from reputable companies such as banks or insurance companies. These messages contain links to spoofed sites that trick victims into providing credit cards or other personal information. Go to the Search Security Web page at http://searchsecurity.techtarget.com/sDefinition/0,,sid14_gci916037,00.html and research this problem from links provided on this page.

3. Internet Security Systems discusses TCP/IP session hijacking at http://www.iss.net/security_center/advice/Exploits/TCP/session_hijacking/default.htm. A link on this page describes the hijacking of a supposedly secure connection that had been authenticated with Kerberos.

4. Robert Graham, on his Web page at http://www.robertgraham.com/pubs/hacking-dict.html, provides brief descriptions of many Internet attacks and exploits. Included are spoofing, man-in-the-middle attacks, replay, hijacking, social engineering, and birthday paradox, as well as many other security-related terms, including those you need to know for other objectives of the Security+ exam. Describe how these attacks were undertaken and distinguish between the different types of attacks. Include some of the common analogies and key points that are mentioned for these attacks.

5. Windows and .NET Magazine describes a man-in-the-middle attack on Windows Terminal Services at http://www.winnetmag.com/Article/ArticleID/38589/38589.html. How was this attack conducted? Another useful but more advanced article on this type of attack appears at http://www.sans.org/rr/papers/60/480.pdf.

6. An article by Brian Posey at http://networking.earthweb.com/netsecur/article.php/624871 discusses replay attacks in Windows 2000 and the use of IP Security (IPSec) to prevent these attacks. What steps must an attacker undertake to perform a replay attack? How can you use IPSec in Windows 2000 to thwart a replay attack?

7. The Encyclopedia of Computer Security discusses mathematical attacks on cryptographic algorithms at http://www.itsecurity.com/asktecs/jun1801.htm. Describe several of their examples of mathematical attacks in your own words. You should also check the description of asymmetric key algorithms provided by Wikipedia at http://en.wikipedia.org/wiki/Asymmetric_key_algorithm. What are several weaknesses of asymmetric key algorithms? We discuss these algorithms in more detail in Chapter 4. These types of algorithms are subject to mathematical attacks.

8. To learn more about software exploitation, go to the article by Gary McGraw in the Software Quality Management Magazine at http://www.sqmmagazine.com/issues/2003-01/bss.html. What are several software security practices that you can undertake to protect your systems? McGraw provides additional references for those interested in knowing more about this subject. Another reference of interest with regard to software exploitation of handheld computers appears at http://www.pnl.gov/isrc/advisory-notices/advis23.stm.

9. Josef Nelissen discusses the buffer overflow attack, which is a common type of software exploitation, at http://www.sans.org/rr/papers/60/481.pdf. Note that a *buffer* is similar to an array and is used to store a sequence of data items within a computer program. What happens when the program attempts to store more data than a buffer can hold? What are some means by which a buffer overflow can occur, and what are several effects of the buffer overflow? Note, in particular, the threat that a buffer overflow can achieve. Nelissen goes into detail about how the most common attack, known as *stack smashing*, can be executed. Although the details of this attack are likely of interest only to mathematically inclined readers, you should note his recommendations for avoiding stack overflows. Above all, security should be a top priority throughout the program development process.

These attacks are not always easy to execute and require that the attacker be knowledgeable on the required methods. The attacker needs to either be on the same subnet or be able to monitor the data being exchanged across the connection. Nevertheless, successful attacks take place all the time.

As you study these references, make particular note about the similarities and differences among the various methods of attack. Think about how successful attackers completed their exploits and what measures could have been taken to thwart them. Be sure that you are able to recognize and distinguish between these attack methods.

What Did I Just Learn?

Now that you have researched and practiced a large number of ways attackers might wreak their havoc on unsuspecting victims, let's take a moment to review all the critical items you've experienced in this exercise:

- A DoS attack consists of flooding a computer with such a large number of packets that it is unable to respond to normal actions and either locks up or crashes. A DDoS attack is similar except that it is launched through a series of compromised machines all directed at a single victim machine.

- A back door is any type of program that allows access to one computer from another. Back door programs range from useful ones, including Microsoft's Terminal Services and Windows XP Remote Desktop, to malicious ones such as Back Orifice. Programmers sometimes leave back doors in programs that can be later abused for unscrupulous purposes.
- Spoofing occurs when an attacker impersonates a trusted entity to gain the victim's confidence. Phishing is a variation of spoofing in which the attacker appears to be a legitimate business requiring information from the victim.
- In a man-in-the-middle attack, the attacker listens in on a conversation between two computers and intercepts or modifies information being transmitted between these computers.
- TCP/IP hijacking involves an attacker taking over a TCP session between two computers, sometimes by using source-routed IP packets. This allows an attacker to take over a connection for which authentication has already been granted.
- Several mathematical attack methods involve the use of various algorithms for cracking encryption. Related to these attacks are those that involve weak keys or birthday attacks. Often, it is not the algorithm that is cracked but the means by which it was implemented; for example, the RC4 algorithm used in wireless local area networks (WLANs).
- Password-guessing methods range from the simplest approach of trying birthdays, phone numbers, children's names, and so on to the use of programs such as L0pht Crack to execute dictionary and brute-force attacks. Birthday attacks use hash functions to perform a type of brute-force attack.

1.5: Recognizing and Mitigating Malicious Code

Malicious code can affect your system in various ways. The problem is that the possibilities are seemingly never-ending. Knowing what virus or worm was making the rounds last week does little to protect you from today's exploits. This lab leads you to several valuable resources of malicious code information that can help you stay up-to-date on the latest attacks.

Don't let our comment about last week's attacks lead you to ignore older malicious code. Attackers are constantly reintroducing old attacks to see who has not patched their software. If an attacker can identify you as having an older vulnerability, he can probably find many ways into your system.

Exercise 1.5.1: Malicious Code Awareness

The absolute first step in addressing the problem of malicious code is to understand the threat. In this exercise, you research the nature of malicious code. Perform this exercise on any computer that is connected to the Internet:

1. Using a Web browser, go to http://www.sophos.com/virusinfo. This is the Web site for Sophos antivirus and antispam software. The Virus Info page contains many links to information on viruses and emerging virus threats.
2. Select the Viruses Explained link to learn about what viruses do and how they can impact your business and everyday activities. This link includes a downloadable e-book that provides detailed information on viruses and their impact. Note in particular their definition of a virus and how it infects your computer.
3. The same e-book defines Trojan horses and worms. What do these types of malicious code do and how do they differ from viruses?

Make sure you know the differences between viruses, worms, and Trojan horses. Note in particular that a worm can replicate by itself without the need for some type of host file. A Trojan horse is additional code within a legitimate program that is designed to perform some malicious task such as emailing confidential information to an unauthorized host.

4. From the same e-book, note three types of viruses, what they do, and how they differ from one another. What are some ways to protect against viruses in addition to the most common types of antivirus software?
5. Return to the Virusinfo page and explore several of the other links found there. In particular, the Top Ten Viruses link summarizes the currently active virus threats. You should visit this page periodically to stay current on threats.
6. Navigate to http://www.clearlybusiness.com/e_business/vs_trojan_horses_worms_&_logic_bombs.jsp for a discussion of Trojan horses, worms, and logic bombs. How does a Trojan horse operate, and what are four malicious acts that it can perform? How does a logic

bomb wreak its havoc, and what are some of its characteristics? What are several methods you can use to protect yourself from the effects of these malicious programs?

7. Navigate to http://searchsecurity.techtarget.com/sDefinition/0,,sid14_gci815177,00.html for a concise definition of a logic bomb. What are some ways in which a logic bomb can be triggered, and how can you detect and eliminate them?

8. For a comprehensive summary of malicious software and other security threats, go to http://www.caci.com/business/ia/threats.html. The table at this link is useful for several other Security+ objectives.

Exercise 1.5.2: Malicious Code Mitigation

After you know what malicious code is, what do you do about it? In this exercise, you explore several competing antivirus software products. The purpose of this exercise is to develop a better understanding of the current product offerings and their general capabilities.

Although many offerings address the malicious code issue, you need to be informed enough to make a wise decision. Many organizations either acquire insufficient features or fail to use them properly. Make sure that you understand how to select, implement, and maintain software that helps protect you from malicious code:

1. Using a Web browser, go to http://www.trendmicro.com. This is the Web site for Trend Micro, a company that offers a free online virus scan. Click Personal to find the online scan and perform the scan on your own computer.

This online scan works only for computers running Microsoft Windows and only when using the Microsoft Internet Explorer or Netscape Navigator Web browsers.

2. While you are on the Trend Micro Web site, try its Trend Micro Outbreak Game at http://www.trendmicro.com/en/products/network/nvw/evaluate/game.htm that teaches you how to stop network viruses.

3. After you explore the Trend Micro scanning page, look at its product offerings, such as the Trend Micro PC-cillin Internet Security virus scanner. Choose a product for your organization and record the basic capabilities and cost.

4. Visit the McAfee site at http://www.mcafee.com/us/ and obtain information about one or more of the products mentioned on this page. You should include enough information to compare the products that will protect your organization from malicious code.

5. Visit the Symantec site at http://www.symantec.com/index.htm and the Computer Associates site at https://www.my-etrust.com/products/Antivirus.cfm?WebRefferalAffiliate=IPE200000001&VDRID=EZ00000006, and repeat Step 4 with these antivirus vendors.

6. Document your findings and make a purchase recommendation for your own organization, based on purchase price, features, and maintainability.

7. As part of your purchase recommendation, document the procedure for keeping the virus signature up-to-date. How often should you update the signature files? How often should you scan? Are there any policy changes your organization will need to make?

Although antivirus software can provide strong controls that protect from malicious code, software alone is not a complete solution. Take some time during your research to consider additional steps your organization could take that would further reduce the threat of malicious code.

Some questions to ask are: What can your users do to reduce the threat of malicious code introduction? How can you teach users to recognize malicious code? What should users do when they suspect malicious code is present?

What Did I Just Learn?

Now that you have looked at several methods of recognizing and addressing different types of malicious code, let's take a moment to review the critical items you've experienced in this lab:

- Malicious code threats change on a daily basis. Diligence is required to properly address the threats. It is imperative to maintain controls for known and emerging threats. (That is, keep your controls updated!)
- A virus is a program that can attach itself to another file and replicate to other computers when the file is executed.
- A Trojan horse is additional code included in another useful program that performs malicious actions such as emailing confidential information to its author.
- A worm is similar to a virus but can replicate itself without activation and without being attached to another program.

- A logic bomb is code that is designed to activate itself when a certain event takes place, such as the arrival of a certain date or the performing of a certain activity.
- Several companies offer software products and services to assist you in protecting your organization from malicious code. Carefully examine the various offerings to choose the right solution for your needs.
- Acquiring and installing software is only the first step in battling malicious code. It is your responsibility to make sure that you understand the nature of the threats and the need for controls.

1.6: Understanding Social Engineering

It is second nature for human beings to try to be helpful to their fellow individuals. An attacker can gain the confidence of someone and con him into giving up information such as usernames and passwords that enable unauthorized access to a network. A few phone calls is often all it takes. Such is the concept of *social engineering*.

Exercise 1.6.1: Understanding Social Engineering

In this exercise, you research the topic of social engineering on the Internet and gain a feeling for how easy it is to dupe your fellow human beings into giving up sensitive information:

1. Sarah Granger of Security Focus provides an excellent review of numerous social engineering tactics at http://www.securityfocus.com/infocus/1527. Note how attackers have impersonated people ranging from maintenance workers to the CEO, playing upon the friendly nature of help desk technicians, watching others enter PINs or passwords, and so on. Attackers might interest victims in some item they have for sale, and send an email that contains a Trojan horse or backdoor program that intercepts passwords and other confidential information. They might even resort to low-tech methods such as dumpster diving (searching through trash for information that leads them to lucrative targets).

2. Sarah Granger continues her discussion with methods of combating social engineering attacks at http://www.securityfocus.com/infocus/1533. Note the table at the end of this page. What are several risk areas, tactics used by hackers, and means that you can use to combat them? For additional information on social engineering attacks and means of combating them, follow the links to references provided in both of these Web pages.
3. The SANS Institute provides references to papers describing methods of social engineering at http://www.sans.org/rr/catindex.php?cat_id=51. Most of these papers were written by individuals seeking the Global Information Assurance Certification (GIAC) security certifications. What are several additional types of social engineering attacks described in these papers?
4. Set up a role-playing exercise with one or more friends or other Security+ candidates, and try out these methods of obtaining information from your fellow human beings.

Intruders can perform social-engineering attacks as a first step in gaining information that will lead to their performing another type of attack on a company's network and information systems.

Educating users about the various risks is the number one method of ensuring a strong defense against social-engineering attacks.

What Did I Just Learn?

Now that you have looked at several types of social engineering attacks, let's take a moment to review all the critical items you've experienced in this exercise:

- Social engineering attacks play on the natural human instinct to help another individual who has a problem.
- Social engineering attacks can take many forms and are often a prelude to another type of attack discussed in this chapter.
- Organizations should have a policy in place and instruct employees on means of reporting and combating social engineering attacks.

1.7: Understanding Auditing, Logging, and System Scanning

You have taken a lot of time to secure your computers and networks against various attacks, but how do you know whether someone is attempting to penetrate your defenses? And how do you know whether your systems are really secure? Information obtained from auditing, logging, and network or system scanning can provide details of exactly what is going on behind the scenes on your machines and networks. In this lab, we look at auditing and logging techniques that provide information on what others, authorized or otherwise, are doing, as well as scanning techniques that you can use to check your computers and networks for vulnerabilities.

Exercise 1.7.1: Configuring Auditing in Windows 2000 Professional

All modern Windows operating systems provide the capability of auditing a large range of actions such as logons, account modifications, and access to files and folders. In this exercise, you configure auditing of logon activity and file access. Perform this exercise on the same Windows 2000 Professional computer you have used previously in this chapter:

This exercise works almost exactly the same on a Windows XP Professional computer and very similarly on a Windows NT 4.0 computer. It does not work on a computer running Windows 9x or Windows XP Home Edition.

1. Log on to the Windows 2000 computer as an administrator.
2. Click Start, Settings, Control Panel, Administrative Tools, Local Security Policy.
3. In the left pane of the Local Security Settings console, expand Local Policies and select Audit Policy. This displays a series of policy settings in the right pane.
4. Right-click Audit Logon Events and choose Security. In the Audit Logon Events Properties dialog box shown in Figure 1.24, select Failure and then click OK. This action logs any failed attempt (such as by an intruder) to log on to the computer.

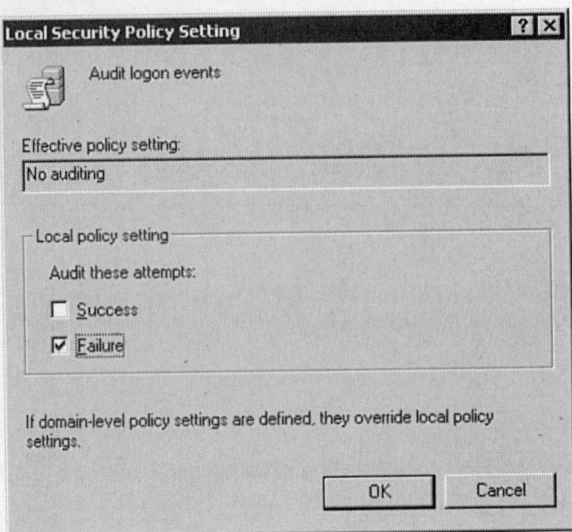

Figure 1.24 Configure the auditing of failed logon attempts.

5. Right-click Audit Object Access and choose Security. Select both Success and Failure and click OK. This action logs successful and failed attempts to access specified objects (files, folders, or printers). To actually perform auditing, we must specify which objects are to be audited.
6. Open My Computer and navigate to the `C:\Data` folder you created in Exercise 1.1.2.2. Right-click this folder and choose Properties.
7. On the Security tab of the folder's Properties dialog box, click Advanced.
8. In the Advanced Security Settings for Data dialog box that opens, select the Auditing tab.
9. Click Add. In the Select User, Computer, or Group dialog box that opens (see Figure 1.25), type **User1** and then click OK.

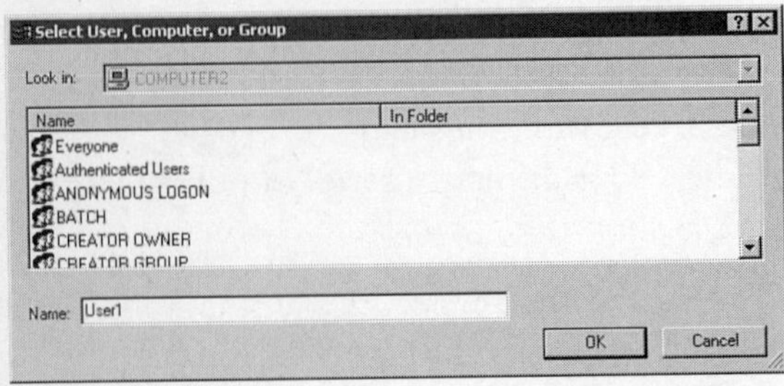

Figure 1.25 Specify a user whose actions will be audited.

10. The Auditing Entry for Data dialog box allows you to select what types of access will be audited. For this example, select List Folder/Read Data, Create Files/Write Data, and Create Folders/Append Data under the Successful and Failed columns to audit all access to this folder. Then click OK.

On a Windows XP computer, you can simply select the Full Control entry under both columns in Step 10.

11. As shown in Figure 1.26, an entry summarizing what you have done appears on the Auditing tab of the Advanced Security Settings dialog box. Click OK, and then click OK again to close the Data Properties dialog box.

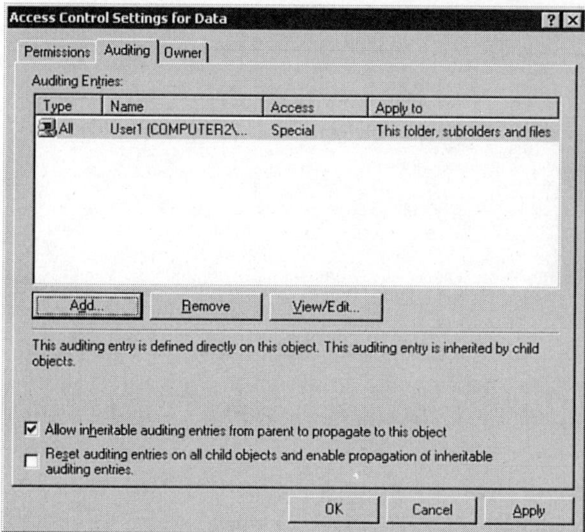

Figure 1.26 The Auditing tab of the Advanced Security Settings dialog box shows which actions by User1 will be audited.

12. To perform some actions that will be audited, log off and log on as User1. Do not specify a password.

13. You receive a message that the system could not log you on. Click OK and try again, specifying `Hello123` as the password.

14. Navigate to and open the `C:\Data` folder. You will see the test documents created earlier.

15. Attempt to open `Test1`. You receive an "Access is denied" error.

16. Open `Test2` and save a change to this file. You are able to save a change because User1 is a member of Group1.

17. Log off and log back on as an administrator.

18. Right-click My Computer, and choose Manage.

19. In the Computer Management console, expand Event Viewer and select Security from the logs that are available. As shown in Figure 1.27, a large number of entries appears in the right pane.

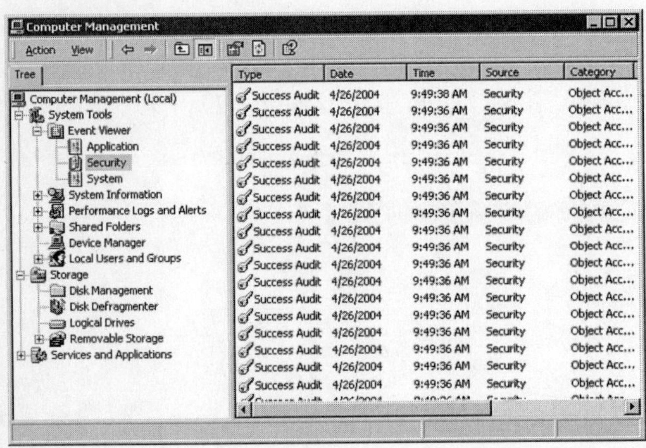

Figure 1.27 The Security log in Event Viewer records all actions you have configured for auditing.

20. Scroll to the bottom of the list and double-click a failure event labeled Logon/Logoff in the Category column. As shown in Figure 1.28, you see a Properties dialog box specifying that an error occurred during logon by User1. This is the type of message you see if you are tracking attempts by unauthorized users to log on to the system. Click OK.

21. Scroll back upwards and double-click an event labeled Failure Audit with a category of Object Access. You should be able to find a failed attempt to read the file `C:\Data\Test1.txt`.

22. Use the up and down arrows in the upper-right corner of the Event Properties dialog box to access the properties of other events. Note that every action performed on the `C:\Data` folder is logged. You should be able to find a successful access to the `C:\Data\Test2.txt` file. Note how an event log can fill rapidly with entries if you log all types of access.

23. Close all dialog boxes when you are finished.

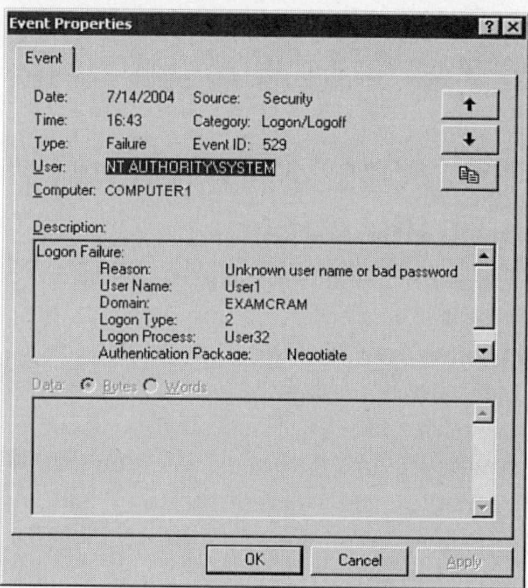

Figure 1.28 The Event Properties dialog box for a failed logon event shows detailed event properties, including the username who attempted to log on.

Exercise 1.7.2: Configuring Auditing on a Domain

You can configure a GPO to audit actions across an entire Active Directory domain or OU from a domain controller running Windows Server 2003 or Windows 2000 Server. In this exercise, you observe the actions that you can audit but do not actually configure any auditing. Perform this exercise on the computer from which you performed Exercise 1.3.2 earlier in this chapter:

1. Log on to a domain controller or to a server running the complete set of administrative tools as an administrator.
2. Open the Group Policy console focused on the GPO you want to configure.
3. Navigate to the Computer Configuration\Windows Settings\Security Settings\Local Policies\Audit Policy node.
4. Note that you can configure the same series of auditing polices that were available on the Windows 2000 Professional computer. The main difference here is that auditing will be enabled on all computers that are subject to the GPO you are configuring.
5. Close the Group Policy console and all other dialog boxes.

On a real network, plan your auditing strategy very carefully. Exercise 1.7.1 shows the large number of events that are generated by auditing only a small number of objects. This number will multiply extremely rapidly when you audit an entire network!

Exercise 1.7.3: Configuring Logging

In this exercise, you look at the logging capabilities included in Internet Information Services (IIS). Logging on a computer hosting a Web site is important because it allows the administrator or Webmaster to track visits to her site and look for problems users have in accessing the site or attempts to unauthorized access. IIS is a complete Web and FTP (File Transfer Protocol) server included with recent Windows versions. Although Windows 2000 Server and Windows Server 2003 include a full version of IIS, Windows 2000 Professional and Windows XP Professional include a mini version that allows these computers to host a single Web site. In this exercise, you look at the logging capabilities of a Windows 2000 Professional computer.

Exercise 1.7.3.1: Installing IIS

In this exercise, you install IIS on a Windows 2000 Professional computer. You can also do this exercise on a Windows XP Professional computer:

1. Log on to the Windows 2000 computer as an administrator.
2. Click Start, Settings, Control Panel, Add/Remove Programs.
3. Click Add/Remove Windows Components.
4. In the Windows Components Wizard that starts, select Internet Information Services (IIS) and then click Next.
5. When prompted, insert the Windows 2000 Professional CD-ROM and click OK.
6. Click Finish when the completion page appears.
7. Close Add/Remove Programs.

Exercise 1.7.3.2: Configuring IIS Logging

In this exercise, you study the logging properties available with IIS on a Windows 2000 Professional computer. You then access the computer's default Web site and note the information that was logged. You can also perform this exercise from a Windows XP Professional computer:

1. Control Panel should still be open from the previous exercise. Click Administrative Tools, and then double-click Internet Services Manager.

On a Windows XP computer, the Control Panel Administrative Tools icon is called Internet Information Services.

2. Expand the local computer entry, right-click Default Web site, and choose Properties.
3. On the Web Site tab of the Default Web Site Properties dialog box, ensure that the Enable Logging check box is selected. This check box is selected by default. Then click Properties.
4. In the Extended Logging Properties dialog box that opens, select Daily for the log time period if it is not already selected. Note the default log file directory (see Figure 1.29), and then click OK.

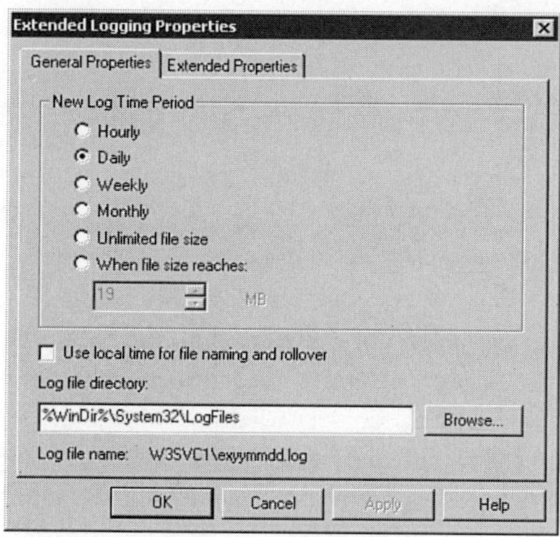

Figure 1.29 IIS logs all visits to the Web site to the **LogFiles** folder by default.

5. Select the Home Directory tab. Ensure that the Log Visits option is selected, and then click OK. This option logs all visits to your computer's Web site.
6. To test logging of visits to the Web site, click Start, Run, and type `http://localhost` in the Run dialog box. Click OK.
7. Internet Explorer opens with a default Windows 2000 message informing you that no default page is specified. This appears because you have not configured any Web pages for the site running on your computer. Close Internet Explorer.

8. Open My Computer and navigate to the location of the log files that was specified on the Extended Logging Properties dialog box (by default, `C:\Winnt\System32\LogFiles`). You will see a `W3SVC1` folder.

9. Open this folder and open the log file contained therein. As shown in Figure 1.30, the log file opens in Notepad and displays information about your visit to the local Web site.

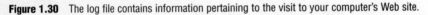

```
ex040714.log - Notepad
File Edit Format Help
#Software: Microsoft Internet Information Services 5.0
#Version: 1.0
#Date: 2004-07-14 21:13:28
#Fields: time c-ip cs-method cs-uri-stem sc-status
21:13:28 127.0.0.1 GET /iisstart.asp 302
21:13:28 127.0.0.1 GET /localstart.asp 401
21:13:30 127.0.0.1 GET /localstart.asp 200
21:13:30 127.0.0.1 GET /win2000.gif 304
21:13:30 127.0.0.1 GET /warning.gif 304
21:13:30 127.0.0.1 GET /web.gif 304
21:13:30 127.0.0.1 GET /mmc.gif 304
21:13:30 127.0.0.1 GET /help.gif 304
21:13:30 127.0.0.1 GET /print.gif 304
21:13:31 127.0.0.1 GET /iishelp/Default.htm 304
21:13:31 127.0.0.1 GET /iishelp/iis/misc/default.asp 200
21:13:31 127.0.0.1 GET /iishelp/iis/misc/navbar.asp 200
21:13:31 127.0.0.1 GET /iishelp/iis/misc/contents.asp 200
21:13:31 127.0.0.1 GET /iishelp/iis/misc/navpad.gif 304
21:13:31 127.0.0.1 GET /iishelp/iis/htm/core/iiwltop.htm 304
21:13:31 127.0.0.1 GET /iishelp/iis/misc/ismhd.gif 304
21:13:31 127.0.0.1 GET /iishelp/iis/misc/MS_logo.gif 304
21:13:31 127.0.0.1 GET /iishelp/iis/misc/Cont.gif 304
21:13:31 127.0.0.1 GET /iishelp/iis/misc/NoIndex.gif 304
21:13:31 127.0.0.1 GET /iishelp/iis/misc/NoSearch.gif 304
21:13:31 127.0.0.1 GET /iishelp/iis/misc/print.gif 304
21:13:31 127.0.0.1 GET /iishelp/iis/misc/synch.gif 304
21:13:32 127.0.0.1 GET /iishelp/common/coua.css 304
21:13:32 127.0.0.1 GET /iishelp/iis/misc/cohhc.hhc 304
21:13:32 127.0.0.1 GET /iishelp/iis/htm/core/iis_banr.gif 304
```

Figure 1.30 The log file contains information pertaining to the visit to your computer's Web site.

10. For the purposes of this exercise, you are not concerned about the content of the log file. The only important fact is that information pertaining to the visit to your Web site has been recorded. On a production Web site, you could locate information pertaining to any access to the site, including operational problems or attempts at hacking the site.

11. Close all dialog boxes.

12. (optional) Access the Windows 2000 Professional Web site from another computer on the network. You should see an Under Construction page. Then return to the Windows 2000 Professional computer and repeat Steps 8 to 10. You should see details of this visit added to the log file.

Exercise 1.7.4: System Scanning

Although administrators can scan systems and networks to detect security vulnerabilities or weaknesses, intruders can also scan systems and networks to detect weak points that are simple to attack. A free open-source utility originally written by a reformed hacker is available from Insecure.org. In this exercise, you download and test this utility, which is called Nmap, and then look at several other scanning tools:

1. Navigate to http://www.insecure.org/nmap/index.html and study the features provided by Nmap. Follow the various links on this page to obtain additional information about this product.
2. To download Nmap for Windows, proceed to the Windows section on the download page, select the link, and follow the instructions that are displayed. Also download the WinPcap (Windows Packet Capture Library) file from the link provided. You can save both downloads to a floppy disk for extraction to whatever computer you desire.

If you have a computer running Unix or Linux, follow the instructions on this Web page to download an appropriate version of Nmap.

3. Extract the zip file to a folder on the root drive.
4. Double-click the WinPcap folder to start the installation of WinPcap. Then follow the instructions presented by the installation wizard.
5. In the folder containing the extracted Nmap files, double-click the `nmap_performance` Registry file, and choose Yes when asked whether you want to add the information to the Registry. Then click OK to acknowledge that the information was added to the Registry.
6. Open a command prompt, change to the folder in which you installed Nmap, and type **`Nmap`** without any parameters to see the available options.
7. Experiment with the options to see what output is produced.

In addition to Nmap, a large number of port scanning tools are available on the Internet. As an adjunct to this exercise, look at the following options to study a few other available scanners:

1. For an overview of port scanning that is applicable to any computer that communicates using TCP/IP, go to http://www.siterecon.com/PortScanning.aspx as well as the links on this page. How many ports are available on a computer, and what are they used for?
2. Tom Lancaster provides a concise summary of several security scanners at http://searchwin2000.techtarget.com/tip/0,289483,sid1_gci970127,00.html?track=NL-122&ad=484994 and at

http://searchwin2000.techtarget.com/tip/0,289483,sid1_gci970110,00.html?track=NL-122&ad=485487. Note some of the conveniences that he mentions and follow the links provided for further information.

3. Follow the link provided by Lancaster for GFI LANguard, which is a freeware network security scanner that scans computers and networks for NetBIOS information, open ports, shares, and security issues. You might want to download this program and perform similar exercises to those described for Nmap.
4. Nessus is a free, powerful Unix-based scanning tool. Go to http://www.nessus.org and follow the links to research the features of this tool. A Windows-based version of this tool, named NeWT 2.0, is also available. You might want to study the features of this tool.
5. SAINT is a security scanner for Windows-based computers that scans TCP and User Datagram Protocol (UDP) ports on the network for vulnerabilities. It is based on the SATAN (Security Administrator's Tool for Analyzing Networks) Unix scanning tool. Go to http://www.saintcorporation.com/products/saint_engine.html and navigate the links provided to obtain more information about SATAN and SAINT.
6. Internet Security Systems (ISS) offers a Windows-based scanning tool called ISS System Scanner. Navigate to http://www.iss.net/issEn/delivery/prdetail.jsp?type=ISS&oid=14558 and study the features of this tool. Compare the various tools profiled in this section, including their usefulness as tools for scanning networks for security holes.

What Did I Just Learn?

Now that you have studied auditing, logging, and system scanning, let's take a moment to review all the critical items you've experienced in this lab:

- You can configure computers and networks for auditing of logon attempts, configuration changes, file and folder access, and other security-related events. Be sure that you configure auditing carefully because logs can fill up large amounts of disk space rapidly. Remember that logs only serve their purpose if you review them regularly.
- Web server applications like IIS provide for logging of access to a Web site and other actions performed by visitors to the site.

- Many port scanners are available both as free tools and commercial versions. You can use them to scan computers and networks for vulnerabilities. Intruders use scanners to identify vulnerable ports on computers from which they can use other tools to launch attacks.

Need to Know More?

For further information on access control, see the following:

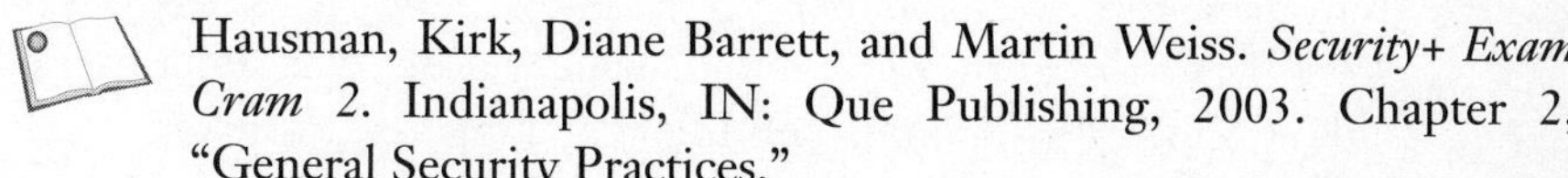
Hausman, Kirk, Diane Barrett, and Martin Weiss. *Security+ Exam Cram 2*. Indianapolis, IN: Que Publishing, 2003. Chapter 2, "General Security Practices."

King, Todd. *Security+ Training Guide*. Indianapolis, IN: Que Publishing, 2003. Chapter 2, "General Security Concepts."

For further information on Windows 2000 Professional access control lists, consult the following:

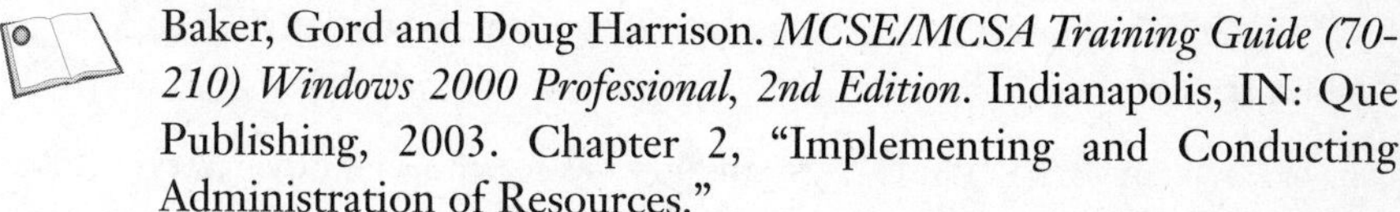
Baker, Gord and Doug Harrison. *MCSE/MCSA Training Guide (70-210) Windows 2000 Professional, 2nd Edition*. Indianapolis, IN: Que Publishing, 2003. Chapter 2, "Implementing and Conducting Administration of Resources."

For further information on Windows XP Professional access control lists, consult the following:

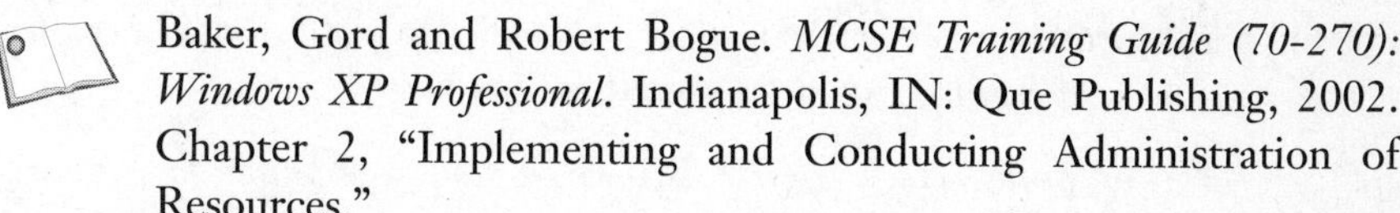
Baker, Gord and Robert Bogue. *MCSE Training Guide (70-270): Windows XP Professional*. Indianapolis, IN: Que Publishing, 2002. Chapter 2, "Implementing and Conducting Administration of Resources."

For further information on general Unix access control, see the following:

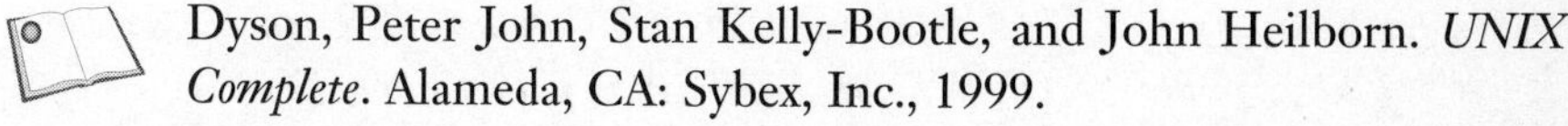
Dyson, Peter John, Stan Kelly-Bootle, and John Heilborn. *UNIX Complete*. Alameda, CA: Sybex, Inc., 1999.

For further information on authentication, consult the following resources:

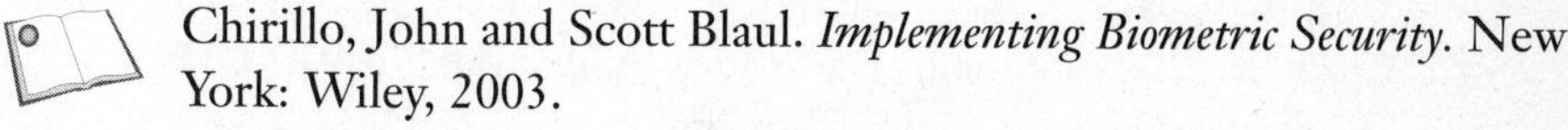
Chirillo, John and Scott Blaul. *Implementing Biometric Security*. New York: Wiley, 2003.

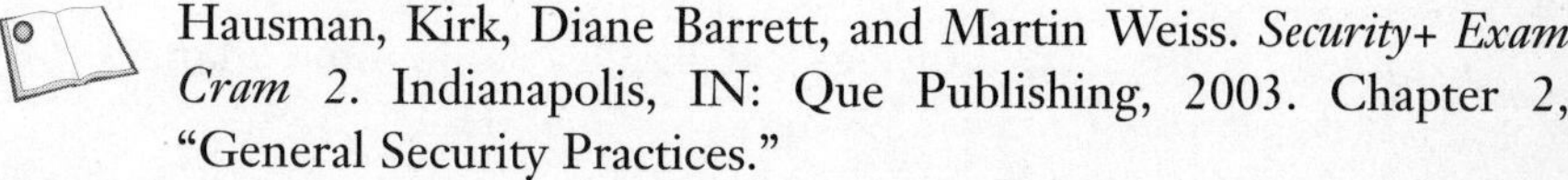
Hausman, Kirk, Diane Barrett, and Martin Weiss. *Security+ Exam Cram 2*. Indianapolis, IN: Que Publishing, 2003. Chapter 2, "General Security Practices."

King, Todd. *Security+ Training Guide*. Indianapolis, IN: Que Publishing, 2003. Chapter 2, "General Security Concepts."

Smith, Ben and Brian Komar. *Microsoft Windows Security Resource Kit*. Redmond, WA: Microsoft Press, 2003. Chapter 3, "Securing User Accounts and Passwords."

For further information on Group Policy, see

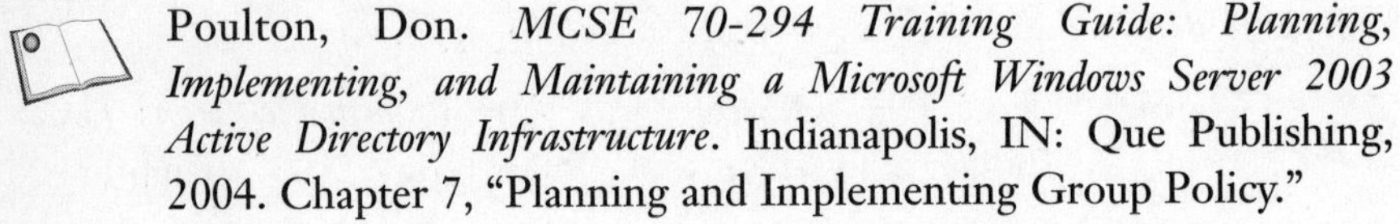

Poulton, Don. *MCSE 70-294 Training Guide: Planning, Implementing, and Maintaining a Microsoft Windows Server 2003 Active Directory Infrastructure*. Indianapolis, IN: Que Publishing, 2004. Chapter 7, "Planning and Implementing Group Policy."

Bersinic, Damir and Rob Scrimger. *MCSE 70-217 Training Guide: Windows 2000 Directory Services Infrastructure, Second Edition*. Indianapolis, IN: Que Publishing, 2003. Chapter 6, "Using Group Policy to Manage Users," and Chapter 8, "Managing Security Using Group Policy."

For further information on services and dependencies, consult the following Web site:

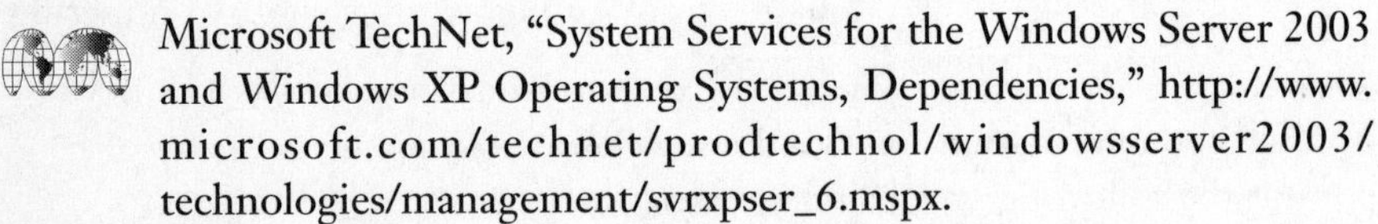

Microsoft TechNet, "System Services for the Windows Server 2003 and Windows XP Operating Systems, Dependencies," http://www.microsoft.com/technet/prodtechnol/windowsserver2003/technologies/management/svrxpser_6.mspx.

For further information on cyberspace attacks, including additional examples of the types of attacks discussed here, see these books:

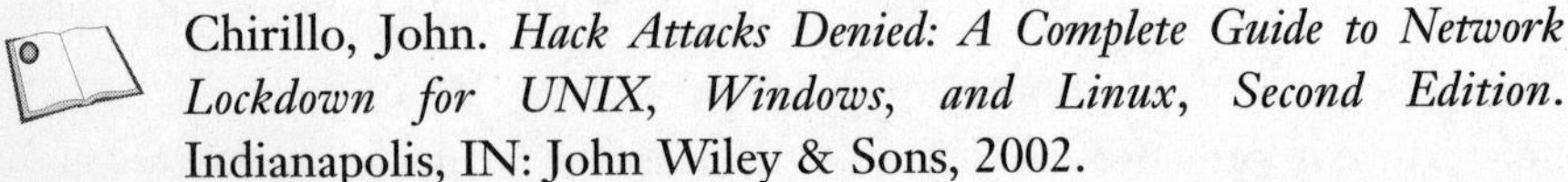

Chirillo, John. *Hack Attacks Denied: A Complete Guide to Network Lockdown for UNIX, Windows, and Linux, Second Edition*. Indianapolis, IN: John Wiley & Sons, 2002.

Chirillo, John. *Hack Attacks Revealed: A Complete Reference to Network Lockdown for UNIX, Windows, and Linux with Custom Security Toolkit, Second Edition*. Indianapolis, IN: John Wiley & Sons, 2002.

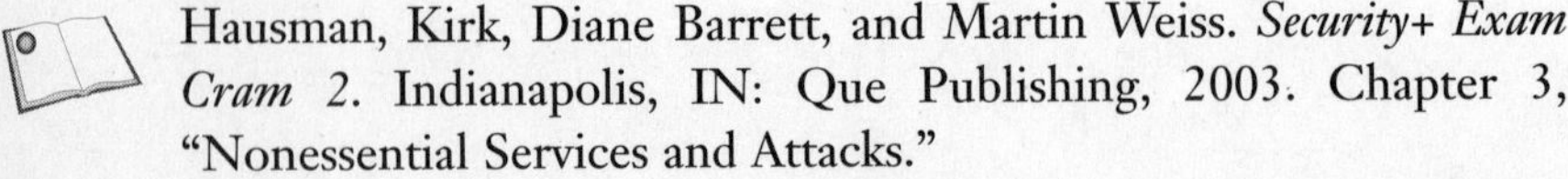

Hausman, Kirk, Diane Barrett, and Martin Weiss. *Security+ Exam Cram 2*. Indianapolis, IN: Que Publishing, 2003. Chapter 3, "Nonessential Services and Attacks."

Jones, Keith, Mike Shema, and Bradley C. Johnson. *Anti-Hacker Toolkit, Second Edition*. New York: McGraw-Hill Osborne, 2002.

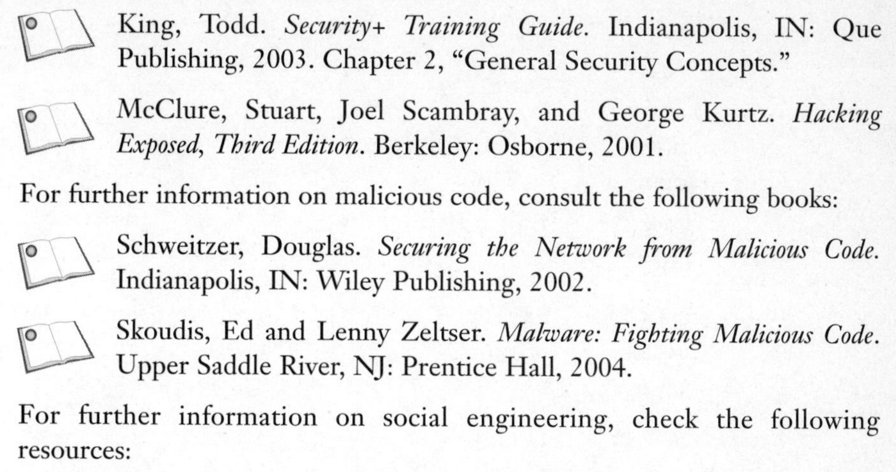

King, Todd. *Security+ Training Guide*. Indianapolis, IN: Que Publishing, 2003. Chapter 2, "General Security Concepts."

McClure, Stuart, Joel Scambray, and George Kurtz. *Hacking Exposed, Third Edition*. Berkeley: Osborne, 2001.

For further information on malicious code, consult the following books:

Schweitzer, Douglas. *Securing the Network from Malicious Code*. Indianapolis, IN: Wiley Publishing, 2002.

Skoudis, Ed and Lenny Zeltser. *Malware: Fighting Malicious Code*. Upper Saddle River, NJ: Prentice Hall, 2004.

For further information on social engineering, check the following resources:

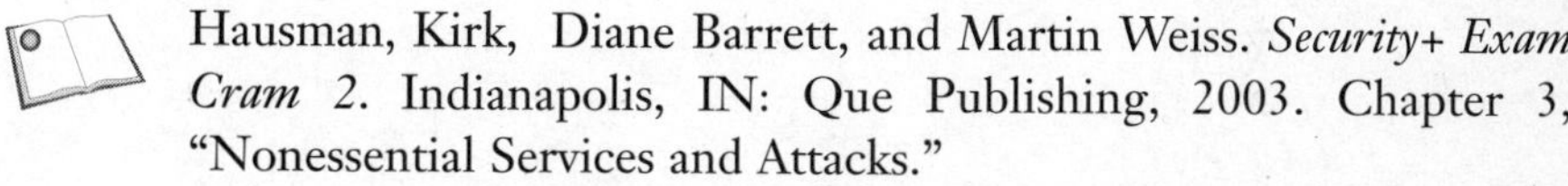

Hausman, Kirk, Diane Barrett, and Martin Weiss. *Security+ Exam Cram 2*. Indianapolis, IN: Que Publishing, 2003. Chapter 3, "Nonessential Services and Attacks."

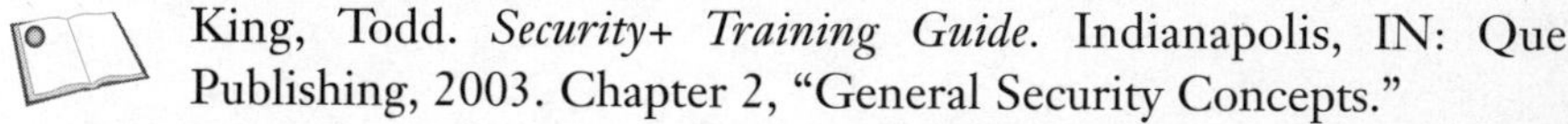

King, Todd. *Security+ Training Guide*. Indianapolis, IN: Que Publishing, 2003. Chapter 2, "General Security Concepts."

SecurityDocs.com provides updated references to articles on social-engineering exploits at http://www.securitydocs.com/Hacks/Social_Engineering.

For further information on auditing, logging, and system scanning, see the following books:

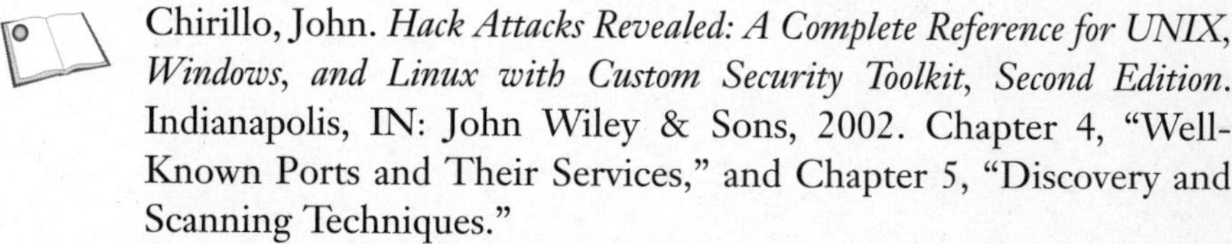

Chirillo, John. *Hack Attacks Revealed: A Complete Reference for UNIX, Windows, and Linux with Custom Security Toolkit, Second Edition*. Indianapolis, IN: John Wiley & Sons, 2002. Chapter 4, "Well-Known Ports and Their Services," and Chapter 5, "Discovery and Scanning Techniques."

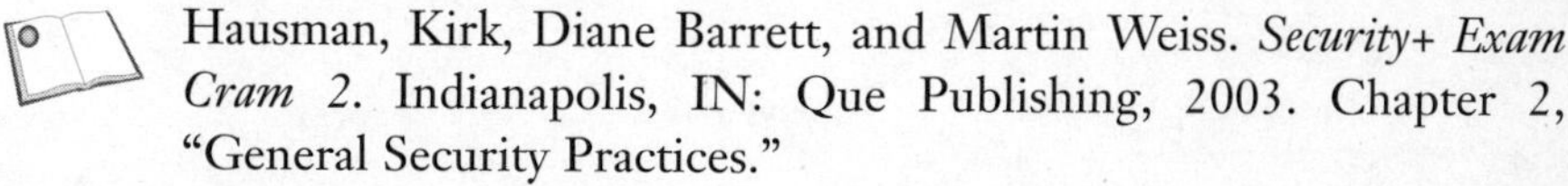

Hausman, Kirk, Diane Barrett, and Martin Weiss. *Security+ Exam Cram 2*. Indianapolis, IN: Que Publishing, 2003. Chapter 2, "General Security Practices."

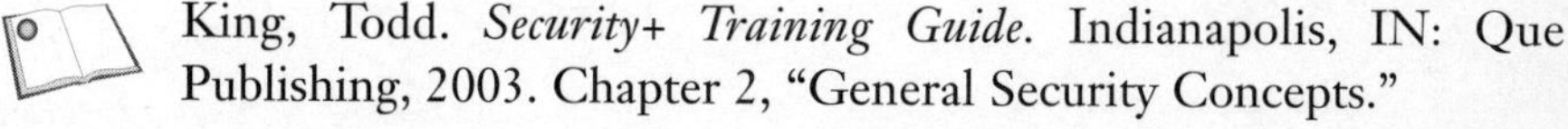

King, Todd. *Security+ Training Guide*. Indianapolis, IN: Que Publishing, 2003. Chapter 2, "General Security Concepts."

Communication Security

In this day and age of a mobile workforce, most companies have employees that need to access the corporate network from locations such as customer offices, hotels, or home. Such remote access to a network brings with it a new set of security problems that you must be familiar with for success on the Security+ exam.

The following is a list of the exam objectives you will be covering in this chapter:

- 2.1 Recognize and understand the administration of the following types of remote access technologies:
  - 802.1x
  - VPN (Virtual Private Network)
  - RADIUS (Remote Authentication Dial-In User Service)
  - TACACS (Terminal Access Controller Access Control System)
  - L2TP/PPTP (Layer Two Tunneling Protocol/Point to Point Tunneling Protocol)
  - SSH (Secure Shell)
  - IPSEC (Internet Protocol Security)
  - Vulnerabilities
- 2.2 Recognize and understand the administration of the following email security concepts:
  - S/MIME (Secure Multipurpose Internet Mail Extensions)
  - PGP (Pretty Good Privacy) like technologies

- Vulnerabilities
  - Spam
  - Hoaxes
- 2.3 Recognize and understand the administration of the following Internet security concepts:
  - SSL/TLS (Secure Sockets Layer/Transport Layer Security)
  - HTTP/S (Hypertext Transfer Protocol/Hypertext Transfer Protocol over Secure Sockets Layer)
  - Instant Messaging
    - Vulnerabilities
    - Packet Sniffing
    - Privacy
  - Vulnerabilities
    - Java Script
    - ActiveX
    - Buffer Overflows
    - Cookies
    - Signed Applets
    - CGI (Common Gateway Interface)
    - SMTP (Simple Mail Transfer Protocol) Relay
- 2.4 Recognize and understand the administration of the following directory security concepts:
  - SSL/TLS (Secure Sockets Layer/Transport Layer Security)
  - LDAP (Lightweight Directory Access Protocol)
- 2.5 Recognize and understand the administration of the following file transfer protocols and concepts:
  - S/FTP (File Transfer Protocol)
  - Blind FTP (File Transfer Protocol)/Anonymous
  - File Sharing

- Vulnerabilities
  - Packet Sniffing
  - 8.3 Naming Conventions
- 2.6 Recognize and understand the administration of the following wireless technologies and concepts:
  - WTLS (Wireless Transport Layer Security)
  - 802.11 and 802.11x
  - WEP/WAP (Wired Equivalent Privacy/Wireless Application Protocol)
  - Vulnerabilities
    - Site Surveys

2.1: Administering Remote Access Security

Remote access refers to connecting to a computer from a remote location. This chapter covers a review of standards that are integral to remote access, creation and administration of remote access connections, and use of common authentication and security protocols. CompTIA included this objective domain because communications between different computers and networks is an important facet of all businesses today and is one of the most exploited areas of vulnerability. The Security+ technician is expected to know how to protect from attack the various areas of communication, including remote access across the Internet, email, dedicated communication lines, and wireless communications.

Exercise 2.1.1: 802.1x and Its Vulnerabilities

The Institute for Electrical and Electronics Engineers (IEEE) provides a series of standards called 802.1x that are related to port-based network access control as it applies to both wired and wireless communications. These standards define the characteristics of authentication and authorization in local area networks (LANs) and metropolitan area networks (MANs) and focus on communications taking place at the Open Systems Interconnection (OSI)

Physical and Data Link layers (Layers 1 and 2 of the OSI model). In this exercise, you focus on researching some attributes of the 802.1x standards.

1. Connect to the Internet and navigate to http://www.ieee802.org/. This site introduces the IEEE 802 series of standards. For more details, select the download link. Those of you who are interested can download the detailed paper on the 802.1x port-based network access control standards.

If the URLs provided in this or other exercises no longer exist, simply use your favorite search engine to locate other sites that contain information pertinent to the topics at hand.

2. For a more readable introduction to 802.1x, navigate to http://www.nwfusion.com/research/2002/0506whatisit.html. This page introduces you to the Point-to-Point Protocol (PPP), which is commonly used for dial-up Internet access. Which protocol was developed to provide additional security for transmissions using PPP? How does this relate to wireless transmissions that are governed by 802.1x?
3. Note and distinguish the three factors that come together in the use of 802.1x: supplicant, authentication server, and authenticator. Also note the procedure used in setting up a communications channel.
4. Another readable introduction to 802.1x appears at http://www.wi-fiplanet.com/tutorials/article.php/1041171. This page introduces Wired Equivalent Privacy (WEP) as it relates to 802.1x. What is the major vulnerability with 802.1x? What extensions to Extensible Authentication Protocol (EAP) are available, and what are their purposes? Explore the links to obtain information about the interoperation of the 802.1x standard with Windows XP.

Remote access refers to connecting to a computer from a remote location. This contrasts with remote control, which refers to the use of a program such as those discussed in Chapter 1, "General Security Concepts" (including Microsoft Remote Desktop) to control a computer remotely.

802.1x utilizes EAP for communicating between the supplicant and the authenticator.

Exercise 2.1.2: Configuring a VPN in Windows 2000 Server

Users connecting to a company network through a public network such as the Internet can use a virtual private network (VPN) that secures traffic by creating a tunnel through which data travels in an encapsulated stream. The data is protected by means of a tunneling protocol such as the Point-to-Point Tunneling (PPTP) or the Layer 2 Tunneling Protocol (L2TP) used in conjunction with IP Security (IPSec).

In this exercise, you configure a server running Windows 2000 Server as a Remote Access Service (RAS) server that can accept VPN connections from a client computer. You can also do this exercise on a computer running Windows Server 2003. The steps are slightly different but accomplish the same result. If you have only one network card in your computer, you can only configure the computer as a dial-up server. If you have two or more network cards, you can select the options to configure a VPN server. The configuration process is similar in both instances.

For more information on setting up and configuring Routing and Remote Access Service (RRAS) on Windows 2000 Server computers, consult the MCSA/MCSE 70-216 training guide referenced in the "Need to Know More?" section:

1. Log on to the computer running Windows 2000 Server as an administrator.
2. Click Start, Programs, Administrative Tools, Routing and Remote Access.
3. If the server is still configured as a router from Exercise 1.1.3 in Chapter 1, right-click the server name and choose Disable Routing and Remote Access. Click Yes to accept the warning that appears.
4. Right-click the server name and choose Configure and Enable Routing and Remote Access. The Routing and Remote Access Server Setup Wizard starts.
5. Click Next to bypass the welcome screen. On the Common Configurations screen, select Remote Access Server, as shown in Figure 2.1. Select the Virtual Private Network (VPN) Server option if you have two or more network interface cards, and then click Next.

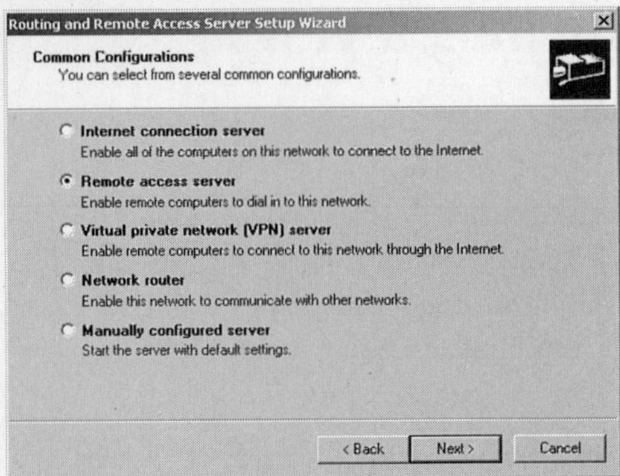

Figure 2.1 The Routing and Remote Access Server Setup Wizard provides several options for configuring a RAS server.

6. On the Remote Client Protocols screen, make sure that TCP/IP is listed in the Protocols field and that Yes, All of the Required Protocols Are on This List is selected. Click Next. If TCP/IP does not appear, select No, I Need to Add Protocols and follow the instructions provided.
7. On the IP Address Assignment screen, select the means by which IP addresses will be assigned on your network. When performing this exercise on a test network without Dynamic Host Configuration Protocol (DHCP), select the From a Specified Range of Addresses option, and then click Next.
8. Supply the IP address information on the Address Range Assignment screen, and then click Next.
9. On the Managing Multiple Remote Access Servers screen, select Yes, Set Up This Server to Work with a RADIUS Server, and then click Next. You configure a Remote Authentication Dial-In User Service (RADIUS) server in the next exercise.
10. On the RADIUS Server Selection screen, type the name of the server in the Primary RADIUS Server text box. Type a password in the Shared Secret text box, and then click Next.
11. Click Finish to complete setting up the RAS server. If you receive a message about supporting the relaying of DHCP messages, click OK to accept this message.

Make sure you understand the difference between PPP and PPTP. PPP is an industry-standard line protocol for data transmission that encapsulates packets being transmitted over a point-to-point link such as a dial-up connection. PPTP is a tunneling protocol that creates a secure tunnel across an insecure medium such as the Internet. It effectively turns the Internet into a VPN for secure data transmission.

The primary purpose of a RADIUS server on the network is to provide centralized authentication for a series of RAS servers. It provides a single point from which you can configure the conditions under which a remote user can connect to your network. You can utilize multiple RADIUS servers for fault tolerance and load balancing.

Exercise 2.1.3: Configuring Remote Access Authentication

Windows 2000 Server provides the Microsoft implementation of RADIUS as a centralized authentication service for remote access clients. This version is known as the Internet Authentication Service (IAS). In this exercise, you configure a computer running Windows 2000 Server for IAS. You can use the same server you used in Exercise 2.1.2 to complete this exercise. Steps on a computer running Windows Server 2003 are similar:

1. Log on to the computer running Windows 2000 Server as an administrator.
2. Click Start, Settings, Control Panel, Add/Remove Programs.
3. Click Add/Remove Windows Components.
4. Highlight Networking Services (do not select the check box, which appears selected but shaded because a portion of these components are installed), and click Details.
5. In the Networking Services dialog box, select the check box for Internet Authentication Service and then click OK. Click Next.
6. If the server is configured as a terminal server from Exercise 1.4.2.2 in Chapter 1, you receive a Terminal Services Setup screen. Remote administration mode should be selected. Click Next to begin installing IAS.
7. When the completion screen appears, click Finish. Close the Add/Remove Programs application and close Control Panel.
8. Click Start, Programs, Administrative Tools, Internet Authentication Service. The Internet Authentication Service console opens.
9. Right-click Clients and choose New Client.

10. In the Add Client dialog box, type a name for the remote access server (which is the RADIUS client). Ensure that RADIUS appears in the Protocol drop-down list, and then click Next.

11. In the Client Information dialog box, type the IP address of the remote access server. Ensure that RADIUS Standard appears in the Client Vendor drop-down list. Type and confirm a password in the Shared Secret and Confirm Shared Secret text boxes and then click Finish. This should be the same password you entered in Step 10 of the previous exercise.

12. The server whose information you entered in Step 9 appears on the right side of the Internet Authentication Service console, as shown in Figure 2.2.

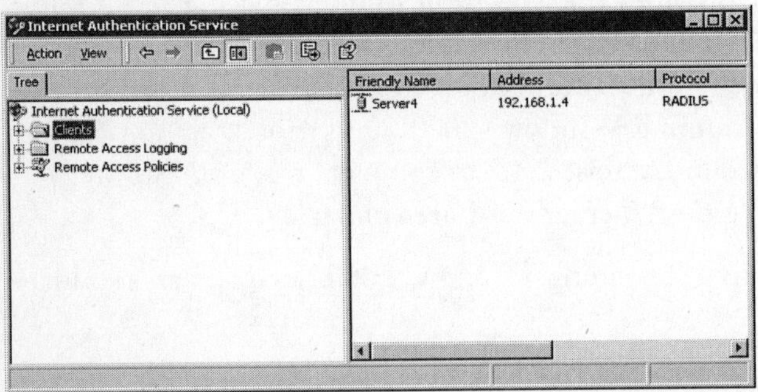

Figure 2.2 You specify information for the RAS server in the Internet Authentication Service console so that the RAS server can use RADIUS.

13. To authenticate the connection, the users that intend to use the connection must be authorized in their account properties. To do this for a domain account in Active Directory, open Active Directory Users and Computers.

14. Right-click the appropriate user account and choose Properties.

15. Select the Dial-in tab.

16. Under Remote Access Permission (Dial-in or VPN), select Allow Access, and then click OK (see Figure 2.3).

You can configure remote access policies on the IAS server that are similar to those we looked at for access to a router under rule-based access control in Chapter 1 (see Exercise 1.1.3). For more information on other properties you can configure for the remote access connection, refer to the training guide for Microsoft Exam 70-216 in the "Need to Know More?" section.

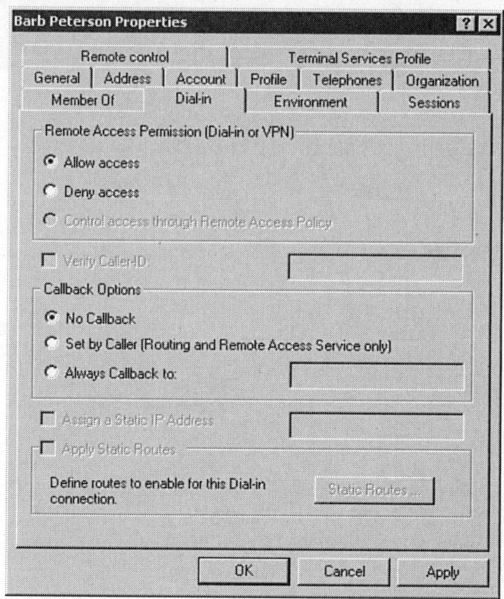

Figure 2.3 Allow a user to connect by means of remote access.

Exercise 2.1.4: Configuring Client Connections

After you configure a RAS server with its authentication process, you are ready to configure client computers for connection to the server. In this exercise, you set up the client side of a VPN connection on a Windows 2000 Professional computer. You can also do this exercise on a Windows XP Professional computer; the steps are slightly different but accomplish the same objective:

1. Log on to the Windows 2000 Professional computer as an administrator.
2. Right-click the My Network Places desktop icon and choose Properties.
3. Double-click the Make New Connection icon. The Network Connection Wizard starts, displaying a welcome screen.

On a computer running Windows XP, click Start, Control Panel, Network and Internet Connections, Network Connections. In the top-left side of the Network Connections window, select Create a New Connection. The New Connection Wizard starts. (The Network Connection Wizard is called the New Connection Wizard in Windows XP Professional.)

4. If a Location Information dialog box opens, type the information requested and then click OK. Click Next.

5. On the Network Connection Type screen (see Figure 2.4), select Connect to a Private Network Through the Internet. Click Next again.

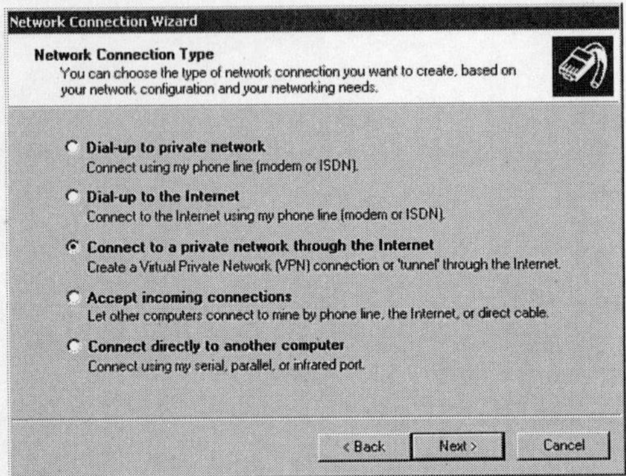

Figure 2.4 The Network Connection Wizard enables you to create several different types of remote access connections in Windows 2000.

6. On the Destination Address screen, type the fully qualified domain name (FQDN) or IP address of the server to which you are connecting, and then click Next.

7. On the Connection Availability screen, select For All Users if you want to make the VPN connection available to anyone who is logged on to the computer. Otherwise select Only for Myself. Click Next.

8. On the completion screen, type a name for the connection such as the name of the company to which you are connecting. Click Finish to complete creating the connection.

9. A Connect [*name*] dialog box opens. To connect now, type the username and password and then click Connect. If you configured the RAS and RADIUS servers properly and authorized the user account for connection, you will receive “Registering your computer on the network” and “Authenticated” messages, and an icon will appear in the Network and Dial-up Connections window (see Figure 2.5).

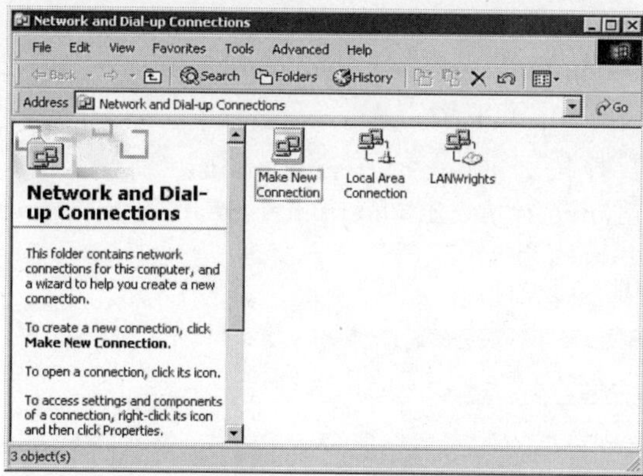

Figure 2.5 Windows 2000 Professional displays an icon for the connection you created in the Network and Dial-up Connections window.

Exercise 2.1.5: Configuring IPSec

IPSec is a series of security protocols that enable encryption, authentication, and data integrity over IP. It is commonly used to secure transmissions that use L2TP for encapsulated transmission across insecure networks such as the Internet. In this exercise, you configure the level of IPSec security required for network and VPN communications in an Active Directory domain. You can do this exercise from a computer running Windows 2000 Server that is configured as a domain controller; the steps are identical in Windows Server 2003:

1. Log on to the computer running Windows 2000 Server as an administrator.
2. Click Start, Programs, Administrative Tools, Active Directory Users and Computers.
3. Right-click the domain and choose Properties.
4. On the Group Policy tab of the domain's Properties dialog box, select the Default Domain Policy Group Policy object (GPO) and click Edit. This opens the Group Policy console focused on this GPO.
5. Navigate to the Computer Configuration\Windows Settings\Security Settings\IP Security Policies on Active Directory node. As shown in Figure 2.6, three default policies appear on the right side. The following policies are available:
   - *Client (Respond Only)*—Uses IPSec when the computer with which it is communicating requests the use of IPSec and supports Kerberos authentication.

- *Secure Server (Require Security)*—Requires that IPSec be used for all inbound and outbound communications and does not communicate with a computer that does not support IPSec.
- *Server (Request Security)*—The computer attempts to use IPSec but permits unsecured communications with computers that do not support IPSec (such as Windows 9x).

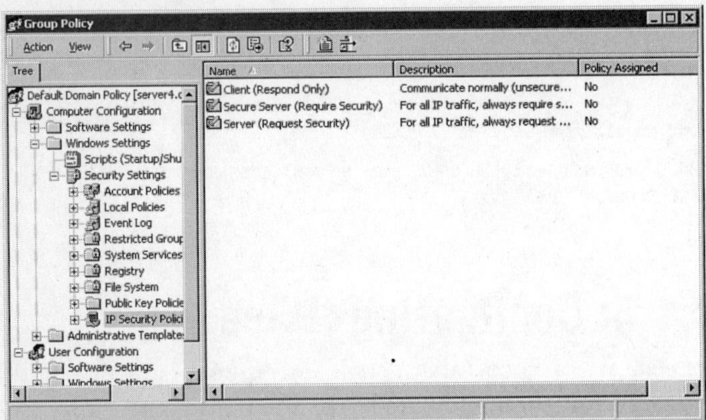

Figure 2.6 Three default security policies are available from the IP Security Policies on Active Directory node in the Group Policy console.

6. To assign a policy, right-click it and choose Assign. You may assign only one policy at any time.
7. To modify a policy's properties, right-click it and choose Properties. Look over the available options. Discussion of these options is beyond the scope of this Security+ lab manual.
8. When you are finished, close the Group Policy Object Editor.

You can also configure a local IP security policy on a local Windows 2000 Professional computer. This setting, available from the Local Security Settings console in Administrative Tools, provides the same security policies as described in this exercise.

IPSec operates at the Network layer (Layer 3) of the OSI networking model, not at the Application layer. Operating at this layer, IPSec is independent of the applications with which it is used. Users do not have to modify every application to suit IPSec's standards.

Exercise 2.1.6: Terminal Access Controller Access Control System (TACACS) and Secure Shell (SSH)

The primary goal of remote access methods is to ensure that only authorized users are granted access to network resources. Each remote access method has its own strengths and weaknesses: Just keeping their differences straight can be challenging. In this exercise, we look at one approach that outlines some strengths and weaknesses of using TACACS+ with SSH:

1. From a Web browser, go to http://www.sans.org/rr. This is the SANS Reading Room Web page. The reading room is a great repository of white papers on nearly every security topic imaginable.
2. Under the Category heading, choose Authentication. This link takes you to papers related to authentication methods, techniques, and issues.
3. Browse through the current papers, looking for TACACS+ and SSH. Take the time to read a couple of papers of interest to you. At the time of writing, two good possibilities are Understanding and Implementing TACACS+ at http://www.sans.org/rr/papers/index.php?id=117 and Implementing Secure Access to Cisco Devices Using TACACS+ and SSH at http://www.sans.org/rr/papers/index.php?id=1041.
4. After reading the papers of your choice, make a diagram of a client/server system using SSH and TACACS+. This diagram can be simple, but it should show where SSH and TACACS+ are used.
5. While still in your Web browser, search for TACACS+ and SSH vulnerabilities. Find at least two additional resources that address issues with these methods.

As you read through different resources, look for any issues that might arise from passing information from a client to server. Specifically, should clients be able to access the TACACS+ server? Where are usernames or passwords sent "in the clear?" What can be done about these or any vulnerabilities?

6. After you have a general understanding of how TACACS+ and SSH work and some of their vulnerabilities, update your diagram with appropriate notes. The notes should list and explain any controls that need to be in place to mitigate potential risks.

SANS (http://www.sans.org) is a great place to start your research. From there, don't forget to look at the bibliography of any papers you read.

Exercise 2.1.7: Remote Access Vulnerabilities

In this exercise, you research the subject of remote access vulnerabilities in general. Some common vulnerabilities include sniffing of packets, modification of data, identity spoofing, and errors or vulnerabilities introduced by users or administrators:

1. Joshua Hill of InfoGard Laboratories presents an analysis of RADIUS and its vulnerabilities at http://www.untruth.org/~josh/security/radius/radius-auth.html. What are some of the ways in which the shared secret or the user/password combination can be compromised? Note the types of attack that we have already investigated in Chapter 1. Hill also presents a link to a document that analyzes the TACACS+ protocol.

2. An article on password security and remote access sniffing vulnerabilities on Unix systems appears at http://unix.about.com/library/weekly/aa010702a.htm. Links include protection of SSH clients from vulnerabilities.

3. A white paper by Sun Microsystems at http://wwws.sun.com/software/whitepapers/solaris9/secureaccess.pdf discusses remote access vulnerabilities and Sun Solaris's solutions to these problems using its SSH extensions. What are some of the threats that this solution guards against? It offers a comparison of its SSH extensions with the protection that IPSec provides.

4. The use of packet filtering on Microsoft RRAS to avoid spoofing attacks is discussed at http://www.garykessler.net/library/nt_packet_filter.html. Although this article is aimed primarily at the Windows NT 4.0 RRAS service, its principles also apply to RRAS in Windows 2000 and Windows Server 2003. You can configure the same packet filters by clicking the Input Filters or Output Filters buttons, as required, on the General tab of the interface's Properties dialog box, as shown in Figure 2.7.

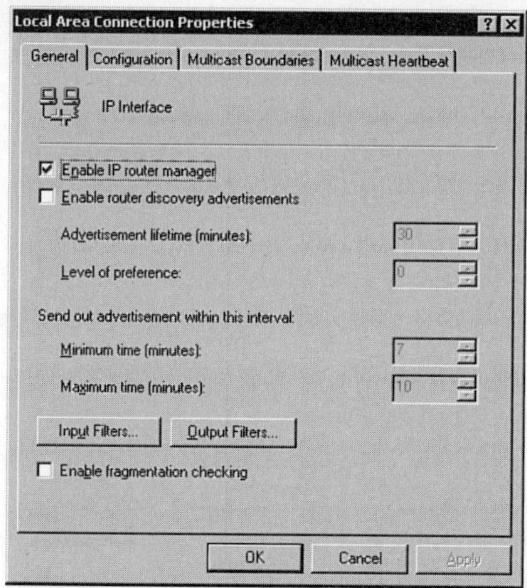

Figure 2.7 The General tab of a connection's Properties dialog box in Windows 2000 or Windows Server 2003 enables you to configure packet filters to help prevent spoofing attacks.

5. Glen Doss of Towson University presents a comprehensive discussion on the security aspects of remote access connections at http://www.gdoss.com/knowledge/ras_1.htm, plus its two sequel pages. Note the multiple system threats including weak passwords, multiple passwords, authentication replay, spoofing, and session hijacking. What are some of the solutions that Doss describes on the next two pages of his article? Look for some advantages and disadvantages of each, and try to decide how you might employ them on a network for which you are responsible.

Keep in mind that unsafe practices in local network computing such as writing passwords on sticky notes or allowing someone to watch while you are entering a username and password can also present vulnerabilities during remote access sessions. An example is a remote logon performed by a sales person from a customer's office location.

What Did I Just Learn?

Now that you have looked at several types of remote access technologies, let's take a moment to review all the critical items you've experienced in this lab:

- The IEEE has defined a series of 802.1x standards that address port-based remote access technologies applied to both wired and wireless communication. These standards define the characteristics of authentication and authorization in LANs and MANs.

- A VPN is a tunneling mechanism used to allow secure transmission of data across an insecure medium such as the Internet.
- RADIUS is a centralized means of authenticating remote access users. Microsoft provides a RADIUS solution called IAS, which is easily set up on a Windows server.
- You can configure Windows-based computers to support either PPTP or L2TP as tunneling protocols for secure remote access connections to remote-based servers.
- TACACS and its TACACS+ enhancement are another means of centralized authentication used by Unix servers.
- The IPSec protocol embraces a series of open standards that ensures private, encrypted IP network communication that can pass securely over any network, including the Internet. You can define policies that require the use of IPSec in Windows-based domains.

2.2: Administering Email Security

Email has become such a common means of communication in recent years that most of us don't think twice about sending messages to individuals and businesses anywhere. But email carries its problems, not limited to spam and viruses. This objective makes sure you understand the principles behind secure transmission of email and avoidance of problems.

Exercise 2.2.1: Secure Multipurpose Internet Mail Extensions (S/MIME) and Pretty Good Privacy (PGP)

S/MIME is an extension of Simple Mail Transfer Protocol (SMTP) that provides the ability to send nontext information such as images and audio in an email message. It adds encryption using the Rivest-Shamir-Adleman (RSA) algorithm to secure email transmission across the Internet. PGP is a scheme for encryption of email messages using ether the RSA or the Diffie-Hellman asymmetric encryption algorithms. In this exercise, you research the similarities and differences of these email security protocols and encryption technologies. You will study the various encryption algorithms in Chapter 4, "Basics of Cryptography."

1. Connect to the Internet and navigate to http://www.rsasecurity.com/rsalabs/node.asp?id=2292 for a concise definition of S/MIME.
2. Navigate to http://www.crazylinux.net/downloads/projects/PGPII.pdf for a summary of S/MIME and PGP that compares and contrasts the two technologies. What are some of the similarities and differences between S/MIME and PGP? In particular, which encryption technologies do S/MIME and PGP use?
3. OpenPGP is a newer extension of the PGP protocol that involves public-key cryptography for encrypting email. Navigate to http://www.openpgp.org/ and the various tabs on this site's home page to obtain information on this standard.
4. The Internet Mail Consortium at http://www.imc.org/smime-pgpmime.html compares OpenPGP to S/MIME. What are the important features of these technologies, and how do they differ? Follow the links on this page to obtain additional information.
5. Although the article is somewhat dated now, Bruce Schneier describes a Windows 95 screensaver that performs a brute-force crack on 40-bit Rivest's Cipher 2 (RC2) keys used by S/MIME. His point is to illustrate the inferiority of this encryption technique compared to Data Encryption Standard (DES) and Triple DES (3DES). Download this tool from http://www.schneier.com/smime.html and examine the instructions that are provided. If you have any email messages that are encrypted using S/MIME with RC2, try to decrypt the message with this tool.

Although S/MIME utilizes a symmetric cipher to encrypt email messages and a public-key algorithm for key exchange and digital signatures, PGP uses public and private keys for encryption and decryption of messages.

Exercise 2.2.2: PGP in Windows 2000

The PGP Corporation makes a free version of PGP available to personal users and students. In this exercise, you install and test the free PGP program. You can do this exercise from a computer running Windows 2000 Professional. (This exercise also works on a computer running Windows XP Home Edition or Professional.)

1. Log on to the computer running Windows 2000 Professional as an administrator.

2. Navigate to http://www.pgp.com/products/freeware.html and click the appropriate link to read the license restrictions of the free PGP product.
3. Accept the license agreement and download the program.
4. Extract the zip file and double-click `PGPx.exe` (where *x* is the version number of the program) to install the program.
5. Follow the instructions in the installation wizard. Be sure to read the Read Me instructions that are presented.
6. Install the component(s) pertinent to the email client(s) you are using (see Figure 2.8). Restart your computer when indicated.

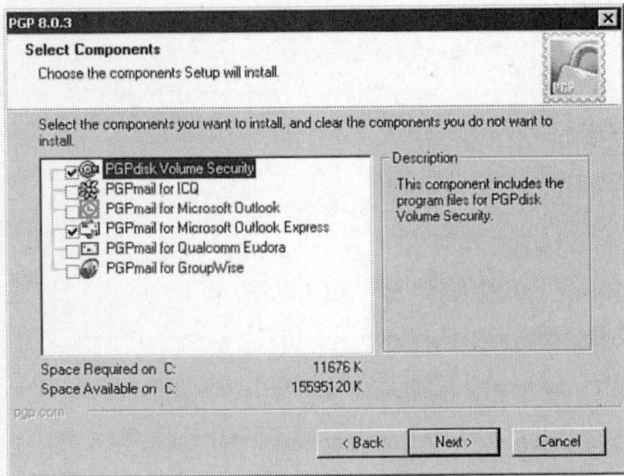

Figure 2.8 The free PGP program contains components for the most popular current email clients.

7. After restarting the computer, PGP presents a license window. For use of the PGP freeware, click Later.
8. Read the information on the PGP Key Generation Wizard welcome screen, and then click Next.
9. The wizard presents a Name and Email Assignment screen (see Figure 2.9). The information on this screen is associated with the public key that is part of the key pair being created. Type the correct name and address, and then click Next.
10. Type and confirm a passphrase that will protect your private key and that you can remember (see Figure 2.10). Click Next.
11. The key is generated. Click Next and then click Finish. PGP installs a padlock icon in the system tray.
12. Click the padlock to display the PGP menu (see Figure 2.11).

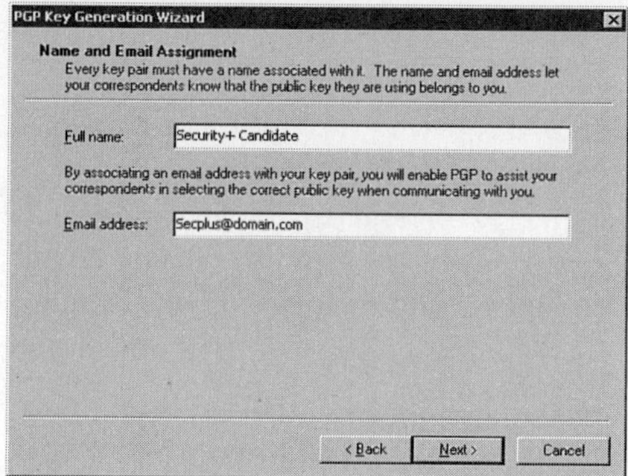

Figure 2.9 The information you provide on the Name and Email Assignment screen is associated with your public key.

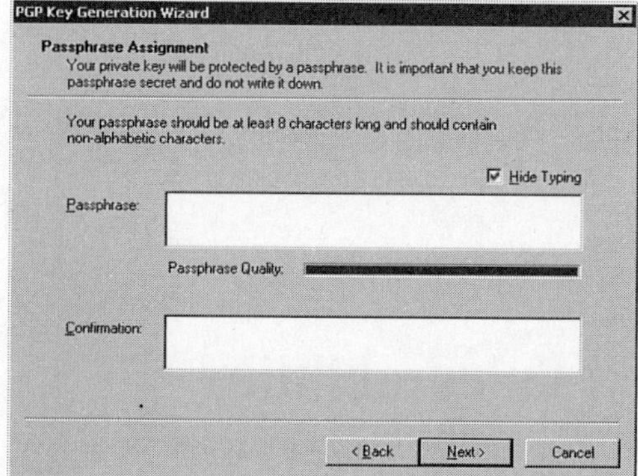

Figure 2.10 The passphrase protects your private key. Be sure to choose a phrase that is complicated but memorable.

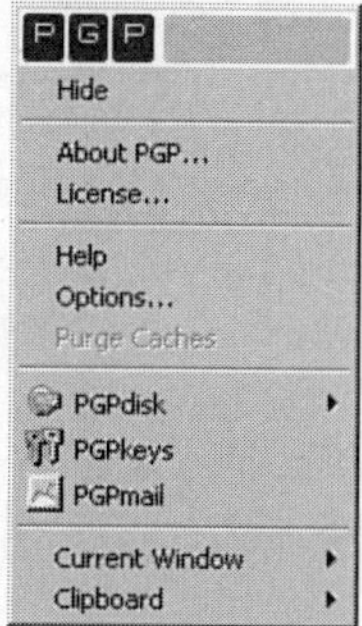

Figure 2.11 PGP provides a menu of available options.

13. By selecting PGPmail, you can display a toolbar with icons representing the tasks that the free PGP program can perform.

14. Select the keys button to display the key you created during installation.

15. Right-click this key and choose Key Properties to display the properties of the key. The dialog box that opens presents information about the key size, algorithm, key length, creation and expiry dates, fingerprint, and so on. You can change the passphrase from this dialog box if required. You can also select the Subkeys tab to replace or revoke subkeys if required.

16. You may exchange encrypted email messages with other users who have installed PGP by exchanging public keys with them.

Because these are public keys available to anyone, you can send them by regular email. Users retain their own private keys and keep them secret.

The passphrase is an important concept that you should understand for the Security+ exam. This phrase is used by PGP to encrypt and decrypt messages.

Exercise 2.2.3: Email Vulnerabilities

The ease of composing and transmitting email messages has led to its use for purposes that are less than honorable, such as the sending of spam, viruses, and hoax messages. In this exercise, you research these vulnerabilities:

1. Many good Web sites exist for finding information about the problem that spam presents to users and senders of email. Navigate to http://spam.abuse.net/ and one of the many links of this page or to the home pages of Internet security companies such as Symantec or McAfee.

2. One reason spammers can send such a large number of messages easily are that open SMTP relays exist on the Internet. They are improperly configured email servers that are vulnerable to being hijacked by spammers. Navigate to http://www.theallineed.com/computers/real_cause_spam.htm for a brief description of open SMTP relay servers. What are some of the consequences of your email server becoming an open SMTP relay?

3. Spam can be more than just a nuisance; it can be a vector for spreading malicious software to victimized computers. Navigate to http://searchsecurity.techtarget.com/tip/0,289483,sid14_gci961150,00.html?track=NL-363&ad=481860 for information on this aspect of the problem. You can find additional information from the links on this page.

4. Those of you who are involved with email servers running Microsoft Exchange Server should go to http://support.microsoft.com/?id=324958 and follow the procedures outlined in this article to test whether your server is operating as an open SMTP relay. You can then configure the server to block open SMTP relaying.

5. Those of you who are involved with Unix email servers running the Sendmail application should go to http://www.tracking-hackers.com/solutions/sendmail.html and follow suggestions on this page for testing and securing the email server. Note how the use of a honeypot can be beneficial in tracking spammers. (We study honeypots in Chapter 3, “Infrastructure Security.”)

6. Hoaxes are email messages that warn users about nonexistent viruses or other problems. They might also promise money, gifts, or other enticements. Some hoaxes instruct you to delete important system files, rendering your computer unbootable if you do so. Navigate to http://www.symantec.com/avcenter/hoax.html for a brief discussion of this problem and a list of hoaxes that have appeared in recent years.

What Did I Just Learn?

Now that you have looked at email security, let’s take a moment to review all the critical items you’ve experienced in this lab:

- S/MIME provides for the ability to send nontext information such as images and audio in an email message. It utilizes a symmetric cipher to encrypt messages and a public-key algorithm for key exchange and digital signatures.

- PGP encrypts email messages using either the RSA or the Diffie-Hellman encryption algorithm. This involves a combination of public and private keys for message encryption. You can easily install a free version on Windows-based computers for securing personal email.

- OpenPGP is a newer extension of the PGP protocol that involves public-key cryptography for encrypting email.

- Spammers can hijack an open SMTP relay machine to easily transmit their email messages.
- Hoaxes are email messages warning about nonexistent viruses or other problems. The message might actually contain a virus or instruct victims to delete important system files or perform other harmful acts on their computers.

2.3: Administering Internet Security

Businesses use Web servers to advertise their products and services on the Internet. If not properly configured, these servers can act as a gateway for intruders to access a company's internal network.

In its basic form, the Web uses Hypertext Transfer Protocol (HTTP) on TCP port 80. To allow for security in Web transactions, Internet vendors make use of Transport Layer Security (TLS), which provides encryption using methods such as DES to protect sensitive data such as credit-card numbers. Secure Sockets Layer (SSL) is a public key–based protocol that secures Web transactions such as credit-card data conducted over TCP port 443 with a 40-bit or 128-bit asymmetric key. Its communication occurs between the Application and Transport layers of the OSI model.

Exercise 2.3.1: Configuring IIS for SSL and HTTP/S

HTTP/S is simply HTTP over SSL. You know that you are connecting to a Web site over HTTP/S when the Web browser address indicates https://*servername* rather than http://*servername*.

In Chapter 1, you installed Internet Information Services (IIS) on a Windows 2000 computer and examined its logging capabilities. In this exercise, you configure the use of SSL and HTTP/S in IIS. Perform this exercise on the same computer you used in Exercises 1.7.3.1 and 1.7.3.2.

Exercise 2.3.1.1: Requesting a Web Server Certificate

The first step in configuring IIS for use of SSL is to obtain a Web server certificate from a certificate server. We look at the use of Windows 2000 Server Certificate Services in Chapter 4:

1. Log on to the Windows 2000 Professional computer as an administrator.

2. Click Start, Settings, Control Panel, Administrative Tools, Internet Services Manager.

3. Expand the entries in the left pane of the IIS console to locate your Web site, right-click the site, and choose Properties.

4. Select the Directory Security tab.

5. To request a certificate, click the Server Certificate command button. The Web Server Certificate Wizard starts.

6. Click Next, and on the Server Certificate screen, select Create a New Certificate. Click Next again.

7. On the Delayed or Immediate Request screen, select Prepare the Request Now, but Send It Later, and then click Next.

8. On the Name and Security Settings screen (see Figure 2.12), type a name for the certificate. Select a bit length and select the other options as required, and then click Next.

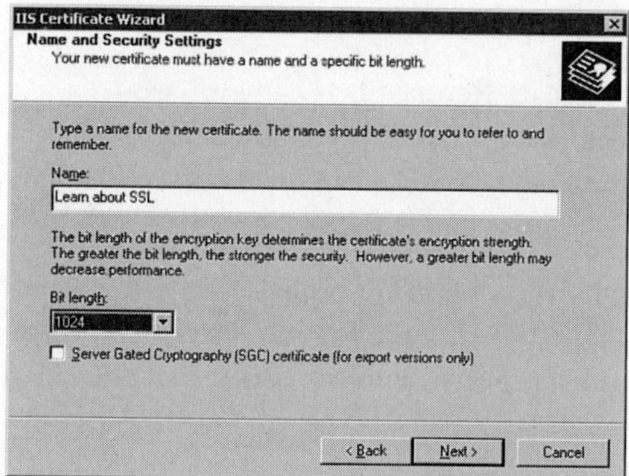

Figure 2.12 The Name and Security Settings screen enables you to provide a name for the requested certificate and configure several security options.

9. On the Organization Information screen, type names for the organization and organizational unit or department, and then click Next.

10. On the Your Site's Common Name screen, type the FQDN of the computer. If the computer is serving only to an intranet, you can use the computer's NetBIOS name. Click Next.

11. On the Geographical Information screen, select your country from the drop-down list. Then type your state or province and your city name. Click Next.

12. Type a filename for the request or accept the default of `c:\certreq.txt`, and then click Next.

13. On the Request File Summary screen, review the information. Click Next and then click Finish to complete the wizard.

14. Copy the request file to a floppy disk or Universal Serial Bus (USB) token and take it to the certificate server.

Exercise 2.3.1.2: Generating a Web Server Certificate

To create a Web server certificate, you need a Windows 2000 or 2003 server running Certificate Services. We install a certificate server in Exercise 4.3.1 in Chapter 4:

1. At the certificate server, click Start, Run, and type **`http://localhost/certsrv`**. This opens the Certificate Services Web pages in Internet Explorer.

2. Select Request a Certificate, and then click Next.

3. Select Advanced Request link, and then click Next.

4. Select the option Submit a Certificate Request by Using a Base-64-Encoded PKCS #10 File or a Renewal Request by Using a Base-64-Encoded PKCS #7 File, and then click Next.

5. Insert the floppy disk or USB token you created in the previous exercise. In Notepad, copy the text of the certificate request file, and paste this text into the Saved Request field of the Certificate Services Web page. Then click Submit. Certificate Services informs you that the certificate request was issued.

6. Use the available link to download the certificate file to the floppy disk or USB token.

Exercise 2.3.1.3: Installing a Web Server Certificate and Enabling SSL

Having been issued a Web server certificate, you install this certificate on the Windows 2000 Professional computer and require the use of SSL:

1. On the Directory Security tab of the Default Web Site Properties dialog box, click the Server Certificate command button to start the Web Server Certificate Wizard again.

2. Click Next. You are informed that a certificate request is pending. Select Process the Pending Request and Install the Certificate, and then click Next.

3. Browse to the floppy disk or USB token, select the certificate file, and then click Next.

4. Review the information on the Certificate Summary screen (see Figure 2.13), and then click Next.

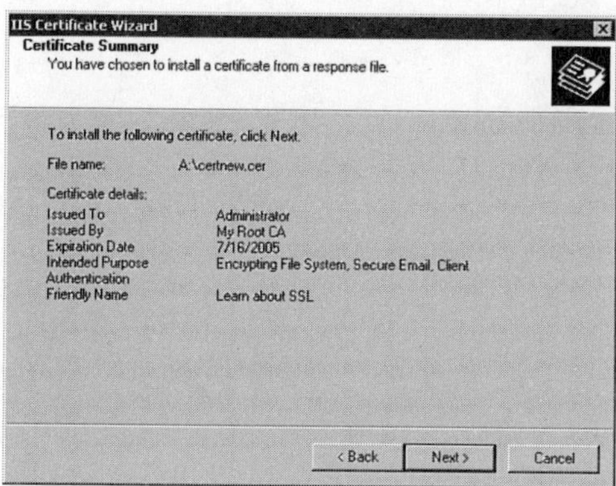

Figure 2.13 The Certificate Summary page provides details of the certificate to be installed on the Web server.

5. Click Finish. You are returned to the Directory Security tab of the Default Web Site Properties dialog box.

6. To require the use of secure communications, click Edit under Secure Communications.

7. On the Secure Communications dialog box, select Require Secure Channel (SSL). To require that all incoming clients have certificates, select Require Client Certificates (see Figure 2.14). If you want to map client certificates to Windows user accounts, select Enable Client Certificate Mapping, and click Edit to configure mappings. If you want to enable a certificate trust list (CTL), select the Enable Certificate Trust List check box and specify the appropriate CTL. Then click OK.

8. Click OK to close the Default Web Site Properties dialog box, and close the IIS console. If an Inheritance Overrides dialog box opens, click OK to dismiss it.

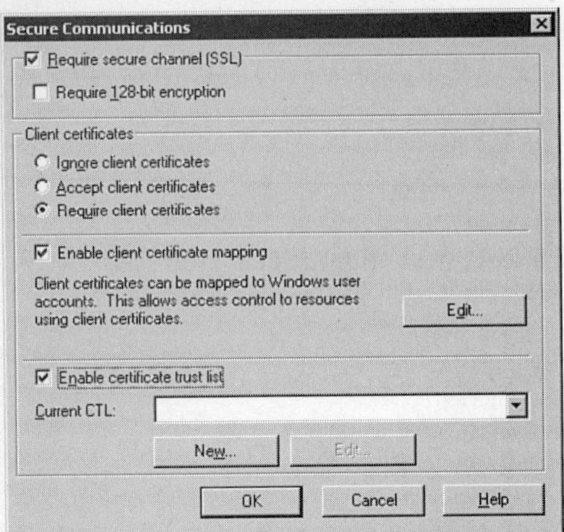

Figure 2.14 The Secure Communications dialog box enables you to configure SSL usage.

Besides HTTP/S, there is another security protocol called Secure HTTP, or S-HTTP. It is a less widely used protocol for secure transmission of individual messages. Unlike HTTP/S, S-HTTP does not establish a session, and only a portion of the traffic is encrypted. S-HTTP does not require the use of a public-key certificate, and it can use symmetric keys that are circulated in advance. Do not confuse these protocols on the Security+ exam.

Exercise 2.3.2: TLS

Similar to SSL, TLS uses a combination of public-key cryptography and symmetric encryption to provide communications security. As an Internet Engineering Task Force (IETF) standard, TLS is considered by many as the probable long-term successor to SSL.

Use of smart cards for access to a RAS server requires TLS in conjunction with EAP. In this exercise, you first research the topic of TLS on the Internet. You then configure the use of EAP-TLS on a RAS server. You should do this exercise on the computer used in Exercises 2.1.2 and 2.1.3:

1. Log on to the Windows 2000 Server computer as an administrator.
2. For a brief definition of TLS and links to further information, connect to the Internet and navigate to http://searchsecurity.techtarget.com/sDefinition/0,,sid14_gci557332,00.html.
3. Click Start, Programs, Administrative Tools, Routing and Remote Access.
4. In the RRAS console, right-click your server and choose Properties.

5. On the Security tab of the server's Properties dialog box, select Authentication Methods.

6. In the Authentication Methods dialog box, select Extensible Authentication Protocol (EAP) and click EAP Methods.

7. The EAP Methods dialog box should list Smart Card or Other Certificate as an installed method in the Methods field (see Figure 2.15). Click OK and then click OK again to close the Authentication Methods dialog box.

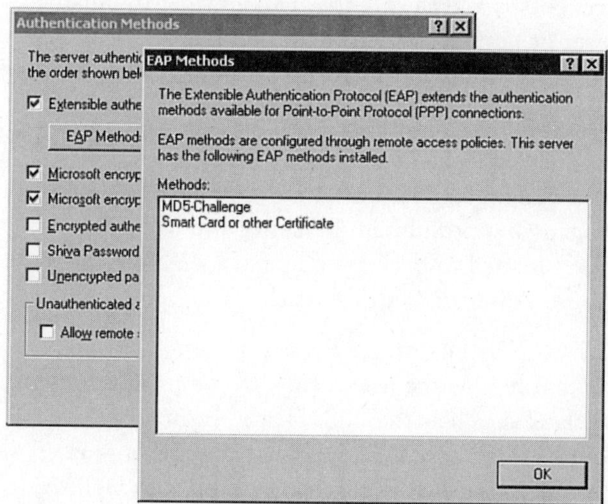

Figure 2.15 When you select EAP as an authentication method for RRAS in Windows 2000 Server, TLS is used for authentication with smart cards or other certificates.

Exercise 2.3.3: Instant Messaging Vulnerabilities

Instant messaging (IM) has evolved from a tool used mainly by teenagers to chat with their friends to a real-time business communication tool. At the same time, however, IM was created without security in mind, and it tends to be more vulnerable than many other communications methods. For example, it allows file attachments that could potentially contain viruses or other malicious code. In addition, most organizations have little control over its use because of its peer-to-peer characteristics. In this exercise, you research the topic of IM vulnerabilities on the Internet:

1. Symantec Ltd. has published a comprehensive paper on IM threats and vulnerabilities at http://securityresponse.symantec.com/avcenter/reference/malicious.threats.instant.messaging.pdf. What are four ways in which IM can propagate worms? What problems can backdoor Trojan horses create for IM clients? Note how large numbers of computers can be infected in seconds by blended threats transmitted by IM. Also note how a blended threat can grow exponentially with time until a plateau is reached and the IM server is forced to be shut down.
2. In the same paper, note how sniffing of session traffic can lead to hijacking of logon credentials and the ability of an attacker to impersonate a legitimate user or perform a man-in-the-middle attack. What are some of the solutions advocated in this paper to thwart the various types of IM attacks?
3. The Pittsburgh Times has published an article at http://www.redsiren.com/pdf/articles/pghbustimesjune21.pdf that describes the reasons why one company has prohibited the use of IM. What are some of the other issues related to business usage of IM? Note the issues related to privacy as discussed in this article.
4. Navigate to http://www.hipaaacademy.net/PressReleases/uncontrolp2p.html and note how the use of IM can compromise privacy as required by legislation such as the U.S. Health Insurance Portability and Accountability Act (HIPAA). What conclusion was drawn with respect to the use of IM by companies subject to HIPAA?

IM is another route of attack for intruders seeking to perpetrate attacks and hoaxes, as well as distribution of spam messages and malicious software.

Exercise 2.3.4: Securing the Web Browser

The Security+ exam tests your understanding of a series of vulnerabilities that affect users visiting Web sites of unknown security levels. When the World Wide Web first became popular, the static pages of the day were relatively secure. Advances in the production of dynamic content, such as Java, JavaScript, and ActiveX, have introduced numerous vulnerabilities. The following is a brief description of these technologies:

- *Java*—A programming language that is used to write applets that are embedded into Web pages. They are executable files and can be used to run malicious code on a computer that can cause buffer overflow or consume system resources. The browser can be redirected to inappropriate hosts.

- *JavaScript*—Similar to Java but not compiled into a program. However, an attacker can still use JavaScript to obtain information about a site or access files and cookies on a client computer.
- *ActiveX*—Pioneered by Microsoft, ActiveX enables applets to be embedded in HTML documents that allow such actions as the viewing of multimedia on a Web page. However, they can also be programmed to perform any type of action, including viewing, modifying, or deleting data on a client computer.

In this exercise, you observe the available security settings in Internet Explorer running on a Windows 2000 Professional computer and secure the browser against common vulnerabilities. You can also do this exercise on a computer running Windows XP Professional or Windows XP Home Edition:

1. Right-click the Internet Explorer icon on the desktop or Start Menu, and choose Internet Properties to open the Internet Properties dialog box.
2. Select the Security tab. As shown in Figure 2.16, four default security levels are available corresponding to the four Web zones. Settings on the Internet zone attempt to balance the ability to browse the Internet with protection against common vulnerabilities.

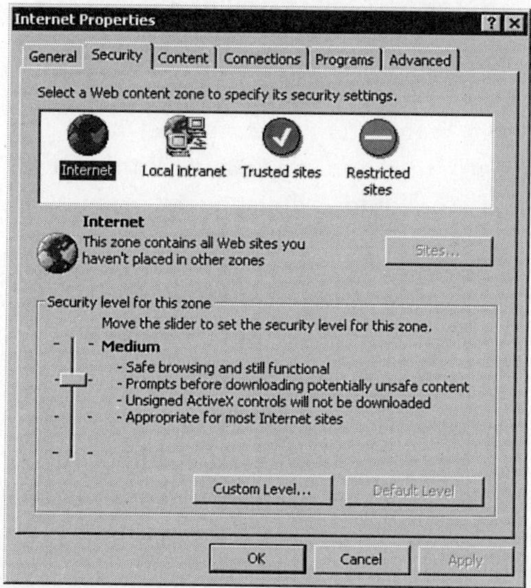

Figure 2.16 The Security tab of the Internet Properties dialog box allows you to configure security properties for each of the four Web content zones.

3. Select each Web content zone in turn, click Custom Level, and then explore the default settings displayed in the Security Settings dialog box. Click Cancel after browsing each set of default settings.

4. After you browse the default settings, you configure modified security settings for the Internet zone. Select this zone and click Custom Level.

5. To control the extent to which ActiveX controls run on Internet Explorer, configure the settings in the ActiveX controls and plug-ins sites. For each of the following options, you may either enable or disable the specified activity or have Internet Explorer prompt you before performing the activity:

   - *Download signed ActiveX controls*—Determines whether you can download signed ActiveX controls from a page in the Internet zone. ActiveX controls can be digitally signed to verify their origin.

   - *Download unsigned ActiveX controls*—Determines whether you can download unsigned ActiveX controls. Such code can be harmful, and this download should be disabled except in the Trusted Sites zone.

   - *Initialize and script ActiveX controls not marked as safe*—Determines whether a script can interact with untrusted ActiveX controls. Untrusted controls can also be harmful. Enabling this option causes Internet Explorer to initialize and script both untrusted and trusted controls. This option should also be disabled except in the Trusted Sites zone.

   - *Run ActiveX controls and plug-ins*—Determines whether ActiveX controls and plug-ins can run from Web pages in the Internet zone. You can choose Administrator Approved to run only controls from a list of approved controls specified for Windows domains in Group Policy.

   - *Script ActiveX controls marked safe for scripting*—Determines whether an ActiveX control that is safe for scripting can interact with a script.

6. Signed applets refer to Java programs that are digitally signed with the aid of a key pair obtained from a commercial certification authority (CA) such as VeriSign. To configure permissions on signed or unsigned Java applets, scroll to the Java permissions section. To permit only certain types of Java applets to run, select the Custom option and then click Java Custom Settings to display the dialog box in Figure 2.17.

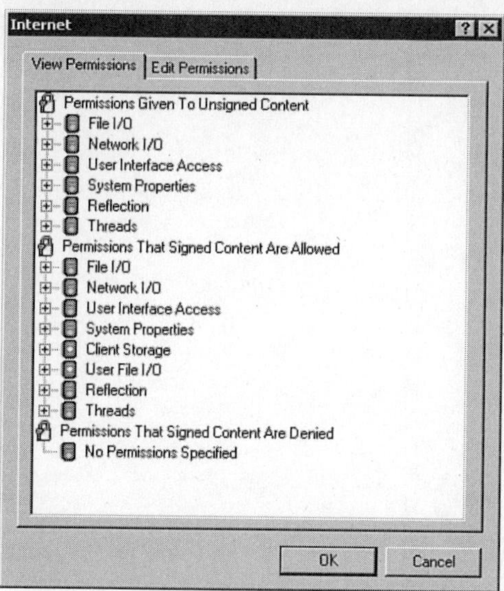

Figure 2.17 You can view and edit permissions on various types of Java applets from the Internet dialog box for each security zone.

7. The View Permissions tab of this dialog box shows the permissions that are currently applied to Java applets. Select the Edit Permissions tab to modify these permissions as required. For details on the available settings, consult the Internet Explorer 6 Resource Kit at http://www.microsoft.com/resources/documentation/ie/6/all/reskit/en-us/part2/c07ie6rk.mspx.

8. To configure the security level for use of cookies by Web sites to which you browse, select the Privacy tab in the Internet Properties dialog box (Internet Explorer 6 only). Cookies can pose a privacy issue because they track information on the client computer such as URLs the user has browsed to. They can also store identification data, credit-card information, and so on that could be exploited by attackers and lead to identity theft. At the same time, cookies can be beneficial for certain reasons, such as saving user preferences when browsing to e-commerce sites. You can select any of six levels ranging from accepting all cookies to blocking all cookies.

9. Click the Advanced tab in the Internet Properties dialog box and scroll to the bottom to configure additional security options, as shown in Figure 2.18. Note that these include the use of SSL and TLS, already discussed in this chapter. Configure these pages as required for your situation.

10. When you are finished, click OK to apply all settings.

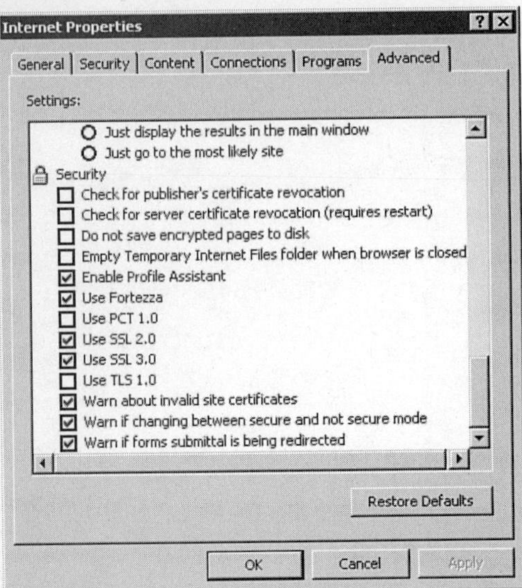

Figure 2.18 The Advanced tab of the Internet Properties dialog box contains additional security options that apply to all security zones.

ActiveX controls from untrusted sources can pose a serious threat to your system. Such controls can exploit weaknesses in your security configuration to perform harmful acts on your computer. When executed, they run with the privilege of the current user account. This fact is a good reason why you should not use an administrator account except when necessary.

The Internet Explorer Administration Kit (IEAK) allows administrators to configure a common set of Internet Explorer settings for all computers on the network, including settings discussed in this section. For more details, go to http://www.microsoft.com/windows/ieak/default.asp.

What Did I Just Learn?

Now that you have looked at Internet security concepts, let's take a moment to review all the critical items you've experienced in this lab:

- You can configure IIS to use HTTP/S by obtaining and installing a certificate from a certification authority.
- TLS, used in conjunction with EAP, allows you to enable the use of smart cards for secure remote access across the Internet to your servers.
- Vulnerabilities of an IM system include sniffing, spoofing, hijacking of a connection, and privacy issues.
- You can improve security of Internet browsing in browsers such as Internet Explorer by enabling a series of security settings.

2.4: Administering Directory Security

We have seen how SSL and TLS are used for securing Web-based and remote access traffic across the Internet. We now look at potential vulnerabilities in these services as well as directory services such as Lightweight Directory Access Protocol (LDAP). Note that LDAP is a hierarchical directory service that provides the foundation upon which Microsoft created its Active Directory service.

Exercise 2.4.1: Vulnerabilities in SSL, TLS, X.500, and LDAP

In the last section, you saw how to configure IIS to use SSL and how to configure a RAS server to use EAP-TLS for smart card certificates. In this exercise, you research several vulnerabilities in these protocols as well as LDAP and the X.500 protocol on which LDAP was built:

1. Connect to the Internet and navigate to http://www.cert.org/advisories/CA-2003-26.html to read a paper prepared by the Computer Emergency Readiness Team (CERT) on vulnerabilities in SSL and TLS. Note that vulnerabilities in Abstract Syntax Notation One (ASN1) might enable intruders to execute code on a victim computer. What is the most common impact? Note the two attack vectors they discuss. Of the types of attack you researched in Chapter 1, which types are used here?

2. Bruce Canvel discusses methods of hijacking passwords in SSL and TLS at http://lasecwww.epfl.ch/memo_ssl.shtml. This discussion begins with a brief review of how SSL and TLS encrypt data such as credit-card numbers. How does an intruder use error messages sent by the server to perform an attack? Of the types of attack you researched in Chapter 1, which types did the intruder use?

3. Those of you who are knowledgeable about programming might be interested in the method used by an enhancement to SSL called OpenSSL to deal with the problem you have just researched. Navigate to http://www.openssl.org/news/secadv_20030219.txt and study the details of the patch described there.

4. CERT discusses vulnerabilities in X.500 and LDAP at http://www.cert.org/advisories/CA-2001-18.html. In particular, they stated that the Microsoft Exchange Server LDAP service and many other email server applications are vulnerable to denial-of-service (DoS) attacks, although the LDAP implementation of Active Directory did not appear to be vulnerable. What other type of attack did they report?

5. Additional information on the exploit against Microsoft Exchange Server LDAP appears at http://www.ciac.org/ciac/bulletins/j-036.shtml. How can intruders access the server to execute arbitrary code?

6. Beth Hemmelgarn discusses hacker exploits in LDAP and X.500 at http://www.giac.org/practical/Beth_Hemmelgarn.doc. This paper concentrates more on Unix than on Windows, but the exploits discussed cover both systems. What six LDAP intrusions does she identify?

7. Wenling Bao introduces several security concerns of LDAP at http://www.giac.org/practical/gsec/Wenling_Bao_GSEC.pdf. What are some directory-oriented and non–directory-oriented exploits discussed in this paper? For more information on LDAP and its security, follow the links provided by this author.

Remember that LDAP directories are built in a hierarchical fashion and arranged like an inverted tree with the root at the start of the LDAP directory structure.

What Did I Just Learn?

Now that you have looked at vulnerabilities in SSL, TLS, X.500, and LDAP, let's take a moment to review all the critical items you've experienced in this lab:

- SSL and TLS present several vulnerabilities, including the ability to sniff passwords from the network. In particular, error messages displayed by the server can lead to clues used by intruders to guess passwords.
- Directory services such as X.500 and LDAP operating on email servers can be vulnerable to DoS attacks.

2.5: Administering File Transfer Security

File Transport Protocol (FTP) is part of the TCP/IP protocol suite and allows users to upload or download data between a client computer and a server running the FTP service. Microsoft IIS is an example of an FTP-capable server.

Exercise 2.5.1: FTP and Its Vulnerabilities

FTP was originally set up to make it easy for users to obtain information from companies by simple downloading. Many companies have set up FTP servers that allow anonymous authentication of users for this purpose. Needless to say, this setup can present many opportunities for improper usage. For example, if anonymous users are given read/write privileges on the FTP server, they might upload items such as unauthorized music files, movies, and software, as well as other undesirable content such as pornography. Numerous vulnerabilities are consequently present. In this exercise, you research some of the vulnerabilities present in FTP and means of combating them:

1. Navigate to http://www.ftpplanet.com/ftpresources/overview.htm for an introduction to FTP. It includes the procedure for anonymous FTP access. If you want additional information on the protocols that form the background of FTP, go to http://www.ftpplanet.com/ftpresources/ftpresource.htm.

2. Laura Taylor introduces the concept of Secure FTP (S/FTP) at http://www.intranetjournal.com/articles/200208/se_08_14_02a.html. What are some of the vulnerabilities introduced by regular FTP that S/FTP attempts to overcome? Note especially how a hacker can use regular FTP to replace the contents of a Web site with anything he wants to insert. What are some ways in which S/FTP can be implemented? Access some of the links from Taylor's second page to learn more about some of the available S/FTP implementations.

3. Blind FTP is a type of anonymous FTP in which users cannot see the listings of files contained on the site. Go to http://www.docendo.se/mspress/msp_online/samplechapter/0735618224.htm and note that software can be uploaded to a blind FTP site. Such sites can become repositories for pirated software and other illegal material such as pornography and pirated music files.

4. For information on FTP vulnerabilities such as packet sniffing, navigate to http://www.robertgraham.com/pubs/sniffing-faq.html. This page discusses sniffing in general and is also useful for other Security+ objectives that relate to this subject.

Because FTP sends its username and password information in clear text, intruders can use packet sniffing to capture this information and obtain unauthorized access.

Exercise 2.5.2: Securing an FTP Server

The FTP service in Microsoft IIS enables you to set up an FTP server. In this exercise, you look at security-based properties of the IIS FTP server. You should do this exercise on a computer running Windows 2000 Server. You can perform the same steps in Windows Server 2003:

1. Log on to the Windows 2000 Server computer as an administrator.

The cut-down version of IIS included with Windows 2000 Professional and Windows XP Professional does not include an FTP server. It is for this reason that you need to do this exercise on a server-based computer.

The default installation of Windows 2000 Server includes IIS with FTP installed by default. If you are performing this exercise on a computer running Windows Server 2003, you need to install IIS from Control Panel, Add or Remove Programs. To include the FTP service, select Details in the IIS server installation, and then select File Transfer Protocol (FTP) Service from the window that appears.

2. Open the IIS console by selecting Start, Programs, Administrative Tools, Internet Services Manager.
3. If necessary, expand the server display in the left pane to reveal the Default FTP site node.
4. Right-click this node and select Properties.
5. To prevent anonymous connections to the FTP site, select the Security Accounts tab. Deselect the Allow Anonymous Connections check box. Doing so requires all visitors to the FTP site to log on with an account in the local database or Active Directory.
6. Read the warning that is displayed (see Figure 2.19), and then click No. You keep anonymous logon enabled to complete the next exercise.

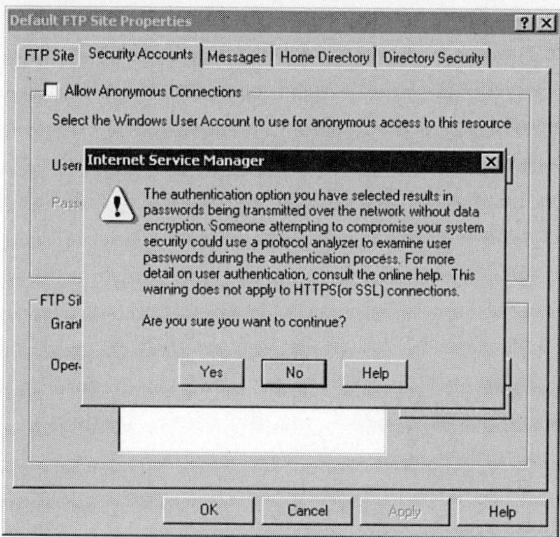

Figure 2.19 You can disable FTP anonymous connections.

7. To limit access to only certain computers, select the Directory Security tab. If you want to restrict only certain computers or networks, leave the default of Granted Access selected and click Add. As shown in Figure 2.20, select either Single Computer or Group of Computers as required, type the IP address or the network ID and subnet mask, and then click OK. If you select the Single Computer option, you'll have the option to specify a DNS domain name by clicking DNS Lookup.

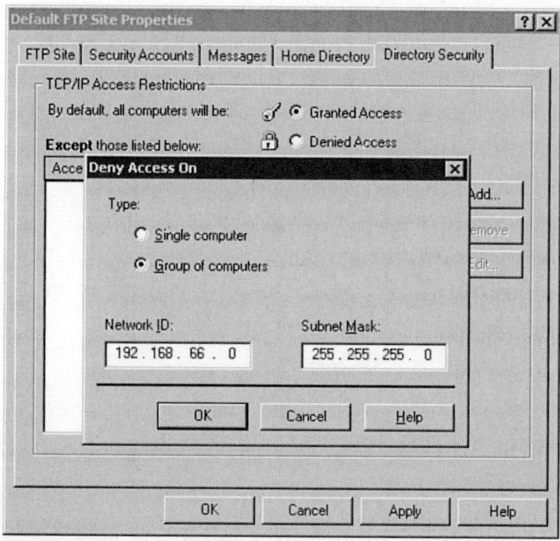

Figure 2.20 Limit access to an IIS FTP server.

8. To enable only certain computers or networks to access the FTP site, select Denied Access on the same tab. Click Add and follow the same procedure as shown in Step 7 and Figure 2.20 to add the IP address of the computer or network to be granted access.
9. To limit the use of the FTP site to reading or writing files, select the Home Directory tab. Select the Read and/or Write check boxes to enable the types of action you want to allow. By default, visits to the FTP site are logged. You should leave this check box selected.
10. When you are finished configuring these properties, click OK.
11. Use My Computer to navigate to the default path (`c:\inetpub\ftproot`), and create and save a test file in Notepad to test the site in the next exercise.

Exercise 2.5.3: Capturing FTP Traffic with a Sniffer

Several protocol analyzers or sniffers are available that enable you to capture traffic to or from an FTP server. In this exercise, you use a sniffer to monitor traffic to the FTP site you configured in Exercise 2.5.2. Perform this exercise from a computer running Windows 2000 Professional. Steps on a computer running Windows XP are similar:

1. Log on to the Windows 2000 Professional computer as an administrator.
2. Navigate to http://www.ethereal.com and read the information on its packet capture tools.
3. Click Download in the left pane and select the Windows package (or other package if you are using a different type of machine).
4. Download the `WinPcap_3_1.exe` and `ethereal-setup-0.10.6.exe` files (or newer releases if available) and save them to an appropriate location on your hard drive. You can download a comprehensive documentation package from http://www.ethereal.com/distribution/docs/user-guide.pdf.

At the time of writing, the documentation package appeared to correspond to an older version of Ethereal. However, the package still provides valuable information related to configuring and running the program.

5. Install the WinPcap program and then the Ethereal program by double-clicking their icons and following the instructions presented. Use the default settings when installing Ethereal.
6. Start Ethereal by clicking Start, Programs, Ethereal, Ethereal.
7. To configure a capture filter, select Start from the Capture menu or click the first toolbar icon. This displays the Ethereal: Capture Options dialog box, from which you may set options such as a capture filter.
8. To capture FTP packets only, type **`tcp port 21`** in the Capture Filter field. This restricts packet captures to those on the default FTP port of 21. (See Figure 2.21.)

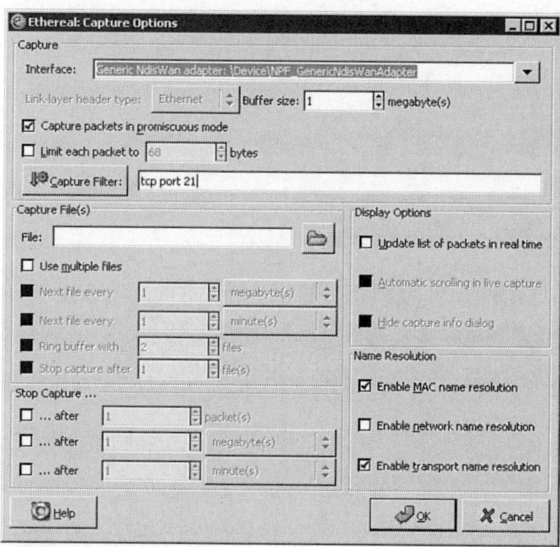

Figure 2.21 Configuring a capture filter in Ethereal.

9. Click OK to begin the packet capture. This displays a Capture dialog box recording the packets that are captured.
10. To capture some FTP data, connect to the FTP server you configured in Exercise 2.5.2. Use an anonymous logon with `hacker@warez.com` for a password. Then download the test file you created in the same exercise to your My Documents folder, and end the FTP session.
11. Back in the Ethereal product, you will have captured approximately 50 packets. Click Stop to stop the capture and display the captured information.

12. Note the types of information displayed. Scroll the upper panel of the displayed information to locate the password you typed in the Info column.

13. As shown in Figure 2.22, you have captured the "anonymous" username entered as well as the password, which appears on the highlighted line and again on the line immediately following.

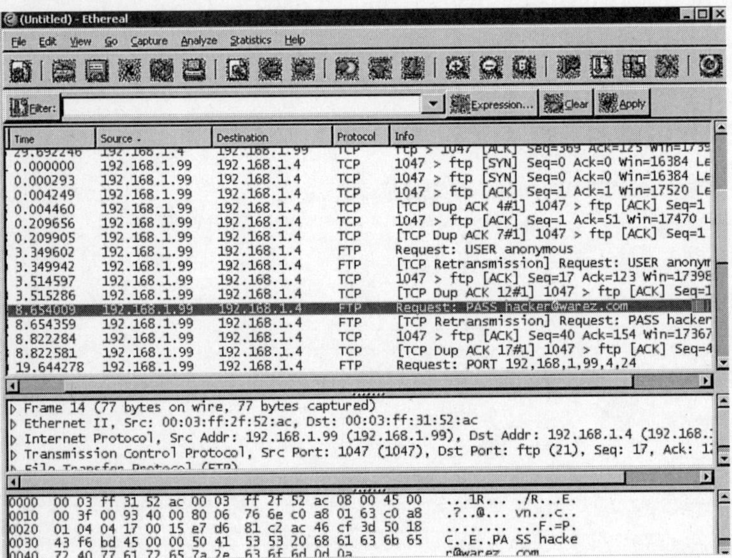

Figure 2.22 The Ethereal packet capture program displays information on data transmitted during an anonymous FTP session, including the password.

14. The next lower panel shows statistics on the number of bytes captured, the source and destination Media Access Control (MAC) addresses and IP addresses, and ports across which data was transferred.

15. The bottom panel shows some of the binary data obtained. Note that the password appears here as well.

16. Experiment further with the Ethereal tool as you desire, and then close the tool when you are finished. If you want, save the captured data to a file of your choice.

Make sure you know the most common port numbers used by typical Internet applications. These include port 21 for FTP, port 22 for SSH, port 23 for Telnet, port 25 for SMTP, port 80 for HTTP, port 143 for Instant Message Access Protocol (IMAP4), port 443 for HTTPS, port 1812 for RADIUS, and so on.

What Did I Just Learn?

Now that you have looked at FTP security, let's take a moment to review all the critical items you've experienced in this lab:

- ➤ Unsecured FTP sites can be exploited by intruders who might upload files such as pirated music or software, pornography, or other undesirable content.
- ➤ FTP traffic is sent in plain-text format, and many packet sniffers are available that can capture passwords, text, and other information during file transfers.
- ➤ The FTP server provided with Microsoft IIS includes a limited set of security configurations that can perform tasks such as preventing anonymous logons and restricting which computers can access the site.

2.6: Administering Wireless Security

Wireless access points have proliferated in recent years and individuals can connect to wireless networks from places as diverse as international airports and coffee shops. Many offices have set up wireless LANs (WLANs), thereby enabling mobility and portability of computers and other networked devices. In addition, many different types of wireless devices have become popular. Besides laptop computers equipped with wireless interfaces, they include cell phones, personal data assistants (PDAs), pagers, and so on. Along with this convenience comes an increased chance of unauthorized access to networks and their data.

Exercise 2.6.1: Understanding Wireless Protocols

Wireless protocols that you need to understand for the Security+ exam include Wireless Transport Layer Security (WTLS), the 802.11x series of specifications, Wireless Application Protocol (WAP), and WEP. In this exercise, you obtain information on each of these protocols and their interrelationships from the Internet:

1. Connect to the Internet and navigate to http://www.windowsecurity.com/articles/Wireless_Security_Primer_101.html. Written as part of a Security+ text, this article introduces WAP as used for mobile wireless

users accessing networks. Using WAP, mobile clients can browse in a manner similar to that of computers using WWW browsers. The authors then introduce WTLS as an extension of the TLS protocol you studied earlier in this chapter.

2. The same article next introduces the 802.11x standards and the two types of wireless networks, ad hoc and infrastructure. How do these two network types differ? Note the use of the Service Set Identifier (SSID) to distinguish different wireless networks. You are then introduced to WEP as a security mechanism for 802.11x networks. What is the original purpose of using WEP with 802.11x, and what additional security configurations should be implemented?

3. Sami Jormalainen and Jouni Laine present a comprehensive discussion of the operation and security of WAP and WTLS at http://www.hut.fi/~jtlaine2/wtls/. They approach the security problem of all data transmissions from the viewpoints of privacy, authentication, and integrity. Note the layered architecture of WAP, the position of WTLS within this architecture, and the internal architecture of WTLS. What key exchange and privacy methods are implemented? How is data integrity ensured?

4. Michael Sutton of IDEFENSE presents a white paper discussing 802.11x and WEP insecurities at https://ialert.idefense.com/idcontent/2002/papers/Wireless.pdf. He starts with a comprehensive introduction to the 802.11x standards and how WEP functions to provide confidentiality for data sent across WLANs.

5. Tahir Hashmi discusses 802.11x security and authentication at http://www.codemartial.org/Computers/WLAN/node5.shtml. What two modes of authentication does 802.11x use? What are some advantages and disadvantages of the WEP algorithm?

6. Another valuable introduction to 802.11 networking appears at http://www.cs.umd.edu/~waa/wireless.pdf. They review the authentication and access control modes and present several weaknesses in these mechanisms.

You should be aware that WTLS provides services such as privacy, data integrity, and authentication for handheld devices such as PDAs in the wireless network environment.

Do not confuse WAP with WEP. Remember that WAP uses WTLS to secure its data transmissions and 802.11x uses WEP to secure its data transmissions. You need to be able to distinguish all four wireless access protocols and their usage for the Security+ exam.

Exercise 2.6.2: Wireless Vulnerabilities

Wireless networks, by their very nature, can be open to anyone with a wireless network card who is within receiving distance of an adequate signal. An exploit that has been frequently conducted is that of *war driving*, in which an individual drives around with a laptop equipped with a wireless network card and scanning software until he locates a network to which he can make some kind of connection. The network and all its resources are then available just as if he were wired directly to the servers.

In this exercise, you continue researching the WLAN protocols on the Internet, focusing on their vulnerabilities and the methods that you can use to protect wireless communications:

1. Return to http://www.hut.fi/~jtlaine2/wtls/, which you accessed in Exercise 2.6.1. Which vulnerabilities in WTLS do the authors describe and what means do they suggest for overcoming them?
2. Continue to http://www.cc.jyu.fi/~mjos/wtls.pdf to note how a brute-force attack on a password in WTLS can occur on a letter-by-letter basis. What other security problems can occur when using WTLS?
3. Return to Sutton's white paper, which you also accessed in Exercise 2.6.1. Sutton presents detailed information on vulnerabilities in WEP and 802.11x. Note the procedures that can be used to locate WLANs, including software WLAN scanners such as Net Stumbler, which sends out broadcast packets to locate access points. He refers to these scanners as "the modern equivalent of the police scanner." Using a laptop and Net Stumbler, he conducted a war-driving survey in Manhattan and northern Virginia that identified a large number of unprotected WLANs. Other software tools discussed include AirSnort and WEPCrack. What tips does he offer to improve the security of WLANs? Consult the references in this paper for additional information as required.
4. Jim Geier discusses the vulnerabilities of 802.11x and WEP at http://www.wi-fiplanet.com/tutorials/article.php/1368661. In what portion of the network does WEP not encrypt transmissions? In what way are the initialization vectors (IVs) and keys used by WEP vulnerable? Geier concludes by noting that use of WEP, despite its shortcomings,

does help reduce the threats posed by individuals conducting war-driving searches for WLANs. You can also find a related article on basic WLAN security at http://www.wi-fiplanet.com/tutorials/article.php/953561.

5. Geier also presents a series of articles on planning wireless LAN support at http://www.wi-fiplanet.com/tutorials/article.php/3078061, http://www.wi-fiplanet.com/tutorials/article.php/3093811, and http://www.wi-fiplanet.com/tutorials/article.php/3095581. He discusses all aspects of planning WLANs, including security concerns. For additional information, consult his book referenced in the "Need to Know More?" section.
6. Geier introduces site survey tools that you can use to determine the placement of WLAN access points at http://www.wi-fiplanet.com/tutorials/article.php/953661.
7. Jesse Walker of Intel analyzes the deficiency of WEP encryption at http://www.dis.org/wl/pdf/unsafe.pdf. To what problems does he attribute the failure of WEP to meet its design goal of providing data privacy equivalent to that of a wired network?

Tools used in site surveys are often the same tools that an intruder would use to locate and access a wireless network.

Exercise 2.6.3: Configuring 802.1x Authentication in Windows 2000 Professional

Microsoft provides an 802.1x authentication client that allows computers running Windows 2000 Professional to employ the IEEE 802.1x authentication standard for connecting to wireless networks that are based on IEEE 802.11. 802.11 uses the following two methods for authentication:

- *Open system*—A device-oriented authentication method that grants access according to the identification of the wireless adapter and the use of a WEP secret key.
- *Shared secret*—A four-step challenge-response authentication method that involves knowledge of a secret key phrase.

IEEE 802.1x authentication makes use of EAP-TLS or Protected EAP (PEAP) for wireless authentication, including certificate-based mutual authentication and encryption.

In this exercise, you configure the use of 802.1x authentication on a Windows 2000 Professional computer. You need a Windows 2000 Professional computer equipped with a wireless network card to perform this exercise:

If you are performing this exercise on a Windows XP Professional computer, you do not need to download any additional client software. You also have the choice of configuring your computer with the Wireless Zero Configuration software, which can configure your computer to automatically connect to available wireless networks.

1. Log on to the Windows 2000 Professional computer as an administrator.
2. Connect to the Internet and navigate to http://www.microsoft.com/windows2000/server/evaluation/news/bulletins/8021xclient.asp. This page describes the Microsoft 802.1x Authentication Client that is used for authenticating Windows 2000 computers by means of the IEEE 802.1x protocol.
3. Click the link provided, which directs you to Microsoft Knowledge Base Article 313664. This article provides more information on the use of 802.1x authentication on Windows 2000 computers. On this page, scroll down and select the English language download.
4. When the download is complete, double-click the downloaded file and follow the instructions provided to install the 802.1x authentication client. You might need to restart your computer.

If you receive a message that your computer must have Windows 2000 Service Pack 3 installed, navigate to http://www.microsoft.com/Windows2000/downloads/servicepacks/sp3/download.asp and follow the instructions provided on this page to download and install Service Pack 3. Then repeat Step 4 to install the authentication client.

5. Right-click My Network Places and choose Properties.
6. In the Network and Dial-Up Connections dialog box, right-click the wireless connection and choose Properties.
7. Select the Authentication tab to obtain the options shown in Figure 2.23.

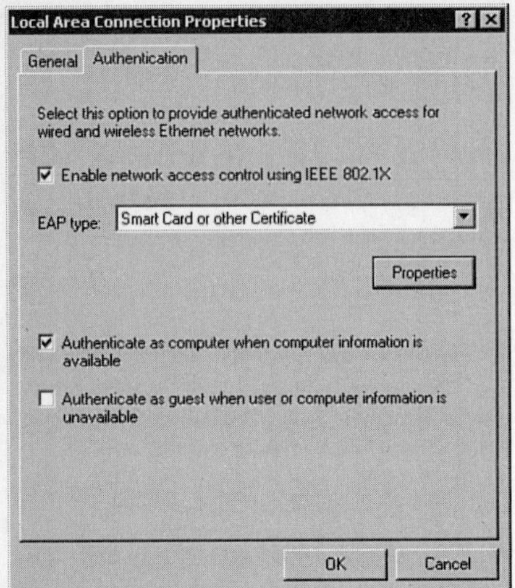

Figure 2.23 The Authentication tab of a connection's Properties dialog box contains options for configuring wireless authentication.

8. To use a smart card or certificate, select Smart Card or other Certificate from the EAP type drop-down list.
9. To configure smart card or certificate options, click Properties and select the smart card or certificate options available on the Smart Card or other Certificate Properties dialog box that appears.
10. If required, select either or both of the following options:
    - *Authenticate as computer when computer information is available*—Client computers can attempt authentication to the network even if a user is not logged on.
    - *Authenticate as guest when user or computer information is unavailable*—Uses the guest account to attempt authentication to the network when user or computer information is not available.

Only Windows XP computers natively support IEEE 802.1x authentication and Wireless Zero Configuration. Microsoft provides an 802.1x Authentication Client download that allows Windows 2000 computers to use the 802.1x standard. Microsoft also provides 802.1x Authentication Clients for Windows 98 and Windows NT 4.0 Workstation to customers with Premier and Alliance support contracts.

What Did I Just Learn?

Now that you have looked at security concerns of wireless networking, let's take a moment to review all the critical items you've experienced in this lab:

- WAP is a standard that enables mobile wireless users to easily access networks and their resources. It uses WTLS to provide a layer of security.
- IEEE 802.11x refers to a series of wireless networking standards developed by the IEEE. These operate at either 2.4GHz or 5GHz and support data transmission rates up to 54Mbps. They use WEP to provide data security.
- All types of wireless data transmission are vulnerable to intrusions ranging from war-driving exploits to brute-force password attacks, man-in-the-middle attacks, and other exploits similar to those occurring on wired networks.
- Microsoft provides Wireless Network Configuration software as an add-on to Windows 2000 for configuring the computer's connection to a wireless network. Wireless configuration software is built into Windows XP Professional and Windows Server 2003.

Exam Prep Questions

Objective 2.1: Remote Access

1. The IEEE 802.1x is a standard for remote access. Which of the following items would the 802.1x standard be concerned with? (Select all that apply.)
   - ❑ A. Authentication for remote access to a centralized LAN
   - ❑ B. SNMP
   - ❑ C. RADIUS server
   - ❑ D. EAP

2. You want a secure connection. You decide on establishing a VPN. Which of the following protocols can you use to accomplish your goal? (Select all that apply.)
   - ❑ A. S/MIME
   - ❑ B. TACACS
   - ❑ C. IPSec
   - ❑ D. L2TP

3. Which of the following remote authentication methods uses a central server for all remote client network access and transports with UDP and can be used with firewalls?
   - ❑ A. TACACS/+
   - ❑ B. 802.1x
   - ❑ C. RADIUS
   - ❑ D. VPN

4. Which of the following remote authentication servers enables a user to change passwords, enables two-factor authentication, and uses and resynchronizes security tokens?
   - ❑ A. DNS server
   - ❑ B. TACACS+
   - ❑ C. RADIUS
   - ❑ D. Proxy server

5. Remote users need to be authenticated and frequently need their data to be encrypted. Which of the following protocols are used together to meet both needs? (Select the two that apply.)
   - ❑ A. L2TP
   - ❑ B. PPTP
   - ❑ C. IPSec
   - ❑ D. AES

6. Which of the following applies to the correct port for Secure Shell?
   - ❑ A. UDP port 16
   - ❑ B. TCP port 22
   - ❑ C. UDP port 25
   - ❑ D. TCP port 136
7. Which of the following are functions of IPSec? (Select all that apply.)
   - ❑ A. Data integrity
   - ❑ B. User authentication
   - ❑ C. Data confidentiality
   - ❑ D. User nonrepudiation
8. IPSec is very popular with organizations that have remote business connections. What types of algorithm does IPSec use? (Select all that apply.)
   - ❑ A. 40-bit DES
   - ❑ B. 56-bit DES
   - ❑ C. 128-bit DES
   - ❑ D. 256-bit DES
9. Remote access users might need to communicate with either TCP or UDP. Which of the following is true about these protocols?
   - ❑ A. UDP is connection-oriented and designed for longer messages.
   - ❑ B. TCP is connection-oriented and corrects errors.
   - ❑ C. TCP does not guarantee delivery, whereas UDP does.
   - ❑ D. UDP guarantees delivery of data.

Objective 2.2: Email

1. S/MIME uses which of the following for authentication? (Select all that apply.)
   - ❑ A. Username
   - ❑ B. Password
   - ❑ C. Private key
   - ❑ D. Public key
2. Which of the following uses passphrases rather than passwords for secure email?
   - ❑ A. SSH
   - ❑ B. SSL
   - ❑ C. PGP
   - ❑ D. IPSec

3. Which of the following protocols transfers email messages in clear text and is a concern or vulnerability?
   - ❑ A. SMTP
   - ❑ B. ICMP
   - ❑ C. SNMP
   - ❑ D. TCP/IP

4. Which of the following statements is false regarding spam mail?
   - ❑ A. The receiver pays so much more for it than the sender does.
   - ❑ B. Spam email targets individual users with direct mail messages.
   - ❑ C. All spam is illegal in all countries.
   - ❑ D. Spam is flooding the Internet with many copies of the same message.

5. Everyone knows that there is nothing like a good joke. When dealing with computer networks, which of the following would be suitable? (Select the best answer.)
   - ❑ A. Playing a hoax for fun can really do no harm.
   - ❑ B. Sending a hidden virus is far more damaging than playing a hoax for fun.
   - ❑ C. Using company resources for gaming and communication is strictly forbidden.
   - ❑ D. By playing a computer hoax, you are still responsible for damages incurred.

Objective 2.3: Web

1. Which of the following uses symmetric encryption to increase Web site security?
   - ❑ A. S/MIME
   - ❑ B. PGP
   - ❑ C. SSL
   - ❑ D. HTTP/S

2. Which of the following protocols uses port 443 to encrypt traffic from a client's browser to a Web server?
   - ❑ A. HTTP/S
   - ❑ B. SSH
   - ❑ C. LDAP
   - ❑ D. IPSec

3. In today's quest for immediate access to information and communication, instant messaging has become popular at some places of work. Which of the following is a realistic vulnerability of IM?

- ❑ A. Programmed applications being offered in pop-up screens
- ❑ B. Advertisements being offered in pop-up screens
- ❑ C. Spam mail being delivered without request
- ❑ D. Malicious code being delivered during file transfers

4. Which of the following statements are true about packet sniffing? (Select all that apply.)
   - ❑ A. The primary purpose of using packet sniffing is to resolve network problems.
   - ❑ B. Packet sniffing can be useful for network administrators as well as crackers.
   - ❑ C. Packet sniffing allows you to view the packets going through the network.
   - ❑ D. A switch is better than a hub in preventing computer data from being sniffed.

5. Your boss wants to host a new secure Web site for the company. What are some of the potential vulnerabilities that you as a network administrator should be concerned about? (Select all that apply.)
   - ❑ A. Malicious scripting
   - ❑ B. Rogue Web servers
   - ❑ C. Browser exploits
   - ❑ D. Web spoofing

6. Which of the following security services do secure cookies provide? (Select all that apply.)
   - ❑ A. Authentication
   - ❑ B. Determination
   - ❑ C. Integrity
   - ❑ D. Confidentiality

7. Spam is considered unsolicited email. Which of the following allows forwarding of spam through multiple mail servers to multiple clients?
   - ❑ A. SMTP relay
   - ❑ B. SMTP forwarding
   - ❑ C. Email relay
   - ❑ D. Email forwarding

Objective 2.4: Directory—Recognition, Not Administration

1. Which of the following standards applies to directory services?
   - ❑ A. X.800
   - ❑ B. X.509
   - ❑ C. X.505
   - ❑ D. X.500

2. Which of the following protocols was the basis for the TLS protocol?
   - ❑ A. SSH
   - ❑ B. SSL
   - ❑ C. PPTP
   - ❑ D. L2F

3. What port must be open for LDAP to work?
   - ❑ A. 139
   - ❑ B. 389
   - ❑ C. 698
   - ❑ D. 1024

4. When configuring a network using LDAP, what is the first network computer known as?
   - ❑ A. The forest trunk
   - ❑ B. The first tree
   - ❑ C. The primary domain controller
   - ❑ D. The root

5. Your company is growing and has many different operating systems. You want to encrypt authentication traffic and use LDAP. Which of the following is the best choice for this situation?
   - ❑ A. SSL
   - ❑ B. SSH
   - ❑ C. HTTP/S
   - ❑ D. LDAP/S

Objective 2.5: File Transfer

1. Which of the following is a valid way to offer security when transferring files or data?
   - ❑ A. FTP
   - ❑ B. FTP/S
   - ❑ C. S/FTP
   - ❑ D. Blind FTP

2. Which of the following apply to anonymous accounts on FTP servers?
   - ❑ A. Crackers can use these accounts to overwrite files.
   - ❑ B. Anonymous FTP accounts are still very popular.
   - ❑ C. To increase security, anonymous FTP logins should be allowed.
   - ❑ D. There is no serious security concern when using anonymous FTP accounts.

3. You host an FTP server that clients log on to. To process files quickly, this server is designed to transfer files to other computers for the clients that log on. What is this process also known as?
   - ❑ A. File transferring
   - ❑ B. Proxy server
   - ❑ C. File sharing
   - ❑ D. Exchange server

4. Which of the following protocols are concerns because they use cleartext passwords? (Select all that apply.)
   - ❑ A. FTP
   - ❑ B. HTTP
   - ❑ C. SSH
   - ❑ D. Telnet

5. Which of the following is very vulnerable to packet-sniffing attacks? (Select all that apply.)
   - ❑ A. Usernames when using FTP
   - ❑ B. Usernames when using SSH
   - ❑ C. Passwords when using HTTPS
   - ❑ D. Passwords when using FTP

Objective 2.6: Wireless

1. In a wireless environment, which of the following is designed to identify clients that are attempting to connect to the network?
   - ❑ A. WAP
   - ❑ B. WEP
   - ❑ C. AP
   - ❑ D. WLAN

2. Several protocols support WAP. Which of the following provides security support for WAP and behaves like SSL?
   - ❑ A. WEP
   - ❑ B. WTLS
   - ❑ C. WSP
   - ❑ D. WTP

3. The wireless 802.11a standard offers much higher rates of transmission than the 802.11b standard. What is the maximum rate of transmission for the 802.11b wireless connection?
   - ❑ A. 5Mbps
   - ❑ B. 11Mbps
   - ❑ C. 16Mbps
   - ❑ D. 24Mbps

4. Your network administrator has chosen to use a WLAN but wants to prevent eavesdropping and guard against unauthorized access to the network. Which protocol should he use?
   - ❑ A. WEP
   - ❑ B. WTLS
   - ❑ C. WAP
   - ❑ D. SSL

5. Which of the following items are *not* required when employing 802.11b wireless networks?
   - ❑ A. A modem
   - ❑ B. A wireless NIC
   - ❑ C. A station
   - ❑ D. An access point
   - ❑ E. SSL

6. One of your employees reported that a strange fellow in a '98 Chevy was using a laptop computer in the employee parking lot. Apparently, the man was in the same spot when the employee arrived at work and when he went to lunch. What kind of threat could this represent to your wireless network?

- ❑ A. None, because the parking lot is not connected to the network
- ❑ B. PC eavesdropping
- ❑ C. War driving
- ❑ D. AP testing

7. How can site surveys apply to WLAN technology?
   - ❑ A. Site surveys are customer equipment satisfaction surveys at a LAN.
   - ❑ B. Site surveys are user satisfaction surveys at a local site (WLAN).
   - ❑ C. Site surveys may include actions used to identify rogue access points.
   - ❑ D. Site surveys may include actions used to identify wireless frequencies.

Exam Prep Answers

Objective 2.1: Remote Access

1. Answers A, B, C, and D are correct. The IEEE 802.1x standard for remote access is concerned with authentication for remote access to a centralized LAN, including RADIUS server connection, SNMP, and encapsulation of EAP.

2. Answers C and D are correct. IPSec and L2TP protocols offer a secure solution for VPNs.

3. Answer C is correct. RADIUS is a remote authentication method that provides a central server for all remote network access. Be aware that TACACS/+ uses TCP and RADIUS uses User Datagram Protocol (UDP).

4. Answer B is correct. Cisco's TACACS+ enables a user to change passwords, enables two-factor authentication, and uses and resynchronizes security tokens.

5. Answers A and C are correct. L2TP and IPSec protocols are used frequently together to offer authentication and encryption.

6. Answer B is correct. SSH uses TCP on port 22.

7. Answers A and C are correct. IPSec offers data integrity and data confidentiality.

8. Answer A is correct. IPSec uses 40-bit, 56-bit, and 128-bit DES algorithms.

9. Answer B is correct. TCP is a connection-oriented transport for guaranteed delivery of data. UDP (nicknamed Unreliable Datagram Protocol) does not offer error correction but is useful for shorter messages.

Objective 2.2: Email

1. Answers C and D are correct. S/MIME uses a private key and a public key for authentication.

2. Answer C is correct. PGP uses passphrases rather than passwords for secure email.

3. Answer A is correct. SMTP transfers or relays email messages in clear text.

4. Answer C is correct. Spam is *not* illegal in all countries.

5. Answer D is correct. By playing a computer hoax, you are still responsible for damages incurred. A hoax can be as lethal as a virus.

Objective 2.3: Web

1. Answer C is correct. SSL stands for Secure Sockets Layer; it is used to increase Web site security by symmetric encryption.

2. Answer A is correct. HTTP/S uses port 443 to encrypt traffic from a client's browser to a Web server.

3. Answer D is correct. Delivery of malicious code through file transfers is a realistic vulnerability of IM.

4. Answers A, B, C, and D are correct. All the listed statements are true for packet sniffing.

5. Answers A, B, C, and D are correct. You should consider all the items listed when hosting a secure Web site.

6. Answers A, C, and D are correct. Secure cookies provide authentication, integrity, and confidentiality.

7. Answer A is correct. SMTP relay allows forwarding of spam through multiple mail servers to multiple clients.

Objective 2.4: Directory—Recognition, Not Administration

1. Answer D is correct. X.500 applies to directory services.

2. Answer B is correct. The TLS protocol is based on SSL. However, TLS and SSL are not compatible with each other.

3. Answer B is correct. Port 389 must be open for LDAP to work.

4. Answer D is correct. When you configure a network using LDAP, the first network computer stores the root.

5. Answer A is correct. SSL can be used to encrypt authentication traffic and can be used with LDAP.

Objective 2.5: File Transfer

1. Answer C is correct. S/FTP is a valid way to offer security when transferring files or data because it is similar to SSH.

2. Answers A and B are correct. Although anonymous FTP accounts are still popular, crackers can use these accounts to overwrite files.

3. Answer C is correct. File sharing is a security concern and feature of the FTP server.

4. Answers A, B, and D are correct. FTP, HTTP, and Telnet are security concerns because they use clear-text passwords.

5. Answers A and D are correct. Usernames and passwords are vulnerable to packet-sniffing attacks when using FTP.

Objective 2.6: Wireless

1. Answer C is correct. In a wireless network, AP stands for access point; WAP stands for Wireless Application Protocol; WEP stands for Wired Equivalent Privacy; and WLAN stands for Wireless Local Area Network.

2. Answer B is correct. The WTLS protocol provides security support for WAP and behaves like SSL.

3. Answer B is correct. The 802.11b wireless connection transmits at a maximum of 11Mbps.

4. Answer A is correct. The WEP protocol prevents eavesdropping and guards against unauthorized access through shared-key authentication.

5. Answer A is correct. A modem is not required for a WLAN or 802.11b wireless network.

6. Answer C is correct. This is an example of war driving.

7. Answer C is correct. Site surveys may include actions taken to identify rogue access points on a WLAN.

Need to Know More?

For further information on remote access technologies, consult the following books:

Bixler, Dave. *MCSA/MCSE 70-216 Training Guide: Windows 2000 Network Infrastructure, 2nd Edition*. Indianapolis, IN: Que Publishing, 2002. Chapter 3, "Configuring, Managing, Monitoring, and Troubleshooting Remote Access in a Windows 2000 Network Infrastructure."

Hausman, Kirk, Diane Barrett, and Martin Weiss. *Security+ Exam Cram 2*. Indianapolis, IN: Que Publishing, 2003. Chapter 4, "Communication Security."

King, Todd and David Bittlingmeier. *Security+ Training Guide.* Indianapolis, IN: Que Publishing, 2003. Chapter 3, "Communication Security."

For further information on setting up a Windows XP Professional computer to connect to a RAS server, see the following:

Baker, Gord and Robert Bogue. *MCSE Training Guide (70-270): Windows XP Professional.* Indianapolis, IN: Que Publishing, 2002. Chapter 6, "Implementing, Managing, and Troubleshooting Network Protocols and Services."

For further information on installing and configuring VPN servers in Windows 2000 Server, visit the following Web site:

"How to Install and Configure a Virtual Private Network Server in Windows 2000 Server" at http://support.microsoft.com/default.aspx?scid=kb;en-us;308208.

For further information on implementation of IPSec, see the following:

Smith, Ben and Brian Komar. *Microsoft Windows Security Resource Kit.* Redmond, WA: Microsoft Press, 2003. Chapter 9, "Implementing TCP/IP Security."

Taylor, Laura, "Understanding IPSec," http://www.intranetjournal.com/articles/200206/se_06_13_02a.html.

For further information on Internet security, see the following:

Hausman, Kirk, Diane Barrett, and Martin Weiss. *Security+ Exam Cram 2*. Indianapolis, IN: Que Publishing, 2003. Chapter 4, "Communication Security," and Chapter 5, "Online Vulnerabilities."

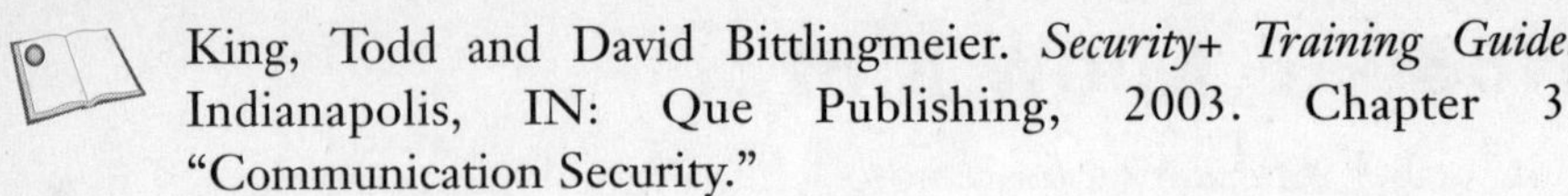

King, Todd and David Bittlingmeier. *Security+ Training Guide.* Indianapolis, IN: Que Publishing, 2003. Chapter 3, "Communication Security."

For more information about Internet Explorer security zones, visit the Web site http://www.microsoft.com/resources/documentation/ie/6/all/reskit/en-us/ie6rkit.mspx.

For further information on TACACS+ and how it works in a Cisco environment, see the following:

Khan, Umer, Vitaly Osipav, Mike Sewwney, and Woody Weaver. *Cisco Security Specialist's Guide to PIX Firewall.* Rockland, MD: Syngress Publishing, Inc., 2002.

For further information on SSH, check the following book:

Barrett, Daniel J., and Richard E. Silverman. *SSH: The Secure Shell.* Sebastopol, CA: O'Reilly & Associates, Inc., 2001.

For further information on protocol vulnerabilities, consult the following books:

Hausman, Kirk, Diane Barrett, and Martin Weiss. *Security+ Exam Cram 2.* Indianapolis, IN: Que Publishing, 2003. Chapter 5, "Online Vulnerabilities."

King, Todd and David Bittlingmeier. *Security+ Training Guide.* Indianapolis, IN: Que Publishing, 2003. Chapter 3, "Communication Security."

For an introduction to X.500 and LDAP as used by Microsoft in building Active Directory, see the following:

Poulton, Don. *MCSE 70-294 Training Guide: Planning, Implementing, and Maintaining a Microsoft Windows Server 2003 Active Directory Infrastructure.* Indianapolis, IN: Que Publishing, 2004. Chapter 1, "Concepts of Windows Server 2003 Active Directory."

For further information on FTP security, see the following books:

Hausman, Kirk, Diane Barrett, and Martin Weiss. *Security+ Exam Cram 2.* Indianapolis, IN: Que Publishing, 2003. Chapter 5, "Online Vulnerabilities."

King, Todd and David Bittlingmeier. *Security+ Training Guide.* Indianapolis, IN: Que Publishing, 2003. Chapter 3, "Communication Security."

For further information on wireless technologies and their vulnerabilities, consult the following books:

Geier, Jim. *Wireless LANs (2nd Edition)*. Indianapolis, IN: Sams, 2002.

King, Todd and David Bittlingmeier. *Security+ Training Guide*. Indianapolis, IN: Que Publishing, 2003. Chapter 3, "Communication Security."

Weber, Chris and Gary Bahadur. *Windows XP Professional Security*. Emeryville, CA: McGraw Hill/Osborne, 2002. Chapter 9, "Wireless Networking Security."

For further information on securing wireless networks in Windows 2000, see the following Web site:

Making IEEE 802.11 Networks Enterprise-Ready, by Arun Ayyagari and Tom Fout, http://download.microsoft.com/download/2/3/d/23d936a3-b294-48ac-a9a5-e9ef1e95c66d/wirelessec.doc.

Infrastructure Security

Companies invest millions of dollars annually in their computing infrastructure on items such as networking equipment and its maintenance, workstation and server hardware and software, and security devices, among many others. Security professionals must be familiar with the latest products and understand the security implications of their use in a particular environment.

The following is a list of the exam objectives you will be covering in this chapter:

- 3.1 Understand security concerns and concepts of the following types of devices:
  - Firewalls
  - Routers
  - Switches
  - Wireless
  - Modems
  - RAS (Remote Access Server)
  - Telecom/PBX (Private Branch Exchange)
  - VPN (Virtual Private Network)
  - IDS (Intrusion Detection System)
  - Network Monitoring/Diagnostics
  - Workstations
  - Servers
  - Mobile Devices

- 3.2 Understand the security concerns for the following types of media:
  - Coaxial Cable
  - UTP/STP (Unshielded Twisted Pair/Shielded Twisted Pair)
  - Fiber Optic Cable
  - Removable Media
    - Tape
    - CD-R (Recordable Compact Disks)
    - Hard Drives
    - Diskettes
    - Flash Cards
    - Smart Cards
- 3.3 Understand the concepts behind the following kinds of security topologies:
  - Security Zones
    - DMZ (Demilitarized Zone)
    - Intranet
    - Extranet
  - VLANs (Virtual Local Area Network)
  - NAT (Network Address Translation)
  - Tunneling
- 3.4 Differentiate the following types of intrusion detection, be able to explain the concepts of each type, and understand the implementation and configuration of each kind of intrusion detection system:
  - Network Based
    - Active Detection
    - Passive Detection
  - Host Based
    - Active Detection
    - Passive Detection

- Honey Pots
- Incident Response

- 3.5 Understand the following concepts of security baselines, be able to explain what a security baseline is, and understand the implementation and configuration of each kind of intrusion detection system:
  - OS/NOS (Operating System/Network Operating System) Hardening
    - File System
    - Updates (Hotfixes, Service Packs, Patches)
  - Network Hardening
    - Updates (Firmware)
    - Configuration
      - Enabling and Disabling Services and Protocols
      - Access Control Lists
  - Application Hardening
  - Updates (Hotfixes, Service Packs, Patches)
  - Web Servers
  - Email Servers
  - FTP (File Transfer Protocol) Servers
  - DNS (Domain Name Service) Servers
  - NNTP (Network News Transfer Protocol) Servers
  - File/Print Servers
  - DHCP (Dynamic Host Configuration Protocol) Servers
  - Data Repositories
    - Directory Services
    - Databases

3.1: Understanding Device Security

Many different types of components make up the present day computer network infrastructure. Every hardware device you incorporate into the network has its security concerns. They include firewalls, routers, switches, modems, various types of servers, workstations, mobile devices, and much more. You must adequately secure each of these components because a network is only as secure as its weakest link. The Security+ exam tests your knowledge of the security issues of all the common network devices.

Exercise 3.1.1: Configuring a Firewall in Windows 2000

A *firewall* is a device designed to shield internal network components from threats originating from the outside world. Firewalls work by capturing and analyzing data entering the network from external points and then rejecting undesirable types of data according to rules configured on the firewall. The major types of firewalls are as follows:

- *Packet-filtering*—Operating at the Network layer (Layer 3) of the Open Systems Interconnection (OSI) model, this type of firewall filters packets based on IP addresses, ports, or protocols. This type of firewall is frequently configured on a router.
- *Proxy service firewall*—A proxy server acts as an intermediary between internal networks and the Internet. One type of proxy service firewall is the circuit-level gateway, which operates at the Session layer (Layer 5) of the OSI model and ensures that sessions established with the internal network are legitimate. Another type is the application-level gateway, which operates at the Application layer (Layer 7) of the OSI model and checks for which application-layer protocols are allowed.
- *Stateful-inspection firewall*—This type of firewall combines the best of the other firewall technologies by using algorithms to process data at the OSI Application layer while monitoring communication states. In this manner, it operates at all layers of the OSI model. The Windows Firewall included with Windows XP Service Pack 2 (SP2) and Windows Server 2003 SP1 is an example of a stateful-inspection firewall.

Many businesses utilize some type of server or other hardware device as a firewall. Several companies produce software firewalls that can be used to protect single computers or small networks. In this exercise, you install and configure ZoneAlarm, which is a software firewall that is well suited to protecting home- or small-office computers or networks. Perform this exercise on a computer running Windows 2000 Professional:

1. Log on to the Windows 2000 Professional computer as an administrator.
2. Connect to the Internet and navigate to http://www.zonelabs.com/store/content/home2.jsp.
3. Click the Free Downloads and Trials link.
4. Click the ZoneAlarm Free Download link, and then click Download FREE ZoneAlarm.
5. When the download completes, click Open and follow the instructions presented by the installation wizard.
6. When requested, click Yes to start ZoneAlarm.
7. In the Zone Labs Security Options window, click the Select ZoneAlarm option, click Next, and then click Finish.

If you want to try out the ZoneAlarm Pro option for 14 days, choose the Select ZoneAlarm Pro option on this window. You can purchase this program later if you want.

8. Follow the instructions in the configuration wizard that next appears.
9. When requested, click OK to restart your computer.
10. When the computer restarts, log back on as administrator. You see the tutorial shown in Figure 3.1.
11. Click Next to display the Do I Need to Change the Default Firewall Settings to Be Secure page. Note the options and then click Next again.
12. Note the actions performed by ZoneAlarm on each page of this wizard, including their definition of “zones,” which is simpler than that used by Internet Explorer. When you reach the end of the wizard, click Done.
13. You can modify all options provided by ZoneAlarm from its control panel. (See Figure 3.2.)

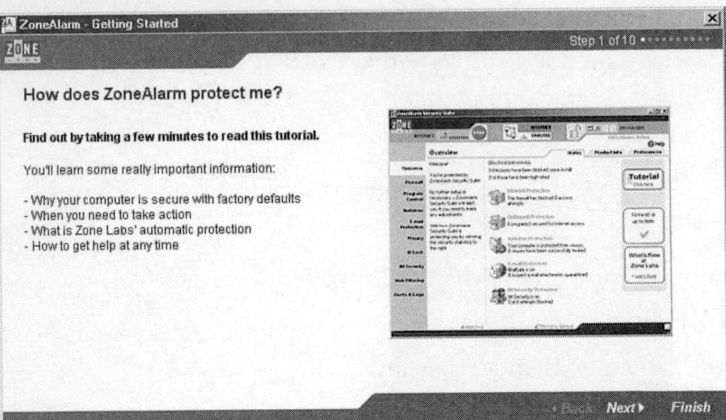

Figure 3.1 The ZoneAlarm tutorial provides information on the available options and configuration settings that serve to protect your computer.

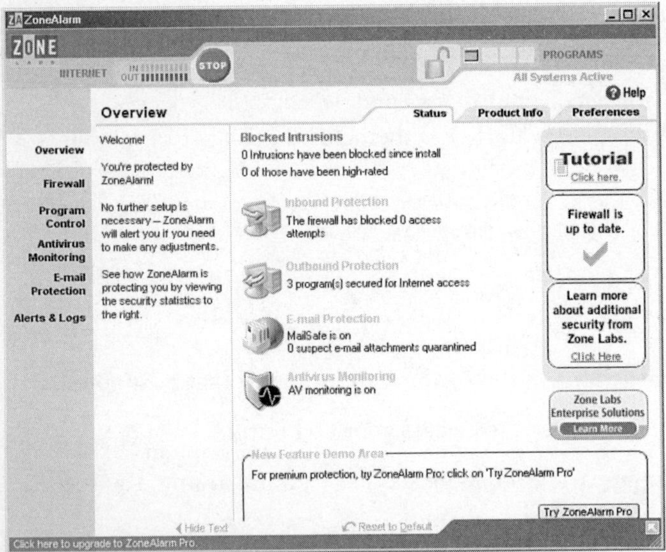

Figure 3.2 You can display intrusion information and configure all available options from the various pages presented by the ZoneAlarm control panel.

14. Select the various pages provided from the left side of the ZoneAlarm control panel. These pages are as follows:

   - *Overview*—As shown in Figure 3.2, provides an overview of the actions that ZoneAlarm has performed.

   - *Firewall*—Allows you to select the security levels for the two zones provided by ZoneAlarm.

- *Program Control*—Determines whether applications are able to access the Internet.
- *Antivirus Monitoring*—Displays the status of your antivirus software.
- *E-mail Protection*—Allows you to turn on MailSafe, which is a supplement to antivirus software that helps to protect you from email-borne viruses.
- *Alerts & Logs*—Allows you to decide whether to display messages on the screen when ZoneAlarm blocks an intrusion. Click Advanced to configure logging properties.

15. Close the ZoneAlarm control panel when you finish exploring and configuring the available options.

You need to know the major well-known ports for the Security+ exam. Knowledge of these ports is vital for answering questions related to firewalls or network access. Be sure you know the following TCP ports as a minimum: 20, File Transfer Protocol (FTP) control; 21, FTP data; 22, Secure Shell (SSH); 23, Telnet; 25, Simple Mail Transfer Protocol (SMTP); 80, Hypertext Transfer Protocol (HTTP); 110, Post Office Protocol 3 (POP3); 119, Network News Transfer Protocol (NNTP); 143, Internet Message Access Protocol (IMAP4); 443, Secure Sockets Layer (SSL and HTTPS); 1812, Remote Authentication Dial-In User Service (RADIUS); and 3389, Microsoft Remote Desktop.

Exercise 3.1.2: Understanding Vulnerabilities in Routers, Switches, Modems, RAS, Telecom, and VPN

The most secure computer system is one not connected to a network. However, isolated systems have few uses in today's environments. The reality is that your computers will most likely be accessible from remote clients in some manner. Be aware that every access path to your system has inherent vulnerabilities.

This exercise directs you to uncover some of the general risks with each type of remote access. Although each of the remote access approaches we discuss is more secure than wide-open access, there are still vulnerabilities you must be aware of and address.

In this exercise, you take a look at a few network access devices and security vulnerabilities associated with each one. Let's start with switches. Although a switch can make it harder for attackers to sniff networks for valuable information, they can also make it easier to launch some attacks. Next, we'll look at virtual private networks (VPNs). Although a VPN is a method to increase connection security, careless implementation can decrease your overall system's security. Then we'll look at modems. The modems you know about aren't the ones that will hurt you. It's the ones you don't know about that someone has connected to your network that will cause problems:

1. Connect to the Internet and browse to http://networking.earthweb.com/netsysm/article.php/933801. This article by Joseph Sloan discusses security problems inherent with switches. Although switches provide some protection from sniffing of network traffic, this protection can be circumvented. What are three ways in which this can occur?

If the URLs provided in this or other exercises no longer exist, simply use your favorite search engine to locate other sites that contain information pertinent to the topics at hand.

2. Continue to Sloan's second article and summarize several methods by which you can overcome these problems in a Unix environment.
3. Navigate to http://www.winnetmag.com/Articles/Index.cfm?ArticleID=8878. This article discusses a tool named Arpredirect, which is an Address Resolution Protocol (ARP) poisoning tool that can sniff traffic across switches. How does this tool work? What capabilities does it provide for an intruder who uses it to access data on your network? For more information, you might want to follow the link provided to Dug Song's Web site, which in turn links to additional articles related to security concerns of switched networks.
4. For an account of programming code that enabled hackers to launch denial of service (DoS) attacks against Cisco routers and switches, go to http://www.computerworld.com/securitytopics/security/story/0%2C10801%2C83820%2C00.html. What can happen if this code is run against a router to send a series of IP packets with a special format? What do network administrators have to do if this happens? Describe two actions that the networking team must perform to mitigate this vulnerability.

The use of switches is a good method for limiting hostile sniffing across the LAN.

5. In Chapter 2, "Communication Security," you learned how to configure RAS and VPN from a Microsoft perspective. Navigate to

http://www.ticm.com/info/insider/old/dec1997.html for a discussion of RAS and VPN vulnerabilities. What are several vulnerabilities inherent in these technologies? Describe how you would mitigate each vulnerability.

6. Matthew Mitchell presents another view of VPN vulnerabilities at http://www.giac.org/practical/matthew_mitchell_gsec.doc. How does encapsulation protect the data on the VPN? We will discuss the encryption algorithms mentioned in this article in Chapter 4, "Basics of Cryptography." What is the limitation of VPN data encryption? How can an unprotected network share become a vulnerability, and what are several consequences of such vulnerabilities? How can an attacker compromise a corporate network through computers used by telecommuters working from home and connected by DSL or cable modems, and what consequences can occur? Summarize the seven-step procedure outlined by Mitchell for protecting users accessing the network by means of a VPN.

7. Mark Collier discusses telecom, Voice over IP (VoIP), and PBX security at http://nwc.networkingpipeline.com/22104067. What are several possible VoIP deployment scenarios, and how can they be attacked? Summarize the types of vulnerabilities inherent in these devices, and note how they include many of the types of attacks you studied in Chapter 1, "General Security Concepts."

8. Another vulnerability associated with RAS and VPNs is that of war dialing. Navigate to http://searchsecurity.techtarget.com/sDefinition/0,,sid14_gci546705,00.html for a concise definition of this term and how a war dialer can be used to penetrate networks.

9. For more information on war dialing and how to mitigate this threat, continue to http://www.sans.org/rr/papers/60/471.pdf. What are several dangers associated with dial-up connections? How does a war dialer work, and what data can it provide? How can an intruder using a war dialer cover up his actions? Describe some components of a policy that should be applied to a company's dial-up users. How can a security professional test her network's vulnerability to the threat of war dialing?

The SANS Reading Room (http://www.sans.org/rr) is a good place to look for papers on many topics you need to know for the Security+ exam. The idea in the situation discussed here is to research problems associated with allowing a secure connection to terminate on an insecure client.

10. Unauthorized hardware such as modems presents another threat to the security of the network infrastructure. Go to http://www.cert.org/security-improvement/practices/p097.html and summarize the reasons why unauthorized hardware can be of concern. What are several means that you can use on a daily or monthly basis to detect unauthorized modems and other peripherals?

Exercise 3.1.3: Windows Network Monitor

Microsoft provides several support tools that help administrators monitor network traffic. A *network monitor* is a tool that sniffs data packets being transmitted across the network and allows an individual to display and analyze the contents of packets. This individual could be a hacker or a network administrator who is searching for evidence of intrusion or other network problems. Specifically, Microsoft Network Monitor provides visibility into what types of traffic are traveling across network segments. The version of Network Monitor depends on the version of Windows you are using. For this exercise, we use the Network Monitor Capture Utility for Microsoft Windows 2000 Server:

Network Monitor is available for Microsoft Systems Management Server, and the Network Monitor Capture Utility, a command-line implementation with similar basic capture capabilities, is available for Windows XP Professional. To make this exercise available to the largest number of installations, we use the Network Monitor Capture Utility for Windows 2000 Server.

In this exercise, you will install Network Monitor. You will also install Dynamic Host Configuration Protocol (DHCP) so that you can capture packets from the four-step DHCP process occurring at a client computer seeking TCP/IP configuration. You will use two computers, one running Windows 2000 Server and the other running Windows 2000 Professional or Windows XP Professional. Steps on a computer running Windows Server 2003 are similar:

1. Click Start, Settings, Control Panel, Add/Remove Programs.
2. Select Add/Remove Windows Components to start the Windows Components Wizard.
3. Select Management and Monitoring tools and click Details.
4. In the Management and Monitoring Tools dialog box, select Network Monitor Tools, click OK, and then click Next.

5. When prompted, insert the Windows 2000 Server CD-ROM, and then click OK.
6. Click Finish when the completion page appears.
7. Click Add/Remove Windows Components again, select Networking Services, and then click Details.
8. In the Networking Services dialog box, select Dynamic Host Configuration Protocol (DHCP), click OK, and then click Next.
9. When the completion page appears, click Finish, and then close Add/Remove Programs and Control Panel.
10. Click Start, Programs, Administrative Tools, Network Monitor. The Microsoft Network Monitor utility opens.
11. If a dialog box opens that discusses selecting a network adapter, click OK to allow Network Monitor to select a network adapter for your system. The initial Network Monitor window is shown in Figure 3.3.

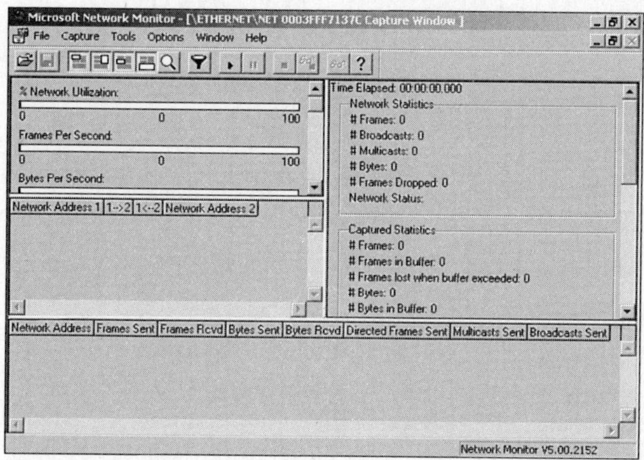

Figure 3.3 Network Monitor provides details of packets captured at the local computer.

12. Click Start, Programs, Administrative Tools, DHCP.
13. In the DHCP console, right-click your server and choose New Scope.
14. Click Next, provide a name for a test scope, and click Next again.
15. Type **192.168.1.101** and **192.168.1.200** for a range of addresses that the DHCP server will assign to clients, and then click Next twice.

16. On the Configure DHCP Options page, select No, I Will Configure These Options Later, and then click Next again until you reach the completion page.
17. Click Finish and close the DHCP console.
18. To capture some network traffic from the network adapter, click Capture, Start.
19. To generate some network traffic, start a DHCP session with a computer running Windows 2000 Professional. Log on to the Windows 2000 Professional computer as an administrator.
20. Right-click My Network Places and choose Properties.
21. In the Network and Dial-Up connections dialog box, right-click Local Area Connection and choose Properties.
22. In the Local Area Connection Properties dialog box, select Internet Protocol (TCP/IP) and then click Properties.
23. In the Internet Protocol (TCP/IP) Properties dialog box, click Obtain an IP Address Automatically and then click OK.
24. Close the Internet Protocol (TCP/IP) Properties and Local Area Connection Properties dialog boxes.
25. Return to the server. Network Monitor should now indicate that some packets have been captured. Click Capture, Stop.
26. Click Capture, Display Captured Data. This displays a summary capture window.
27. Scroll this window, watching the columns labeled Protocol and Description. You should be able to locate packets for the DHCP protocol with descriptions labeled Discover, Offer, Request, and ACK (as shown in Figure 3.4). They represent the four steps of the DHCP process and show how you can use Network Monitor to capture and analyze data on the network.

After you capture a file of network traffic, you need the complete Network Monitor tool to view its contents. This tool is available on Microsoft Systems Management Server.

Consult the Windows Support Tools help file for a complete description of the Network Monitor Capture Utility.

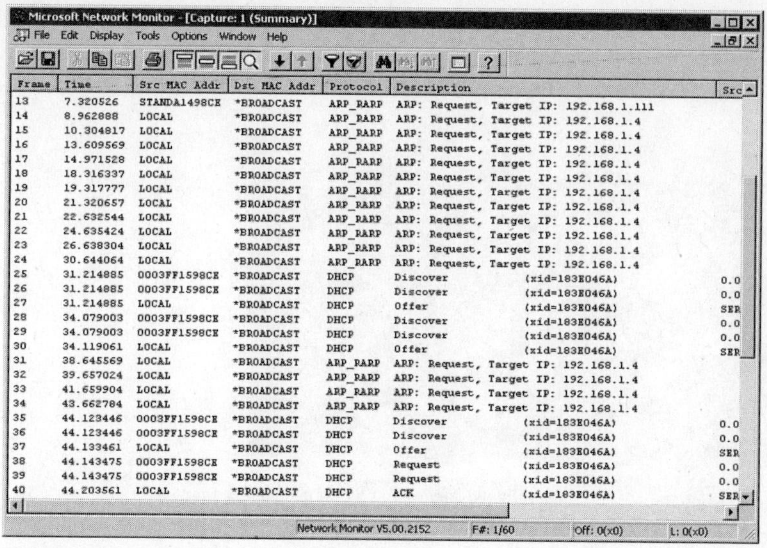

Microsoft Network Monitor - [Capture: 1 (Summary)]

File Edit Display Tools Options Window Help

Frame	Time	Src MAC Addr	Dst MAC Addr	Protocol	Description		Src
13	7.320526	STANDA1498CE	*BROADCAST	ARP_RARP	ARP: Request, Target IP: 192.168.1.111		
14	8.962888	LOCAL	*BROADCAST	ARP_RARP	ARP: Request, Target IP: 192.168.1.4		
15	10.304817	LOCAL	*BROADCAST	ARP_RARP	ARP: Request, Target IP: 192.168.1.4		
16	13.609569	LOCAL	*BROADCAST	ARP_RARP	ARP: Request, Target IP: 192.168.1.4		
17	14.971528	LOCAL	*BROADCAST	ARP_RARP	ARP: Request, Target IP: 192.168.1.4		
18	18.316337	LOCAL	*BROADCAST	ARP_RARP	ARP: Request, Target IP: 192.168.1.4		
19	19.317777	LOCAL	*BROADCAST	ARP_RARP	ARP: Request, Target IP: 192.168.1.4		
20	21.320657	LOCAL	*BROADCAST	ARP_RARP	ARP: Request, Target IP: 192.168.1.4		
21	22.632544	LOCAL	*BROADCAST	ARP_RARP	ARP: Request, Target IP: 192.168.1.4		
22	24.635424	LOCAL	*BROADCAST	ARP_RARP	ARP: Request, Target IP: 192.168.1.4		
23	26.638304	LOCAL	*BROADCAST	ARP_RARP	ARP: Request, Target IP: 192.168.1.4		
24	30.644064	LOCAL	*BROADCAST	ARP_RARP	ARP: Request, Target IP: 192.168.1.4		
25	31.214885	0003FF1598CE	*BROADCAST	DHCP	Discover	(xid=183E046A)	0.0
26	31.214885	0003FF1598CE	*BROADCAST	DHCP	Discover	(xid=183E046A)	0.0
27	31.214885	LOCAL	*BROADCAST	DHCP	Offer	(xid=183E046A)	SER
28	34.079003	0003FF1598CE	*BROADCAST	DHCP	Discover	(xid=183E046A)	0.0
29	34.079003	0003FF1598CE	*BROADCAST	DHCP	Discover	(xid=183E046A)	0.0
30	34.119061	LOCAL	*BROADCAST	DHCP	Offer	(xid=183E046A)	SER
31	38.645569	LOCAL	*BROADCAST	ARP_RARP	ARP: Request, Target IP: 192.168.1.4		
32	39.657024	LOCAL	*BROADCAST	ARP_RARP	ARP: Request, Target IP: 192.168.1.4		
33	41.659904	LOCAL	*BROADCAST	ARP_RARP	ARP: Request, Target IP: 192.168.1.4		
34	43.662784	LOCAL	*BROADCAST	ARP_RARP	ARP: Request, Target IP: 192.168.1.4		
35	44.123446	0003FF1598CE	*BROADCAST	DHCP	Discover	(xid=183E046A)	0.0
36	44.123446	0003FF1598CE	*BROADCAST	DHCP	Discover	(xid=183E046A)	0.0
37	44.133461	LOCAL	*BROADCAST	DHCP	Offer	(xid=183E046A)	SER
38	44.143475	0003FF1598CE	*BROADCAST	DHCP	Request	(xid=183E046A)	0.0
39	44.143475	0003FF1598CE	*BROADCAST	DHCP	Request	(xid=183E046A)	0.0
40	44.203561	LOCAL	*BROADCAST	DHCP	ACK	(xid=183E046A)	SER

Network Monitor V5.00.2152 F#: 1/60 Off: 0(x0) L: 0(x0)

Figure 3.4 Network Monitor provides information on the contents of frames captured from the network adapter.

Exercise 3.1.4: Diagnostics and Utilities Used for Monitoring Networks, Workstations, Servers, and Mobile Devices

Many utilities allow you to monitor various system events and activity. With respect to network activity, we'll look at a few common utilities in this exercise. This exercise focuses on Microsoft Windows, but these utilities are commonly found on other operating systems as well.

The basic purpose of monitoring utilities is to take a snapshot of activity so you can improve the performance or security of a system. The utilities generally provide raw data for you to analyze. The more you can request very specific data, the quicker you will be able to zero in on pertinent information. Take the time to learn how to use monitoring utilities and their common features. You will be rewarded with the information to adjust your systems to perform the way you intend:

1. Launch a Windows command prompt by choosing Start, Programs, Accessories, Command Prompt. If you are using Unix or Linux, these commands are accessible from the command line in any shell.
2. Use the `ping` command to test a remote computer to see whether it is reachable. Type **`ping`** ***`IP address`***. (You can also use a fully qualified

domain name [FQDN]; for example, we used `ping www.foxnews.com`.) The `ping` command shows the amount of time it takes to reach the target system and for the target system to respond (see Figure 3.5).

```
Command Prompt
Microsoft Windows 2000 [Version 5.00.2195]
(C) Copyright 1985-2000 Microsoft Corp.

C:\>ping www.foxnews.com

Pinging a20.g.akamai.net [207.61.136.35] with 32 bytes of data:

Reply from 207.61.136.35: bytes=32 time=62ms TTL=57
Reply from 207.61.136.35: bytes=32 time=62ms TTL=57
Reply from 207.61.136.35: bytes=32 time=62ms TTL=57
Reply from 207.61.136.35: bytes=32 time=46ms TTL=57

Ping statistics for 207.61.136.35:
    Packets: Sent = 4, Received = 4, Lost = 0 (0% loss),
Approximate round trip times in milli-seconds:
    Minimum = 46ms, Maximum =  62ms, Average =  58ms

C:\>
```

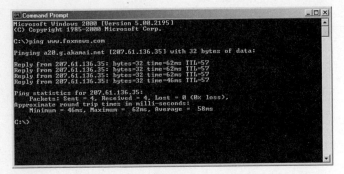

Figure 3.5 The **ping** command verifies the existence of and connectivity to a remote machine on the Internet.

The `ping` command sends special network packets—Internet Control Message Protocol (ICMP) echo packets—to remote computers. If the remote computer allows and responds to ICMP packets, you should get a response from the `ping` command. However, some firewalls block or drop ICMP packets so the `ping` command doesn't always report back correctly. When it doesn't provide a response from the target system, you have to use other, more sophisticated, diagnostic tools. All `ping` tells you is that the target machine responded to an ICMP echo packet.

3. Use the `tracert` command to show how many machines, or hops, exist between your computer and the target (see Figure 3.6). This utility is useful to diagnose performance issues by showing the path between two machines. Type **`tracert`** ***`IP address`*** or **`tracert`** ***`FQDN`*** (for example, we used `tracert www.foxnews.com`).

   The `tracert` command is similar to the `ping` command in that it sends ICMP echo packets. The difference is in the use of the Time to Live (TTL) field in the ICMP packet. A router decrements the TTL value when it receives an ICMP packet and most routers return a "TTL expired in transit" message when the TTL value reaches 0. The `tracert` command sends out many ICMP packets, with TTL values ranging from 1 to some maximum value. At each hop along the way, routers decrement the TTL values. The first router in the path returns the TTL packet that started with a TTL value of 1. The second router returns the packet whose TTL value started with 2. The sender listens for returned ICMP packets and constructs the route all the way to the destination.

```
Command Prompt
C:\>tracert www.foxnews.com

Tracing route to a20.g.akamai.net [207.61.136.35]
over a maximum of 30 hops:

  1    63 ms    47 ms    46 ms  64.230.254.62
  2    47 ms    47 ms    46 ms  dis8-hamilton14-Vlan102.in.bellnexxia.net [64.23
0.236.233]
  3    47 ms    46 ms    47 ms  core1-hamilton14-Gigabite2-0.in.bellnexxia.net [
64.230.236.241]
  4    47 ms    47 ms    62 ms  64.230.241.121
  5    63 ms    46 ms    63 ms  64.230.240.17
  6    46 ms    63 ms    62 ms  64.230.240.2
  7    47 ms    63 ms    62 ms  207.61.136.35

Trace complete.

C:\>
```

Figure 3.6 The **tracert** command provides information on all routers through which the signal passes to reach a target machine.

4. Use the `netstat` command to show the status of ports on your machine. Type **`netstat -a`** to show all ports that are listening for connections (see Figure 3.7). You can also use `netstat` to show which process is listening to a port. This option is nice when you are trying to find unknown or hostile programs installed on a machine. When you know that a port is open, you can use other utilities to determine what program opened the port. In Windows, you need to install third-party utilities, such as Inzider (http://ntsecurity.nu/toolbox/inzider/) or Foundstone's FPortNG tool (http://www.foundstone.com/knowledge/zips/FPortNG.zip).

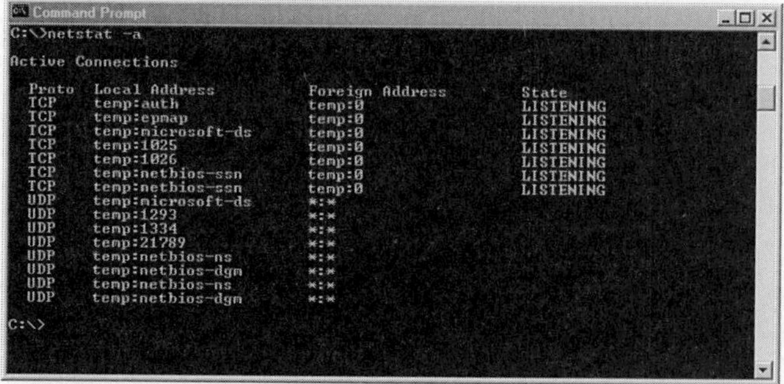

```
Command Prompt
C:\>netstat -a

Active Connections

  Proto  Local Address          Foreign Address        State
  TCP    temp:auth              temp:0                 LISTENING
  TCP    temp:epmap             temp:0                 LISTENING
  TCP    temp:microsoft-ds      temp:0                 LISTENING
  TCP    temp:1025              temp:0                 LISTENING
  TCP    temp:1026              temp:0                 LISTENING
  TCP    temp:netbios-ssn       temp:0                 LISTENING
  TCP    temp:netbios-ssn       temp:0                 LISTENING
  UDP    temp:microsoft-ds      *:*
  UDP    temp:1293              *:*
  UDP    temp:1334              *:*
  UDP    temp:21789             *:*
  UDP    temp:netbios-ns        *:*
  UDP    temp:netbios-dgm       *:*
  UDP    temp:netbios-ns        *:*
  UDP    temp:netbios-dgm       *:*

C:\>
```

Figure 3.7 The **netstat –a** command displays a list of all ports that are listening for connections on your machine.

These are just a few of the many monitoring utilities that exist for capturing and analyzing the status and activity of your systems. Look at your system's administration documentation for additional utilities. In addition, check the following sites on the Internet for suitable monitoring utilities:

- Labmice at http://labmice.techtarget.com/Utilities/networkmonitor.htm offers a range of freeware and shareware administrative tools with brief descriptions of each.
- Adle Enterprises at http://www.adlenterprises.com/Utilities/Network/linux-network-monitoring.php offers Linux network monitoring shareware tools.
- NetSaint is a network monitoring tool primarily designed for Linux. Information and downloads, as well as links to other monitoring utilities, are available at http://www.netsaint.org/docs/0_0_6/about.html.
- Monitor Tools at http://www.monitortools.com/cat_networksystem/ offers a comprehensive list of links to network and system monitoring utilities for all operating systems.

What Did I Just Learn?

Now that you have looked at device security, let's take a moment to review all the critical items you've experienced in this lab:

- A firewall is a hardware or software device that stops unwanted network or Internet traffic from entering a computer or network. ZoneAlarm is a popular software firewall that is easily configured for home- or small-office computers.
- Every network device has some kind of vulnerability associated with it. We looked at ARP poisoning as it affects switches, unauthorized modems, and VPN vulnerabilities.
- The Microsoft Support Tools includes a simple Network Monitor Capture Utility that you can use to capture and analyze traffic from the network adapter of a Windows computer. Although Microsoft makes it easy to capture network data, it is more important to understand how to interpret network activity.
- Several TCP/IP utilities allow you to monitor system activity and connectivity on Windows, Unix, or other computers.

3.2: Understanding Media Security

The essence of a network is that a series of computers are connected in some fashion to one another and transmitting information across some type of media. Although you might have secured your computers and other devices to the strongest extent possible, attackers might still be able to access information as it flows across the wires or from removable media such as CDs, tapes, and disks and use this information for their benefit or for pursuing more potent attacks on your network.

Exercise 3.2.1: Understanding Media Security Concepts

Networking cable types whose security concerns you need to be familiar with include coax (thinnet or 10Base-2 and thicknet or 10Base-5), twisted pair (UTP and STP), and fiber optic. In this exercise, you research the security concerns of these networking media.

1. From a Web browser, connect to the Internet and navigate to http://www.enterasys.com/support/techtips/tk0399-9.html. This document provides a background of the specifications of the various networking media, which should all be familiar to anyone who has taken the Network+ exam.

2. Continue to http://c0vertl.tripod.com/text/ethernet.htm and note some problems that exist with the various types of networking cable. Which troubleshooting device do the authors claim can detect tapping of a network cable?

3. Continue to http://www.puredata.com/supports/faqs/fiber/faqs.html and find out why eavesdropping of fiber-based networks is virtually impossible.

4. Note the table comparing characteristics of network media at http://website.lineone.net/~paulcon/70-58-2.html. Which type of media is most subject to eavesdropping?

5. You might want to conduct a search on Google or Yahoo! for additional articles that relate to security concerns of Ethernet media, but be forewarned that not much relevant material is present.

In addition to these sources, review the material provided in the *Exam Cram 2* and the *Training Guide* for the Security+ exam for additional information on networking media security concerns. (See the "Need to Know More?" section at the end of this chapter.)

Keep in mind other properties of network media when it comes to assessing security of the different media types. For example, cabling located in a location subject to electromagnetic interference should be shielded in some manner. STP or fiber optic cable is more suitable to such a location than UTP cable such as standard 10Base-T or 100Base-T installations.

Exercise 3.2.2: Securing Removable Media

Unauthorized users who can remove disks or tapes from a network can steal information from the network; they can also insert disks containing viruses, Trojan horses, sniffers, or other unauthorized software to facilitate other attacks. In this exercise, you look at some of the concerns of removable media security:

1. Rick Cook discusses the security of backup tapes at http://searchstorage.techtarget.com/tip/1,289483,sid5_gci756807,00.html. What method does he suggest for improving the security of these tapes?
2. A good source for information on data security management is http://www.degaussing.net/security-issues-in-data-facility-management.html. They review degaussing of magnetic media, including tapes and hard disks, and offer a large number of links to additional sources. Study this reference and enumerate all the issues they discuss related to security of data stored on tapes and disks. Also locate as many reasons as possible for performing complete data erasure on tapes and disks that are no longer required.
3. Threats to data stored on removable media can come from within the company as well as outside. Note some of the precautions you should observe when planning backup strategies in http://www.nss.co.uk/WhitePapers/data_storage_mment/data_storage_mment.htm. Follow the two "Security" links in the article's table of contents. What is a potential loophole associated with an unattended backup taking place at a user's desktop? What is a potential security breach associated with members of the Backup Operators group also being able to restore data?
4. Thanks to readily available hardware and software solutions, recordable CDs can present a security problem because it is easy to copy data to a CD and remove it from the premises. Data Link Associates sells a CD/optical media eraser, which they claim can erase all types of CDs. For information on this product, go to http://www.datalinksales.com/degaussers/1200.htm. A hand-cranked device described at http://www.datalinksales.com/degaussers/shredder434355.htm completely destroys CDs and DVDs.

5. David White discusses systems security at http://www.dbmsmag.com/9711d13.html. His article includes smart card and PCMCIA card security concerns. What is one way in which an unauthorized user can obtain information from a smart card? He also discusses topics of interest related to several other Security+ objectives.

6. Stephen Wilson discusses smart card and hardware key security at http://www.sans.org/rr/papers/20/763.pdf. We discuss certificate and hardware key security in Chapter 4. What are some of the security features that Wilson mentions? What is the biggest limitation regarding the use of smart cards, and what solution does he advocate for this limitation?

Exercise 3.2.3: Using the Encrypting File System to Encrypt Data in Windows 2000 Server

Starting with Windows 2000, Microsoft made available an easily implemented system of encrypting data on a hard disk with the Encrypting File System (EFS). This method of encryption is especially useful for portable computers that are subject to loss or theft and prevents data from being copied after removing the disk to another computer or by an intruder who does not know the username or password under which the data was encrypted. In this exercise, you encrypt a test file and then attempt to access it as an unauthorized user. Perform this exercise on a computer running Windows 2000 Server. You can also do this exercise on a computer running Windows XP Professional or Windows Server 2003. In any case, the hard disk must be formatted with the NTFS file system:

1. Log on to the computer running Windows 2000 Server as an administrator.

2. Open My Computer and navigate to the C: drive.

3. Create a new folder named `Encrypt`.

4. Right-click this folder and choose Properties.

5. On the General tab of the Encrypt Properties dialog box, click Advanced.

6. In the Advanced Attributes dialog box that opens, select the Encrypt Contents to Secure Data check box (see Figure 3.8), and then click OK.

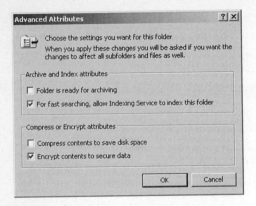

Figure 3.8 Encrypt a folder in Windows 2000 Server.

7. Click Apply to apply the change.

If you are using Windows XP Professional or Windows Server 2003, you must select the Security tab of the Encrypt Properties dialog box, select the Users entry, select the Full Control permission under the Allow column, and then click OK. Granting this permission is necessary so that you can distinguish the effect of data encryption from that of the application of NTFS permissions, as we discussed in Chapter 1.

8. Open the `Encrypt` folder and create a text document by selecting File, New, Text Document and then typing **`Text1.txt`** as the filename.
9. Open this document and type something in the body of the document that identifies the document. Save the document and close Notepad.
10. Log off and log on as the User1 user you created in Chapter 1.
11. Navigate to and attempt to open the text document in the `C:\Encrypt` folder. What happens? You receive an "Access is denied" message because the document was encrypted by the administrator. Any user can create an encrypted document according to permissions specified on the folder in which the document is created.
12. To prove this point, repeat Steps 8 and 9 to create another document as the User1 user. Then log off and log back on as the administrator and try to open this document. You receive the same message because this document was encrypted by the User1 user. EFS provides this second level of security that is valuable in situations where the computer might be vulnerable to theft or other unauthorized access.

What Did I Just Learn?

Now that you have looked at media concerns, let's take a moment to review all the critical items you've experienced in this lab:

- You need to keep your network cabling media secure from intrusions such as eavesdropping by means of wiretapping, which can occur on coaxial and twisted-pair networking configurations.
- Fiber optic cable is more difficult to compromise than coaxial or twisted-pair networking media. However, it is more expensive and difficult to work with. Its usage is mainly in places where physical security is difficult to achieve or where the need for large bandwidth or freedom from electromagnetic interference is required.
- Removable media such as tapes, CDs, disks, flash cards, and smart cards can present security problems because of the ease of removal from work premises. The same is true with regard to hard disks, although these take more time to remove except in hot-swap configurations.
- EFS in Windows 2000/XP/2003 provides an additional layer of data security that is especially valuable in situations where theft or loss of portable computers is possible.

3.3: Security Topologies

A *security topology* is the arrangement of hardware devices on a network with respect to internal security requirements and needs for public access. For example, an Internet order firm will need Web servers that can be accessed by the public for placing orders. In turn, the Web servers will need access to internal database servers, and internal users (employees) will need access to the various servers and possibly to the Internet.

Exercise 3.3.1: Understanding Security Zones

As discussed in the *Security+ Exam Cram 2* book, several types of security zone topologies exist, and they include features such as bastion hosts, screened host gateways, and screened subnet gateways. You can place resources that require access from both external and internal locations in a DMZ. An intranet is an internal network that is built using Web servers to disseminate information on an internal basis only. An extranet is a portion of a network set up to allow access by a specified external location only, such as a business partner. In this exercise, you research these topics on the Internet:

1. Connect to the Internet and navigate to http://www.sharkbelly.org/ebooks/security_plus/0789728362_ch03lev1sec4.html#ch03fig04. This reference provides a comprehensive overview of all topics in Objective 3.3 of the Security+ exam. Review the information provided and in particular the following:

    - Where is a bastion host placed, and how does it protect an internal network?
    - What is the attack surface, and how should it be set up for the highest level of security?
    - How does a screened host gateway differ from a bastion host, and in what ways is it similar to a bastion host?
    - What is the function of an application gateway?
    - How does a screened subnet gateway differ from the other types of security topologies? What types of servers are placed in the DMZ that this gateway defines?
    - What are two different DMZ configurations? Note how these configurations differ from one another and when you should use one configuration or another.
    - What components of a network can constitute an intranet?
    - How does an extranet differ from an intranet, and what components normally appear in an extranet?
    - What is a virtual LAN (VLAN), and in what situations is it advantageous to employ one?
    - How does Network Address Translation (NAT) work? What are the private IP address ranges, and what purpose do these address ranges serve?
    - Which vulnerability is presented by VPN tunneling, and what topological solutions do the authors suggest to overcome this problem?

A VLAN is a good solution when the need arises to implement a hardware-based implementation that restricts internal access within a network to certain portions as needed for performance of users' tasks. This technology is also beneficial in reducing the likelihood of data compromise by sniffers.

2. TechSmiths provides an additional point of view on these topics at http://www.techsmiths.com/wapug/exch03/white_papers/webspeed/securing_firewall.htm. What is the major weakness of a bastion host-based security topology? In what two ways is a screened host topology better than a bastion host? Note that the screened subnet topology includes the DMZ concept. Note that a version of the screened subnet topology exists that embraces the concept of an extranet. Finally, note their preferred version of a DMZ configuration and the advantages provided by this configuration.

3. Yet another viewpoint on security topologies appears at http://www.interhack.net/pubs/fwfaq/. This article contains information of special interest to those of you who are running Cisco routers. It answers many questions related to firewall and topology basics, various intrusions, and methods of making server-based applications work across a firewall. That said, it is a valuable reference for several Security+ objectives in all five objective domains.

4. A concise report on what bastion hosts do appears at http://www.sans.org/resources/idfaq/bastion.php. What types of bastion hosts are used, and what methods are used to harden or secure these systems?

You should be able to distinguish the types of security topologies and know when to implement a given topology.

Exercise 3.3.2: The Use of VLANs

Two situations often arise when working with LANs. First, as LANs become more popular and faster, they tend to grow larger. As a result, any broadcast messages reach a larger audience than was common even in recent history. Additionally, as more companies adopt organizational structures that are less hierarchical, employees can move from location to location more frequently.

One solution to both of these issues is the VLAN. A *VLAN* allows a group of computers to be virtually configured as a separate LAN. A VLAN can simply define a subset of a larger LAN or can include computers from various existing LANs.

Figure 3.9 shows a simple VLAN configuration.

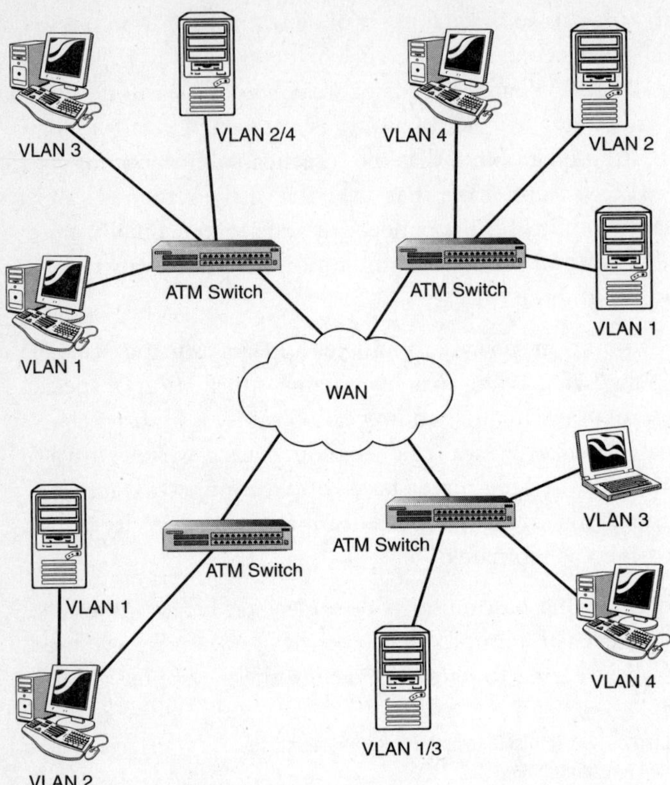

Figure 3.9 A VLAN connects groups of computers, forming a separate network.

This exercise directs you to research VLANs and answer some questions about what you learned:

1. From a Web browser, visit the Candela Technologies Web page at http://www.candelatech.com/~greear/vlan.html and the University of California–Davis Web page at http://net21.ucdavis.edu/newvlan.htm. These Web sites and the links within them contain a lot of information on VLANs. How does a VLAN differ from an ordinary LAN? What are some drawbacks of ordinary routed networks that are solved by the use of a VLAN? Summarize the benefits and limitations of VLANs as described in the University of California page.
2. Write a brief summary that explains what VLANs are, what benefits they provide over standard LANs, and how you might use one in your environment. Also answer the following questions:

- What standard defines VLANs?
- What factor influences VLAN designs more, physical location or logical grouping?
- Can VLAN devices belong to different physical LANs, or must they all belong to the same LAN?
- Do VLANs normally increase or decrease network performance?

Exercise 3.3.3: Configuring Internet Connection Sharing in Windows 2000

Internet Connection Sharing (ICS) is a simplified form of Network Address Translation (NAT) available in Windows 2000, Windows XP, and Windows Server 2003. ICS allows users in a home- or small-office environment to connect to the Internet through a host computer on which it is enabled. Like the full version of NAT, ICS hides the internal computers from anyone attempting to access them externally. In the following exercise, you configure a computer running Windows 2000 Professional for ICS. Perform this exercise on a computer that is not joined to a domain. The steps are slightly different, depending on the service pak level in use.

1. Right-click My Network Places and choose Properties.
2. Right-click the network connection on which you want to enable ICS and choose Properties.
3. On the Sharing tab of the Properties dialog box that opens, select Enable Internet Connection Sharing for This Connection (see Figure 3.10).
4. To ensure that the connection will be dialed when another computer on the network attempts to connect to the Internet, select the Enable On-Demand Dialing check box.
5. To configure additional ICS settings, click Settings. You can specify which applications are enabled for networking as well as which services will be provided to computers on the network.
6. Click OK.

When running ICS, client computers receive IP addresses on the 192.168.0.0/24 network. You should configure these computers to use DHCP to obtain IP addresses.

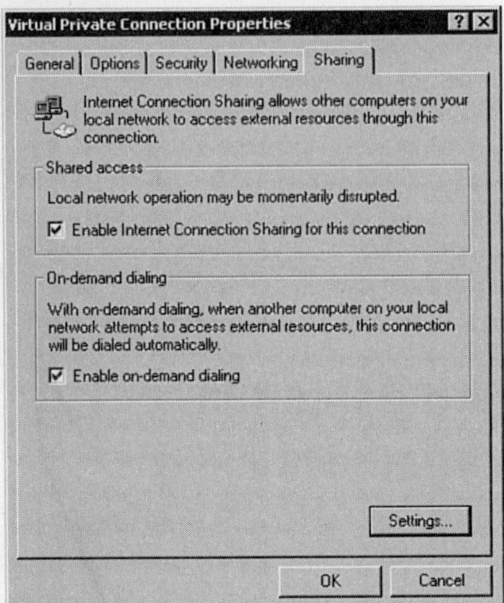

Figure 3.10 Enable ICS in Windows 2000 in the Virtual Private Connection Properties dialog box.

What Did I Just Learn?

Now that you have looked at security zone topologies, let's take a moment to review all the critical items you've experienced in this lab:

- Security zone topologies include bastion hosts, screened host gateways, and screened subnet gateway.
- A DMZ is a small network located between the local network and the Internet on which services such as Web servers are located. Several configurations for a DMZ are available.
- An intranet is an internal network configured with a locally available Web server that facilitates exchange of information.
- An extranet is similar to an intranet but allows access to another trusted network, such as that of a business partner.
- A VLAN combines computers on the network into a single logical network that can span multiple switches. It is used to provide logical groupings of computers.
- NAT enables multiple computers to connect to the Internet through a single gateway computer. ICS is a simplified form of NAT available in Windows 2000, Windows XP, and Windows Server 2003.

3.4: Implementing and Configuring IDSs

An important part of a security administrator's job is to detect attacks in progress as early as possible so he can minimize the damage and prevent further attacks. An intrusion detection system (IDS) is a software or hardware tool that alerts the administrator to the possibility that an attack is in progress and enables him to take appropriate steps.

Exercise 3.4.1: Understanding IDSs

IDSs can be either network-based or host-based; in other words, they might operate across an entire network or be centered on a specific host. Either type of IDS uses two methods: knowledge-based (also known as signature-based), which identifies known attack signatures similar to the method of virus signatures used by antivirus programs, and behavior-based (also known as anomaly-based), which watches for unusual network behavior that might indicate an attack is in progress. In this exercise, you research these topics and study several commercially available IDSs:

1. SANS maintains an FAQ site at http://www.sans.org/resources/idfaq/ that answers several hundred questions related to intrusion detection. Peruse the answers to as many questions as you can, but in particular, look for answers to the following:

   - What is intrusion detection, and why is it needed?
   - What is a honeypot?
   - What are host-based and network-based intrusion detection? For more information, access the links provided on these topics.
   - What are some advantages and disadvantages of a knowledge-based IDS? A behavior-based IDS?
   - Why are false positives observed?
   - What are some methods used by attackers to evade IDSs?
   - What are some methods used for intrusion detection on wireless networks? See the paper by David Dobrotka.
   - Note briefly the various types of scans and probes that are discussed.
   - What are some indications of attack on a Unix system?

- Summarize the types of intrusion-detection products referred to, and note which types of products are most useful under which circumstances.
- Study and summarize several examples of attacks that they discuss in the last section of their list.
- You will return to the same site in Exercise 3.4.3 to learn about incident response.

A *false positive* refers to an event that is detected as an intrusion when in fact it is a normal occurrence. A *false negative* refers to a real intrusion that is passed off as a normal occurrence. False negatives can be dangerous because you are not aware that something is going on while the attacker is obtaining data or creating havoc on your systems.

Be sure that you can compare and contrast the types of IDSs and the circumstances in which each one should be used.

2. Lawrence Halme and Kenneth Bauer provide a paper on Anti-Intrusion Taxonomy (AINT) at http://www.sans.org/resources/idfaq/aint.php. This paper, which you can reach from the SANS FAQ site, discusses six approaches to IDSs and three means of intrusion prevention. Compare these methods and ask yourself which are the most and least likely means of achieving results.
3. Another approach to IDSs is a statistical method. Jamil Farshachi presents several types of statistical-based systems at http://www.sans.org/resources/idfaq/statistic_ids.php. Review them and take a look at the Spade anomaly detector. Note in particular how you can set the threshold adjustment. What are the consequences if you set this adjustment too high or too low?
4. Greg Shipley contrasts network-based and host-based IDSs at http://www.networkcomputing.com/1023/1023f1.html. What are some advantages and disadvantages of each approach, and how does Shipley's solution combine the best of both?
5. Edward Yakabovicz discusses IDS recommendations at http://searchsecurity.techtarget.com/originalContent/0,289142,sid14_gci779268,00.html. What recommendations for IDS tools and products deployment does he present? In addition, which project management tasks should be undertaken? What are the three tiers that he advocates for deployment of network-based IDSs?

6. An additional resource for brief Q&A–style information on IDSs and other topics relevant to the Security+ exam appears at http://www.windowsecurity.com/faqs/Intrusion_Detection/. Compare their answers to those obtained from other sources.

7. Roger Grimes discusses the purpose of honeypots and reviews several commercial honeypots at http://www.winnetmag.com/Articles/Index.cfm (enter `41976` in the InstantDoc ID text box). What are some of the characteristics of attacks that have been uncovered using honeypots? How does a real honeypot differ from a virtual honeypot, and what are some of the advantages and drawbacks of each?

8. For another viewpoint on real and virtual honeypots, go to Brian Posey's article at http://techrepublic.com.com/5100-6264_11-5195024.html?tag=e064. Summarize his opinions on the advantages and disadvantages of real and virtual honeypots. What conclusion does he draw?

You should be aware that an IDS is unable to detect attacks directed at the network or computer from spoofed email messages.

Although a honeypot is a single computer set up to attract attacks, a *honeynet* is a network that is set up for the same purpose. You should be able to compare and contrast honeypots with honeynets for the Security+ exam.

Exercise 3.4.2: Configuring an IDS

In this exercise, you download, install, and configure the trial version of a representative host-based IDS, Tripwire for Servers. Perform this exercise on a computer running Windows 2000 Server. The exercise will also work on a computer running Windows 2000 Professional, Windows XP Professional, or Windows Server 2003:

1. Go to http://www.tripwire.com/products/index.cfm# and read about Tripwire's products.

2. Select the Find Out More link under Tripwire for Servers.

3. To obtain information on Tripwire for Servers, select the download of Tripwire for Servers from the right side of the Tripwire for Servers page.

4. After reading the information presented, click the Go link under Evaluation Downloads.

5. Click Download Trial Kit Software. You will need to fill out an information form, including a valid email address, to receive a trial license by email and download the product. Follow the instructions provided and click Submit.

6. In a few minutes, you should receive an email message with instructions and license files. Save these files and download the Windows executable file.

7. Follow the instructions presented by the installation wizard, and provide the path to the license files when prompted. Click Finish when the installation completes.

8. Click Start, Programs, Tripwire 4.0 Trial, Trial Guide. Internet Explorer displays the page shown in Figure 3.11. This page contains information on what the trial version does, including a guide that walks you through the performance of several simulated actions.

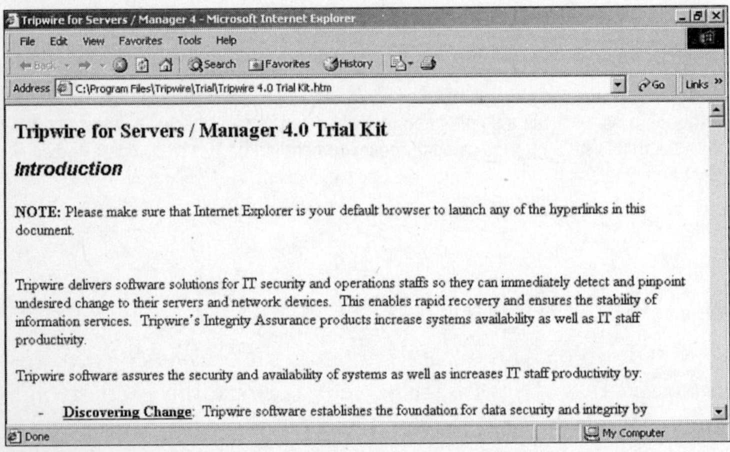

Figure 3.11 The demo version of Tripwire Manager contains a Web page from which you can perform a series of simulated actions.

9. Select the link to run Tripwire Manager.

10. If you are running Windows XP SP2, you might receive a security alert message. Select Unblock This Program to allow Tripwire Manager to proceed.

11. Follow instructions on the Web page to perform simulated actions that include adding agent machines to the list, editing the configuration and policy files, creating a baseline, running integrity checks, installing an application, upgrading an existing application, compromising an application, and attacking with a worm.
12. Note how Tripwire reports on the installation of an unapproved application, as shown in Figure 3.12. This capability enables you to monitor client computers for such activity.

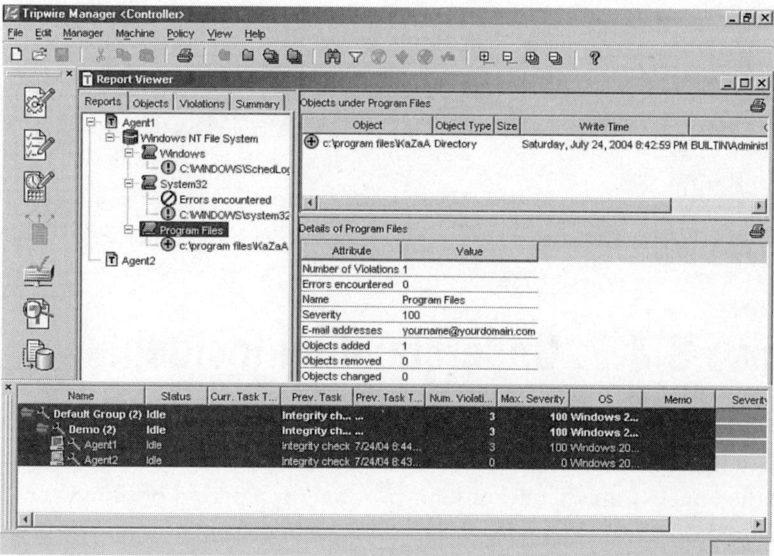

Figure 3.12 An IDS can alert you to activity such as installation of an unapproved program.

13. In the last part of the demo exercise, Tripwire reports on a simulated worm attack, as shown in Figure 3.13.
14. When you are finished, run the last script and observe the conclusions at the bottom of the Web page. Think about how you can use an IDS program like Tripwire to detect changes occurring on a network for which you are responsible.

Many different commercial IDSs are available, and a Web search can provide a lot of information and trial downloads. Downloading and running another IDS or two will prove useful in both advancing your knowledge and preparing you for the Security+ exam.

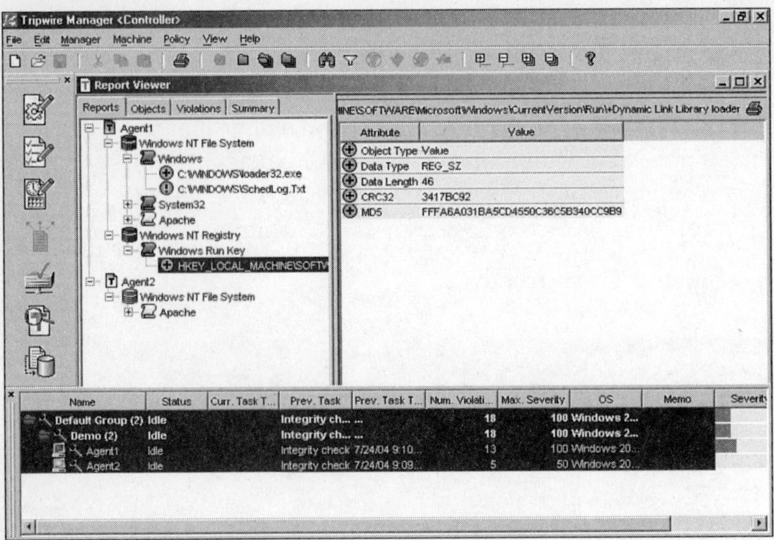

Figure 3.13 Tripwire reports on changes made to the Registry by a simulated worm attack.

Exercise 3.4.3: Understanding Incident Response Systems

After you detect an attack in progress, you need to know how to respond. Do you stop the attack immediately, or let it proceed for a period of time to collect additional evidence? What legal rights do you have, and how do you protect them? In this exercise, you study the methods of responding to an attack:

1. Return to the SANS FAQ site that you accessed in Exercise 3.4.1 at http://www.sans.org/resources/idfaq/. Look at the Incident Handling and Response section and obtain answers to the following:

   - What steps should you take when you suspect that an intrusion is in progress? How should you respond?
   - What legal issues do security administrators need to be aware of?
   - What did we learn from the Melissa virus?
   - How do you preserve the evidence of an attack if you want to pursue legal action? What activities are of questionable legal value?

- Describe several methods of automated responses. Which are most effective, and what are some of the risks or drawbacks?
- What are two methods of active response to an attack?

2. Jim Reavis presents a comprehensive procedure detailing how to respond to an intrusion at http://www.nwfusion.com/newsletters/sec/0913sec1.html. Which utilities does he recommend for detecting intrusion on Unix systems? What information should you collect when documenting intrusions? What steps does he advocate, and what preparations do you need to make beforehand so that you are ready to deal with an intrusion when it happens?

What Did I Just Learn?

Now that you have looked at intrusion detection systems, let's take a moment to review all the critical items you've experienced in this lab:

- An IDS can be either network based or host based. A network-based IDS operates across an entire network, whereas a host-based IDS concentrates on a single computer but provides a higher level of intrusion detection.
- A knowledge-based IDS identifies known attack signatures similar to the method used by antivirus programs.
- A behavior-based IDS watches for unusual behavior on a network that might indicate an attack is in progress.
- An active IDS attempts to perform some task that restricts the intruder's access, such as shutting down a server or terminating a connection. A passive IDS merely informs the administrator that an attack is in progress and does not attempt to stop it.
- A honeypot is a computer that is configured for the purpose of distracting attackers while obtaining information about attacks in progress.

3.5: Establishing Security Baselines

Before you can recognize abnormal system behavior as a sign of attack, you need to know what normal behavior is. In other words, you need a security baseline. In setting a baseline, it is important to harden or lock down your servers and networks at a level where incursions are less likely to occur.

These exercises introduce you to the concepts of operating system, network, and application hardening.

Exercise 3.5.1: Hardening Windows and Unix Operating Systems

Operating system hardening includes locking down files, folders, and applications, as well as the operating system itself. In Chapter 1, you looked at mandatory access control (MAC), discretionary access control (DAC), rule-based access control (RBAC), and role-based access control (also RBAC). Earlier in this chapter, you looked at securing data using EFS. These topics all play a role in the overall picture of hardening the operating system. In this exercise, you look at security baselines in Windows and Unix.

Exercise 3.5.1.1: Microsoft Baseline Security Analyzer

Microsoft provides a tool known as the Microsoft Baseline Security Analyzer (MBSA) that scans Windows-based computers for security vulnerabilities. MBSA scans computers for critical updates and patches and determines the need for further system hardening. In this exercise, you install MBSA and scan your computer for security vulnerabilities. Perform this exercise on a Windows 2000 Professional computer. The steps are the same for Windows XP Professional:

1. Log on to the computer running Windows 2000 computer as an administrator.
2. Navigate to http://www.microsoft.com/technet/security/tools/mbsahome.mspx, select the download link, and download the MBSA setup file to your computer.
3. Double-click the setup file and follow the instructions in the setup wizard that appears. The wizard installs an icon on the desktop.
4. If you receive a message informing you that you need to install the Microsoft XML Parser version 3.0, follow the link provided to install this parser, and then continue the setup.
5. Double-click this icon to start MBSA.
6. On the welcome screen, select the Scan a Computer option to scan your computer.
7. The Pick a Computer to Scan screen (see Figure 3.14) enables you to select a computer (which is your computer by default) as well as the

types of scans that will be performed. Leave all options selected and click Start Scan.

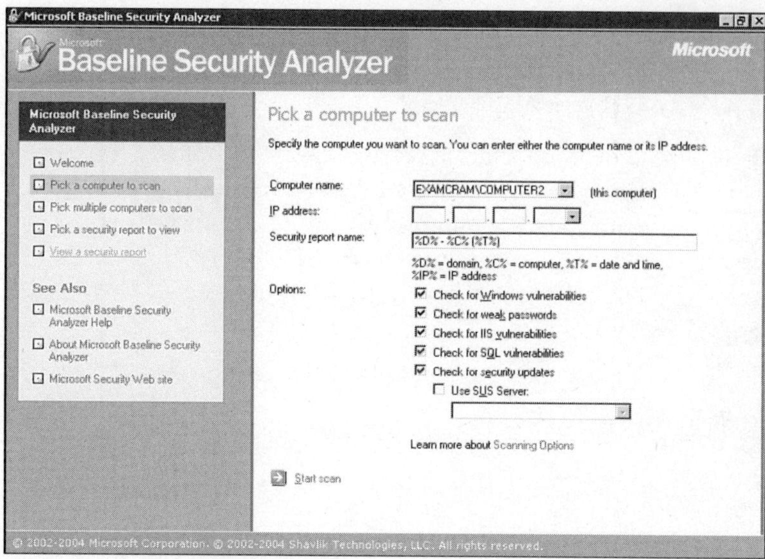

Figure 3.14 MBSA enables you to select from several types of scans.

8. MBSA downloads the latest security update information from Microsoft and performs the scan. It displays a security report, as shown in Figure 3.15, which highlights vulnerabilities present on the system.
9. To obtain information on vulnerabilities, select the Result Details link under the categories of interest. MBSA displays information related to the vulnerabilities present on the system, as shown in Figure 3.16.
10. To obtain information on correcting problems, select the link labeled How to Correct This. This link connects to the Help and Support Center to display information related to the issue at hand as well as procedures for correcting the problem.
11. To revisit previously obtained security reports, select the Pick a Security Report to View option from the left side of the MBSA window (refer to Figure 3.15), and then select the report to be viewed from the list that appears.

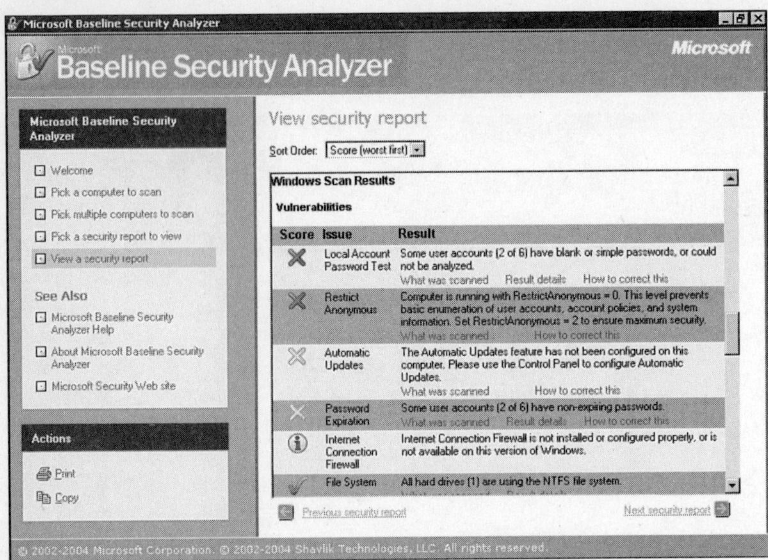

Figure 3.15 The MBSA security report provides information on system security vulnerabilities.

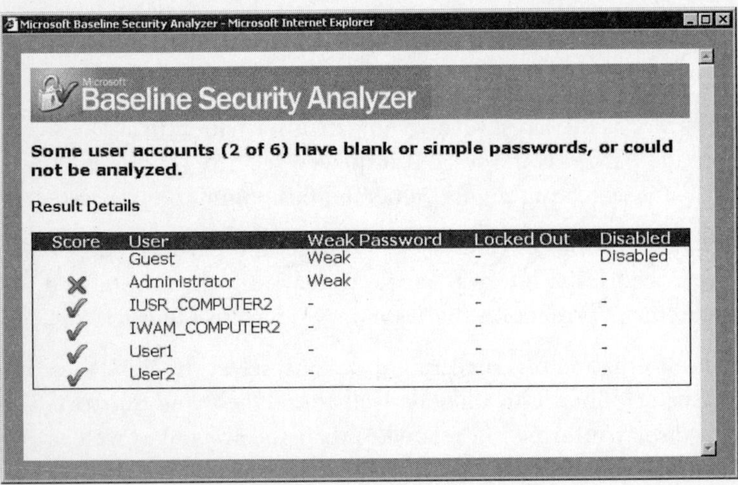

Figure 3.16 A weak password is one type of information that MBSA can display.

Hardening servers and networks involves more than just locating and fixing vulnerabilities using the procedures we have discussed here. You need to pay attention to the general topics we discussed in Chapter 1 as well as physical security recommendations such as locking doors. We discuss physical security in more detail in Chapter 5, "Operational and Organizational Security."

Exercise 3.5.1.2: Security Configuration and Analysis

Another tool provided by Microsoft that analyzes security settings and applies baseline security configurations is the Security Configuration and Analysis (SCA) console. This tool uses a *security template* to analyze a computer against a predefined level of security and apply the security settings against the computer. These templates are useful because they provide the ability to configure a series of computers with consistent security settings and reapply the settings should a problem arise. The security template is a series of configuration settings that affect items such as the following:

- *Account Policy*—Defines settings related to user account logon such as password strength and expiration, lockout of accounts after entering incorrect passwords, and settings related to Kerberos authentication.
- *Local Policy*—Defines which types of events will be audited; which groups are granted which rights on the system; and additional security options, such as the use of digital signing and encryption, the display of legal messages, the installation of unsigned drivers, the use of smart cards, and so on.
- *Event Log*—Defines settings related to the size of and access to security logs as well as their retention methods.
- *Restricted Groups*—Defines the membership of groups that have the capability to administer the system.
- *System Services*—Defines whether certain services running on the system are started, stopped, or disabled (prevented from starting). We discussed the disabling of unnecessary services in Chapter 1.
- *Registry*—Defines access permissions placed on portions of the system Registry.
- *File System*—Defines access permissions placed on files and folders.

Security templates available in Windows XP Professional and Windows Server 2003 include additional security settings such as wireless network policies, public-key policies related to EFS, and trusted root certification authorities.

In this exercise, you use SCA to analyze the baseline security settings and apply a security template to a computer running Windows 2000 Professional. You can also do this exercise on a computer running Windows XP Professional:

1. Log on to the computer running Windows 2000 as an administrator.
2. Click Start, Run; type **mmc**; and press Enter. This opens a blank Microsoft Management Console (MMC).
3. Click Console, Add/Remove Snap-in to open the Add/Remove Snap-in dialog box.
4. Click Add, select the Security Configuration and Analysis snap-in, click Add, and then click Close.
5. Click OK. The Security Configuration and Analysis snap-in is added to the blank console.
6. Click Console, Save As; type a descriptive name such as **Security.msc**; and then click Save. The console is saved in the Administrative Tools folder unless you select another location such as the desktop.
7. To analyze your computer's security settings, you need to create a database. Right-click Security Configuration and Analysis and choose Open Database. Type a name for the database (such as **Test1**) and then click Open.
8. Select a template from the Import Template dialog box that opens (see Figure 3.17). A good template to use is the `securews.inf` template, which applies secure settings to a workstation computer. Click Open.

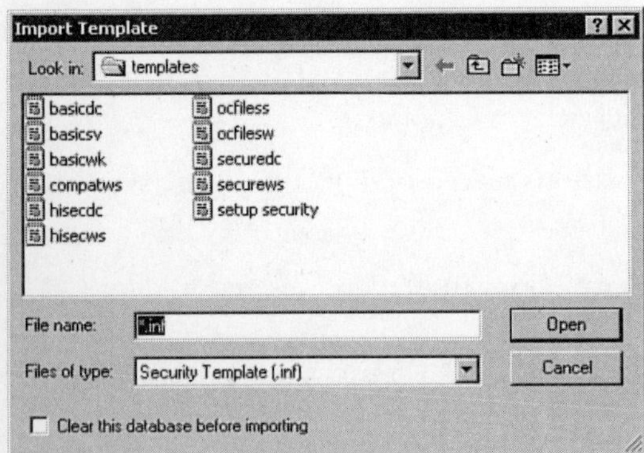

Figure 3.17 To configure a security database in SCA, you need to import a template from those in the template database.

9. To analyze the computer's security settings, right-click Security Configuration and Analysis and choose Analyze Computer Now. Click OK to accept the log file path.

10. The configuration settings are compared against the settings in the security database, and a series of nodes appears in the left pane. To compare the computer settings against those in the database, expand the desired nodes and select the appropriate policy. As shown in Figure 3.18, the settings in a series of policies appear in the right pane. A green check mark indicates that the computer's security settings meet the standard defined by the database, whereas a red X indicates a setting that differs from that in the database.

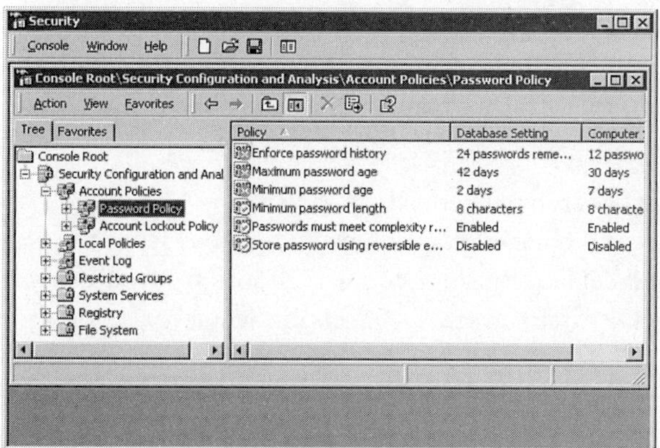

Figure 3.18 SCA indicates policies whose settings differ from those in the template with a red "X."

A red X could indicate a security setting that is actually more secure than that of the database, as well as the more usual security weakness.

11. Select the various nodes in turn and note how the settings differ from those in the database.

12. To configure the computer with the database settings, right-click Security Configuration and Analysis and choose Configure Computer Now. Click OK to accept the log file path.

13. Repeat Steps 9 to 11 and notice that the security settings defined by the database have been applied.

14. When you are finished, close the console. Click No if you are asked whether to save your settings.

Exercise 3.5.1.3: Developing a System Hardening Checklist

The process of hardening an operating system is little more than reducing the number of vulnerabilities that could allow the system to be compromised. Although every system is unique, you should employ certain strategies for all computers.

This exercise directs you to research general Windows and Unix/Linux hardening strategies and start developing a simple hardening checklist:

1. From a Web browser, navigate to http://www.sans.org/top20/. This Web page presents the SANS/FBI 20 Most Critical Internet Security Vulnerabilities list. The list actually contains the top-10 vulnerabilities each for Windows and Unix. It is a great place to start hardening your operating system.

2. Continue to http://staff.washington.edu/dittrich/R870/security-checklist.html and choose several hardening steps from the top of the Unix Security Checklist. Because you can choose from so many options, pick five checklist items from the Account Security section.

3. Continue to http://labmice.techtarget.com/articles/securingwin2000.htm and choose several hardening steps from the Windows 2000 Security Checklist. Pick the top-five checklist items. Note that the top items on the list deal with account security:

   - Do any of the checklist items exist in both operating systems?
   - Why are account issues near the top of most security checklists?
   - Which of the checklist items should be easiest to address?

4. Develop a hardening checklist of at least five items you would address for Windows, based on the information you have found. Provide details for each checklist item. For example, one common checklist item suggests that you disable any unneeded protocols and services.

Although you already have one checklist item, choose several common services that make sense to disable. See whether you can document 10 services. (Refer to Chapter 1 if necessary.) You might need to do more searching.

5. Arrange your security checklist in priority order. Which item should be addressed first? Explain why you chose each item's priority.

6. Add a section to your security checklist that discusses recurring actions. What steps must you take periodically to keep a system secure?
7. Complete your sample operating system hardening checklist by adding a brief discussion of items you have chosen not to include. For example, if your system resides behind several firewalls, you might choose not to implement a firewall on your server. What else would you not implement and why?

Exercise 3.5.2: Hardening a Network

Much of the activity involved in network hardening involves actions that we have already examined. These include configuring access control lists (ACLs) on sensitive files and folders, configuring router access policies, disabling unnecessary services, and configuring auditing, all of which we discussed in Chapter 1, and configuring remote access and VPN access, specifying IPSec policies, securing Web and FTP servers, and configuring wireless network security, all of which we discussed in Chapter 2.

Another part of hardening a network is knowing what is out there that might cause a problem. In Chapter 1, we looked at port scanning tools such as Nmap, which you can use to scan networks for open ports that intruders might use to initiate an attack. Another component of network hardening is the removal of services (including disabling of NetBIOS over TCP/IP), which we discussed in Chapter 1.

In Exercise 3.5.1.2, we looked at using SCA to harden a computer by applying a security template. In this exercise, we harden a Windows-based network by applying the security template to the network in Group Policy. Perform this exercise from a computer running Windows 2000 Server configured as a domain controller:

1. Log on to the server as an administrator.
2. Click Start, Programs, Administrative Tools, Active Directory Users and Computers.
3. Expand the left pane of Active Directory Users and Computers to locate the domain or organizational unit (OU) to which the computers in the network you want to harden belong.
4. Right-click this domain or OU and choose Properties.
5. On the Group Policy tab of the Properties dialog box that opens, select the desired Group Policy object (GPO) and click Edit to open the Group Policy console.

6. Navigate to the Computer Configuration\Windows Settings\Security Settings node.
7. Right-click this node and choose Import Policy.
8. From the dialog box shown in Figure 3.19, select the template you want to apply, and then click Open.

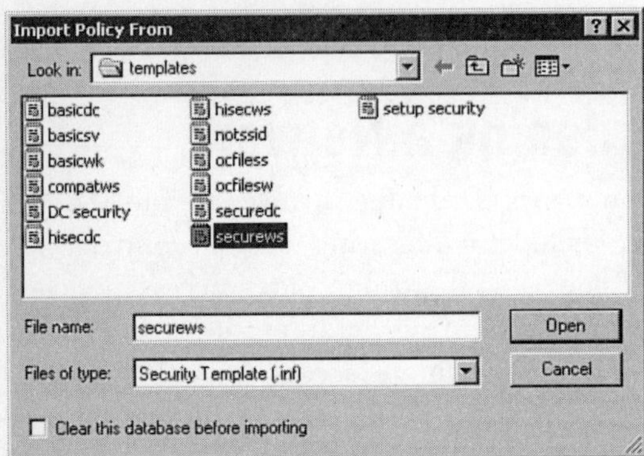

Figure 3.19 You can apply a security template in Group Policy.

9. This action applies the security settings in the template. To check their application, expand the Security Settings node, select the required subnodes, and verify the settings displayed in the right pane.

Exercise 3.5.3: Securing and Hardening Application Servers

The average network runs many types of servers, including Web servers, email servers, FTP servers, DHCP servers, DNS servers, NNTP servers, file and print servers, and database servers. Default installations of these servers are more often set up for convenience rather than security, so it is important that you secure these servers to the level that is appropriate to the services they provide.

MBSA analyzes components of various server applications as part of its installation. In this exercise, you run MBSA on a server configured with one or more of the applications mentioned here and note the results. Perform this exercise on a computer running Windows 2000 Server. The steps are similar in Windows Server 2003:

Performing this exercise on a computer running a default version of Windows 2000 Server with a few services such as Internet Information Services (IIS) will yield more security vulnerabilities than it will on Windows Server 2003. Microsoft has hardened the default settings of server applications considerably with the new server release.

1. Log on to the server as an administrator.
2. If you are working at a test server (which you should be for this type of exercise), you might want to install additional services such as the FTP, SMTP, and NNTP components of IIS and a DHCP server.
3. Use the procedure of Exercise 3.5.1.1 to install and run MBSA on the server.
4. Scroll the security report to note the vulnerabilities and obtain information on correcting them. For example, a default installation of IIS 5.0 on Windows 2000 yields the vulnerabilities shown in Figure 3.20.

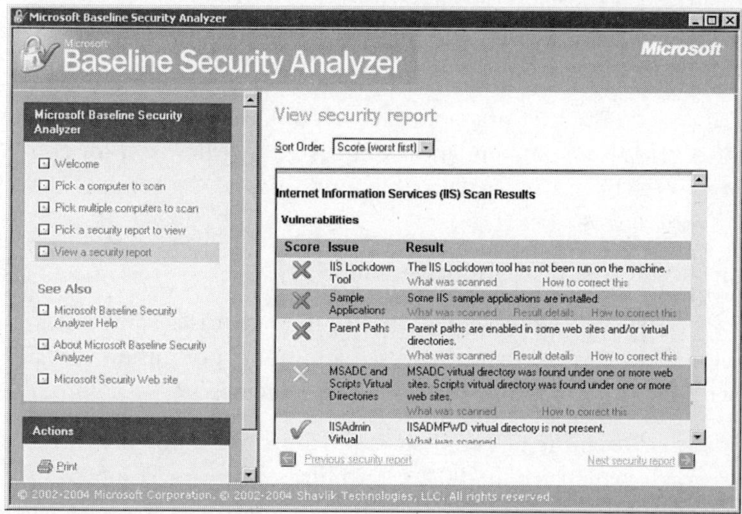

Figure 3.20 MBSA reports several vulnerabilities in the default installation of IIS 5.0 on a computer running Windows 2000 Server.

Application servers hosting specific applications such as email need additional hardening actions. For example, you need to prevent email servers from being used as open relays. You might encounter questions with respect to specific application servers on the Security+ exam. For more information on hardening specific application servers, refer to the *Exam Cram 2* or *Training Guide* books in the "Need to Know More?" section.

Exercise 3.5.4: Securing Data Repositories and Databases

Databases present a special security challenge because users and customers must have the proper level of access for the purpose to which the database has been built, but at the same time you are preventing all types of unauthorized access. In this exercise, you take a look at some of the problems facing administrators of databases running on Microsoft SQL servers:

1. From a Web browser, connect to the Internet and navigate to http://www.sql-server-performance.com/vk_sql_security.asp. The author, Vyas Kondreddi, provides a comprehensive review of SQL Server security. Locate answers to the following questions:

   - What types of authentication does an SQL database accept, and what recommendation is suggested for improving login security?
   - What three roles does SQL Server use for controlling access to objects within the database, and how are these roles used in assigning permissions?
   - In what way do the best practices suggested by Kondreddi correspond to general recommendations suggested by Microsoft for controlling access by users to regular files and folders?
   - What recommendation does Kondreddi make with regard to the default system administrator (sa) account?
   - Note that security recommendations are in many cases similar to those for securing other servers. What additional precaution is available with regard to backups of SQL Server databases?

2. SQL Server has been the target of several worms, most notably the Slammer worm that struck in 2003. Go to http://www.microsoft.com/sql/techinfo/administration/2000/security/securingsqlserver.asp. What are the 10 steps that they recommend for hardening the SQL server? Summarize the types of vulnerabilities that each step is designed to help protect against.

3. Marcin Policht has produced a series of articles on SQL security for *Database Journal*. Navigate to http://www.databasejournal.com/features/mssql/article.php/3334851 for the first article. Note the use of net libraries by SQL Server and the need to balance performance and security concerns. What means can you employ in SQL Server 2000 to encrypt net libraries?

4. Continue to Policht's second article at http://www.databasejournal.com/features/mssql/article.php/3341651. He discusses the need for secure authentication methods, again emphasizing the two authentication modes and the need for securing the sa account password. What are several advantages of operating the SQL server in an Active Directory domain environment? What is impersonation, and how is it used on SQL Server? Summarize the uses and drawbacks of the delegation process.

5. Continue to Policht's third article at http://databasejournal.com/features/mssql/article.php/3349561. Note the services associated with SQL Server. What recommendations does Policht make with regard to these services? Why should you not use the Local System Account when configuring these services?

6. The second segment of Policht's third article, found at http://databasejournal.com/features/mssql/article.php/10894_3349561_2, continues the discussion of accounts used by services. Why should you use a newly created user account for SQL Server Agent Services? What user rights and permissions do you need to assign to this account? Note that you should not add this account to a privileged group such as Administrators or Power Users unless certain actions need to be performed, as detailed in this article.

7. Policht's fourth article, found at http://databasejournal.com/features/mssql/article.php/3357861, discusses authorization, which determines the level of privileges granted to accounts accessing the databases and objects in SQL Server. What are server roles used for? Name the most important server roles and describe the capabilities granted to these roles. Describe some of the factors that determine what access rights are granted to each database. What are the two types of database roles, and what do the default roles provide? Note that you can define your own custom database roles.

8. Policht's fifth article, found at http://www.databasejournal.com/features/mssql/article.php/3363521, defines application roles in SQL Server. How do application roles differ from the database roles discussed in the previous article? Summarize his recommendations regarding the use and management of database roles and application roles.

9. Policht's sixth article, found at http://databasejournal.com/features/mssql/article.php/3370701, focuses on ownership and object permissions. What are two main factors that help determine the access to

objects in SQL Server? Note that ownership of a database object confers a set of rights and permissions. How are these similar to the case of NTFS folders and files? What is ownership chaining, when does it take place, and what potential vulnerability can it introduce?

10. Those of you involved with Oracle database servers should go to http://www.petefinnigan.com/orasec.htm and peruse the links to a large number of papers related to Oracle database security.

What Did I Just Learn?

Now that you have looked at system, network, and database hardening, let's take a moment to review all the critical items you've experienced in this lab:

- Microsoft provides MBSA and SCA, both of which you can use to analyze computers on a network for security vulnerabilities.
- You can use SCA to configure a fixed set of security parameters on an individual computer or import these settings to a GPO for configuring a series of computers on a network.
- Various application servers might present additional vulnerabilities. You can use MBSA to locate these vulnerabilities and obtain recommendations for fixing them.
- Databases such as SQL Server present specific vulnerabilities, some of which have been exploited by worms such as SQL Slammer. You need to follow both general and specific recommendations for hardening database servers.

Exam Prep Questions

Objective 3.1: Devices

1. Your company has a large internal network that you want to subnet into smaller parts. Which of the following devices can you use to separate your LAN and still protect critical resources? (Select all that apply.)

   ❑ A. An internal firewall

   ❑ B. A router between subnets

   ❑ C. A modem between computers

   ❑ D. A switch between departments

2. Your company receives Internet access through a network or gateway server. Which of the following devices is best suited to protect resources and subnet your LAN directly on the network server?

   ❑ A. DSL modem

   ❑ B. A multihomed firewall

   ❑ C. VLAN

   ❑ D. A brouter that acts both as a bridge and a router

3. Stateful firewalls might filter connection-oriented packets that are potential intrusions to the LAN. Which of the following types of packets can a stateful packet filter deny?

   ❑ A. UDP

   ❑ B. TCP

   ❑ C. IP

   ❑ D. ICMP

4. Your primary concern is LAN security. You want to subnet your internal network with a device that provides security and stability. Which of the following devices do you choose to meet these needs?

   ❑ A. Static router

   ❑ B. Dynamic router

   ❑ C. Static switch

   ❑ D. Dynamic switch

5. You manage a company network and the network budget. You want to minimize costs but also prevent crackers from sniffing your LAN. Which of the following devices would you recommend to meet your goals?

   ❑ A. Hub

   ❑ B. Switch

   ❑ C. Router

   ❑ D. Firewall

6. Which of the following are true statements about modems? (Select all that apply.)
   - ❑ A. Modems use telephone lines.
   - ❑ B. Modem stands for modulator and demodulator.
   - ❑ C. Modems are no longer used on secure networks.
   - ❑ D. A modem's fastest transfer rate is 56Kbps.
7. You want to have a private communication between two sites that also allows for encryption and authorization. Which of the following is the best choice in this instance?
   - ❑ A. Modem
   - ❑ B. Firewall
   - ❑ C. VPN
   - ❑ D. Bastion host
8. VPNs transfer encrypted data through tunneling technology. Which of the following performs fast data encryption and may be used with VPNs?
   - ❑ A. Stream cipher
   - ❑ B. RSA
   - ❑ C. DES
   - ❑ D. IPSec
9. What does the acronym IDS stand for?
   - ❑ A. Intrusion detection system
   - ❑ B. Internet detection standard
   - ❑ C. Internet detection system
   - ❑ D. Intrusion detection standard

Objective 3.2: Media

1. Which of the following are types of network cabling? (Select all that apply.)
   - ❑ A. Twisted pair
   - ❑ B. Token ring
   - ❑ C. Fiber optic
   - ❑ D. Coaxial
2. Which of the following is the greatest advantage of coax cabling?
   - ❑ A. High security
   - ❑ B. Physical dimensions
   - ❑ C. Long distances
   - ❑ D. Easily tapped

3. What is the media standard for most local network installations?
   - ❑ A. Fiber
   - ❑ B. CAT 3
   - ❑ C. CAT 5
   - ❑ D. Thinnet
4. Which of the following network cabling would you choose to install around a noisy room where machines are constantly running?
   - ❑ A. Fiber
   - ❑ B. STP
   - ❑ C. Coax
   - ❑ D. UTP
5. Which of the following are examples of magnetic storage media? (Select all that apply.)
   - ❑ A. Zip disk
   - ❑ B. CD-ROM
   - ❑ C. Floppy disk
   - ❑ D. DVD

Objective 3.3: Security Topologies

1. Which of the following are known as the registered ports, according to the IANA?
   - ❑ A. Ports 1 to 255
   - ❑ B. Ports 255 to 1023
   - ❑ C. Ports 1024 to 49151
   - ❑ D. Ports 1025 to 65535
2. Which of the following terms could be considered security zones? (Select all that apply.)
   - ❑ A. Intranet
   - ❑ B. Internet
   - ❑ C. DMZ
   - ❑ D. Extranet
3. You have decided to create a DMZ to allow public access to your business assets. Which of the following could you place within the DMZ? (Select all that apply.)
   - ❑ A. Web server
   - ❑ B. Proxy server
   - ❑ C. Email server
   - ❑ D. FTP server

4. You are in charge of a large network and have been using many devices. You finally want to subnet your network and allow users from the sales department in one office to communicate with sales representatives in another city. Which device should you use to improve connectivity?

- ❑ A. Router
- ❑ B. VLAN
- ❑ C. Brouter
- ❑ D. Bridge

5. Which of the following applies to the networking concept of tunneling? (Select all that apply.)

- ❑ A. Private network data is encapsulated or encrypted.
- ❑ B. Public network data is encapsulated or encrypted.
- ❑ C. Private data is transmitted over a public network.
- ❑ D. Private network data is lost in a black hole.

Objective 3.4: Intrusion Detection

1. An IDS may be configured to report attack occurrences. You just received a notification that an attack occurred, but after checking, you find that it really wasn't an attack at all. What is the term for this type of alarm?

- ❑ A. True positive
- ❑ B. False positive
- ❑ C. True negative
- ❑ D. False negative

2. Which of the following IDSs functions in current or real time to monitor network traffic?

- ❑ A. Network-based
- ❑ B. Host-based
- ❑ C. Gateway-based
- ❑ D. Router-based

3. What tool would you use to monitor for intrusions by reviewing computer system and event logs on a client computer?

- ❑ A. Honeypot
- ❑ B. Client IDS
- ❑ C. Network-based IDS
- ❑ D. Host-based IDS

4. Which type of network device is characterized by the following description: used to fool crackers, allowing them to continue an attack on a sacrificial computer that contains fictitious information?

- ❑ A. Fake firewall
- ❑ B. Rogue router
- ❑ C. IDS
- ❑ D. Honeypot

5. Your network administrator has installed a network-based IDS and a honeypot on the network. What is the written plan called that indicates who will monitor these tools and how users should react once a malicious attack has occurred?
   - ❑ A. Active response
   - ❑ B. Incident response
   - ❑ C. Monitoring and response
   - ❑ D. Security alert and response

Objective 3.5: Security Baselines

1. Which of the following items relates to the fundamental principle of implementing security measures on computer equipment to ensure that minimum standards are being met?
   - ❑ A. Security baselines
   - ❑ B. Security policies
   - ❑ C. Security standards
   - ❑ D. Security countermeasures
2. You have just installed an NOS and want to establish a security baseline. Which of the following tasks should you perform to harden your new NOS? (Select all that apply.)
   - ❑ A. Check the installation CD for a valid expiration date.
   - ❑ B. Check the manufacturer's Web site for any additional service patches for the NOS.
   - ❑ C. Lock the back of the computer with a padlock.
   - ❑ D. Disable any unused services.
3. Even in a large, mixed environment, TCP/IP is the protocol of choice for most networks. Which of the following protocols would you want to *deny* passage over your firewall?
   - ❑ A. TCP
   - ❑ B. IP
   - ❑ C. IPX/SPX
   - ❑ D. NetBEUI

4. Which of the following relates best to application hardening?
   - ❑ A. Buying the most recent application version available
   - ❑ B. Buying the most recent software package available
   - ❑ C. Configuring network applications with the most recent updates and service packs
   - ❑ D. Testing the most recent hotfixes, service packs, and patches after purchasing

5. Which of the following are used as large data repositories? (Select all that apply.)
   - ❑ A. SAN
   - ❑ B. WAN
   - ❑ C. NAS
   - ❑ D. DEN

6. Which of the following databases have this default security vulnerability: The sa account is established with a blank password?
   - ❑ A. LDAP
   - ❑ B. Microsoft SQL Server
   - ❑ C. Proxy
   - ❑ D. Exchange

Exam Prep Answers

Objective 3.1: Devices

1. Answers A, B, and D are correct. Firewalls, routers, and switches will help you protect critical resources and separate your LAN.

2. Answer B is correct. A firewall is best suited to protect resources and subnet your LAN directly on the network or gateway server.

3. Answer B is correct. Stateful firewalls may filter connection-oriented packets such as TCP.

4. Answer A is correct. The static router offers a stable table that you, as the network administrator, generate.

5. Answer B is correct. A switch will meet your goals for this situation.

6. Answers A and B are correct. The term *modem* stands for modulator and demodulator. Modems use telephone lines. DSL and cable modems are faster than 56Kbps.

7. Answer C is correct. A VPN provides for a private communication between two sites that also permits encryption and authorization.

8. Answer C is correct. Data Encryption Standard (DES) performs fast data encryption and may be used with VPNs.

9. Answer A is correct. IDS stands for intrusion detection system.

Objective 3.2: Media

1. Answers A, C, and D are correct. Twisted pair, fiber optic, and coaxial are types of network cabling. Token ring is a type of physical topology.

2. Answer C is correct. Of the choices listed for coax cabling, long distance is the best answer.

3. Answer C is correct. CAT 5 twisted-pair cabling is the media standard for most local network installations.

4. Answer A is correct. Fiber is the best choice in this situation.

5. Answers A and C are correct. Zip disks and floppy disks are magnetic storage media.

Objective 3.3: Security Topologies

1. Answer C is correct. There are three accepted ranges for port numbers: the well-known ports; the registered ports, which are registered by the Internet Assigned Numbers Authority (IANA); and the dynamic (private) ports.

2. Answers A, B, C, and D are correct. All of the items listed are examples of security zones.

3. Answers A, C, and D are correct. You should place your Web servers, FTP servers, and email servers within the DMZ. Web servers, FTP servers, and email servers are typically hosted within the DMZ.

4. Answer B is correct. A VLAN will improve connectivity in this situation.

5. Answers A and C are correct. With tunneling, private network data, which is encapsulated or encrypted, is transmitted over a public network.

Objective 3.4: Intrusion Detection

1. Answer B is correct. This is an example of a false-positive result.

2. Answer A is correct. The network-based IDS monitors network traffic in real time.

3. Answer D is correct. A host-based IDS can review computer system and event logs to detect a successful attack on a client computer.

4. Answer D is correct. A honeypot is a computer configured as a sacrificial lamb so that administrators are aware when malicious attacks are in progress.

5. Answer B is correct. An incident response is a written plan that indicates who will monitor these tools and how users should react after a malicious attack occurs.

Objective 3.5: Security Baselines

1. Answer A is correct. Security baselines relate to the fundamental principal of implementing security measures on computer equipment to ensure that minimum standards are being met.

2. Answers B and D are correct. To harden your NOS, check the manufacturer's Web site for any additional service patches for the NOS and disable any unused services.

3. Answer D is correct. NetBEUI should be denied passage over your firewall for security reasons.

4. Answer C is correct. Of the items listed, configuring network applications with the most recent updates and service packs relates best to application hardening.

5. Answers A, C, and D are correct. Large data repositories may include storage area network (SAN), network attached storage (NAS), and directory enabled networks (DEN).

6. Answer B is correct. SQL has this default security vulnerability because the sa account is established with a blank password.

Need to Know More?

For further information on device and media security, and security topology, consult the following books:

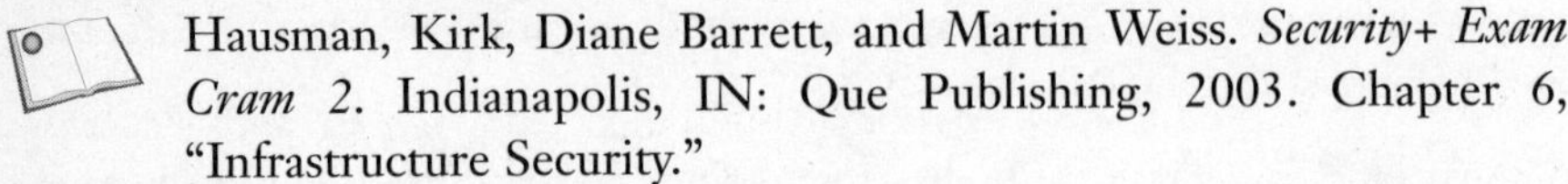
Hausman, Kirk, Diane Barrett, and Martin Weiss. *Security+ Exam Cram 2*. Indianapolis, IN: Que Publishing, 2003. Chapter 6, "Infrastructure Security."

King, Todd and David Bittlingmeier. *Security+ Training Guide*. Indianapolis, IN: Que Publishing, 2003. Chapter 3, "Devices, Media, and Topology Security."

Taylor, Tiffany, ed. *Security Complete*. Alameda, CA: Sybex, Inc., 2002.

For further information on VPNs and their implementation (as well as additional information on general network security), see the following:

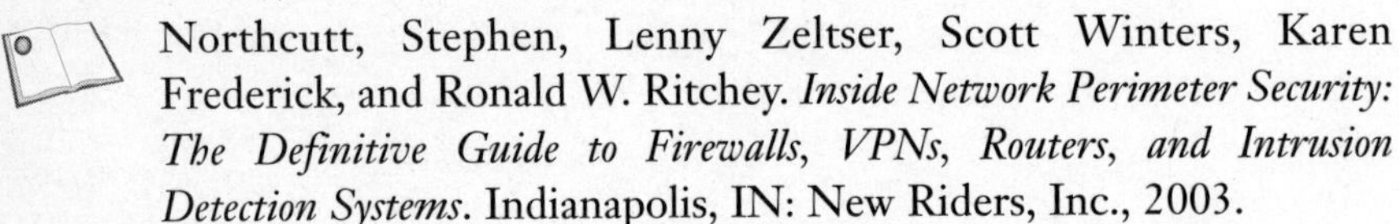
Northcutt, Stephen, Lenny Zeltser, Scott Winters, Karen Frederick, and Ronald W. Ritchey. *Inside Network Perimeter Security: The Definitive Guide to Firewalls, VPNs, Routers, and Intrusion Detection Systems*. Indianapolis, IN: New Riders, Inc., 2003.

For further information on network troubleshooting tools, check out this book:

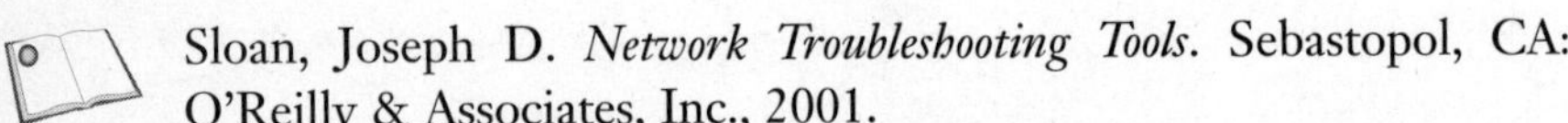
Sloan, Joseph D. *Network Troubleshooting Tools*. Sebastopol, CA: O'Reilly & Associates, Inc., 2001.

For further information on network monitoring and analysis, see the following:

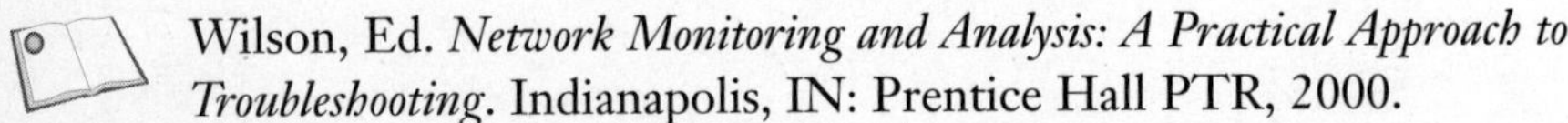
Wilson, Ed. *Network Monitoring and Analysis: A Practical Approach to Troubleshooting*. Indianapolis, IN: Prentice Hall PTR, 2000.

For further information on bastion hosts, consult the following:

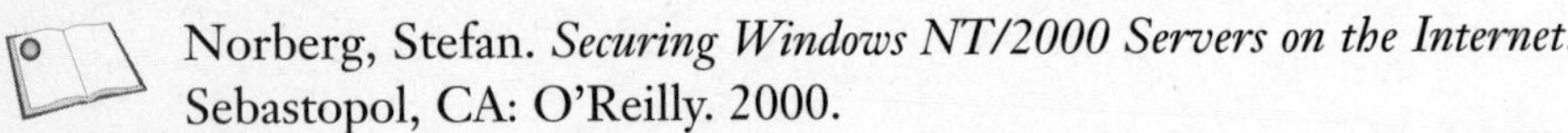
Norberg, Stefan. *Securing Windows NT/2000 Servers on the Internet*. Sebastopol, CA: O'Reilly. 2000.

For further information on VLANs, see this book:

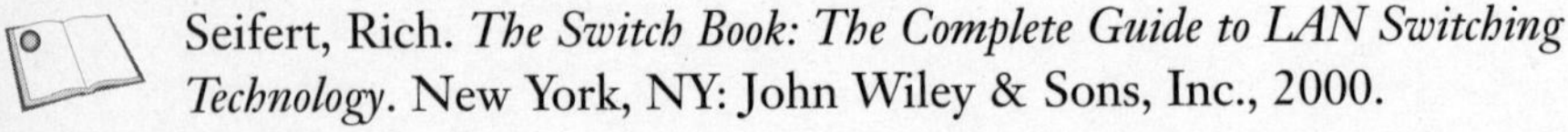
Seifert, Rich. *The Switch Book: The Complete Guide to LAN Switching Technology*. New York, NY: John Wiley & Sons, Inc., 2000.

For further information on intrusion detection and response, see the following books:

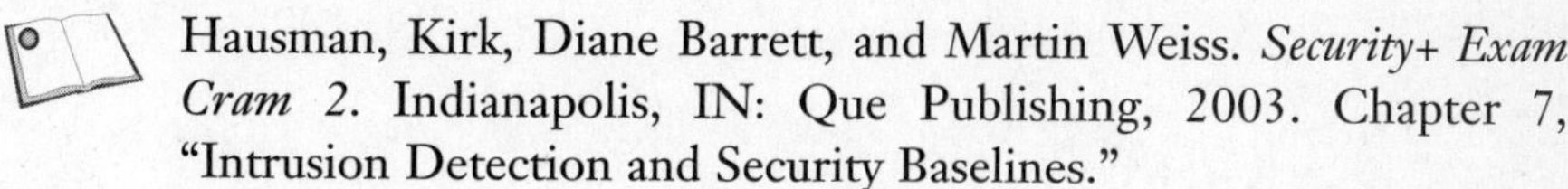
Hausman, Kirk, Diane Barrett, and Martin Weiss. *Security+ Exam Cram 2*. Indianapolis, IN: Que Publishing, 2003. Chapter 7, "Intrusion Detection and Security Baselines."

King, Todd and David Bittlingmeier. *Security+ Training Guide*. Indianapolis, IN: Que Publishing, 2003. Chapter 4, "Intrusion Detection, Baselines, and Hardening."

Pipkin, Donald. *Information Security: Protecting the Global Enterprise, First Edition*. Upper Saddle River, NJ: Prentice Hall, 2002.

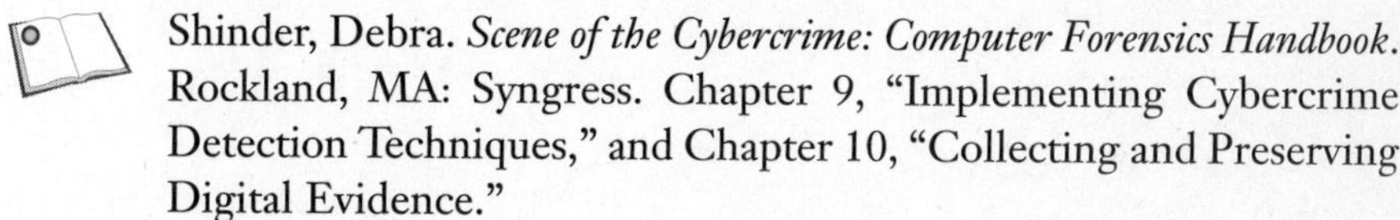
Shinder, Debra. *Scene of the Cybercrime: Computer Forensics Handbook*. Rockland, MA: Syngress. Chapter 9, "Implementing Cybercrime Detection Techniques," and Chapter 10, "Collecting and Preserving Digital Evidence."

For further information on security baselines and system hardening, consult the following resources:

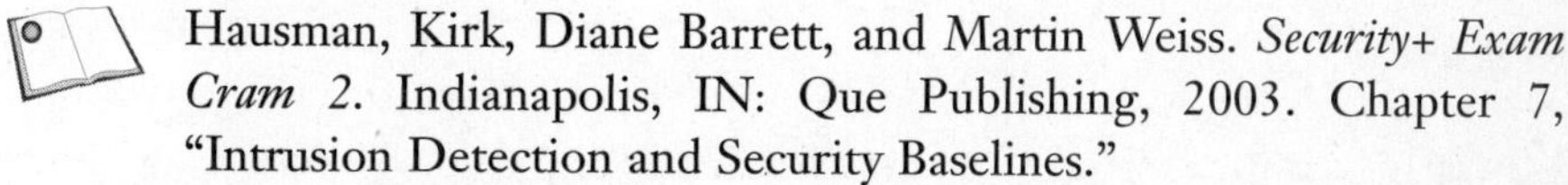
Hausman, Kirk, Diane Barrett, and Martin Weiss. *Security+ Exam Cram 2*. Indianapolis, IN: Que Publishing, 2003. Chapter 7, "Intrusion Detection and Security Baselines."

King, Todd and David Bittlingmeier. *Security+ Training Guide*. Indianapolis, IN: Que Publishing, 2003. Chapter 4, "Intrusion Detection, Baselines, and Hardening."

Chapter 8, Security Baselines, http://www.docendo.se/mspress/msp_online/samplechapter/0735618224.htm.

For further information on MBSA and SCA, see the following:

Smith, Ben and Brian Komar. *Microsoft Windows Security Resource Kit*. Redmond, WA: Microsoft Press, 2003. Chapter 24, "Using Security Assessment Tools."

For further information on system and network hardening, see the following:

Bragg, Roberta. *Hardening Windows Systems*. Emeryville, CA: McGraw Hill/Osborne, 2004.

For further information on application server hardening, check out the following resources:

Smith, Ben and Brian Komar. *Microsoft Windows Security Resource Kit*. Redmond, WA: Microsoft Press, 2003. Part IV: "Securing Common Services."

Chapter 8, Security Baselines, http://www.docendo.se/mspress/msp_online/samplechapter/0735618224.htm.

For further information on Linux security, see the following:

Toxen, Bob. *Real World Linux Security, 2nd Edition*. Upper Saddle River, NJ: Prentice Hall PTR, 2002.

For further information on Unix security, see the following:

Spafford, Gene, Simson Garfinkel, and Alan Schwartz. *Practical Unix and Internet Security, 3rd Edition*. Sebastopol, CA: O'Reilly & Associates, Inc., 2003.

Basics of Cryptography

Cryptography is the science of scrambling or disguising information so that unauthorized individuals are unable to access its contents. Although manual methods of cryptography have existed for centuries, it is only in recent decades that automated cryptography based on mathematical algorithms has become feasible as computing powers have increased.

The following is a list of the exam objectives you will be covering in this chapter:

- 4.1 Be able to identify and explain the following different kinds of cryptographic algorithms:
  - Hashing
  - Symmetric
  - Asymmetric
- 4.2 Understand how cryptography addresses the following security concepts:
  - Confidentiality
  - Integrity
    - Digital Signatures
  - Authentication
  - Nonrepudiation
    - Digital Signatures
  - Access Control

- 4.3 Understand and be able to explain the following concepts of PKI (Public Key Infrastructure):
    - Certificates
        - Certificate Policies
        - Certificate Practice Statements
    - Revocation
    - Trust Models
- 4.4 Identify and be able to differentiate different cryptographic standards and protocols:
- 4.5 Understand and be able to explain the following concepts of key management and certificate lifecycles:
    - Centralized vs. Decentralized
    - Certificates
    - Storage
        - Hardware vs. Software
        - Private Key Protection
    - Escrow
    - Expiration
    - Revocation
        - Status Checking
    - Suspension
        - Status Checking
    - Recovery
        - M-of-N control (Of M appropriate individuals, N must be present to authorize recovery)
    - Renewal
    - Destruction
    - Key Usage
        - Multiple Key Pairs (Single, Dual)

4.1: Identifying Cryptography Algorithms

An *algorithm* is a mathematical formula that can be applied to plain-text data to scramble it. All algorithms have a counterpart that enables the encrypted data to be unscrambled at the other end so that its recipient can read it. The Security+ exam expects you to know three major algorithms: hashing, symmetric, and asymmetric.

Exercise 4.1.1: Understanding Cryptography Algorithms

In this exercise, you look at several types of algorithms to see how they operate and when they are most suitable for use:

1. Connect to the Internet and navigate to http://www.webopedia.com/TERM/h/hashing.html for a definition of hashing. What is the purpose of a hash and how is it used?
2. Corey Hines of Network Security presents a series of articles that introduce cryptography, starting at http://www.2000trainers.com/article.aspx?articleID=263&page=1. This page introduces symmetric cryptography. What is the basis of symmetric cryptography, and what are the two formats used by symmetric encryption algorithms?
3. Follow the link to the second page of Hines's series of articles. How does the length of an encryption key determine the strength of the resulting encryption? Note that brute-force attacks, which you saw in relation to password cracking, can also be used to crack encryption. What method of cracking is more efficient than brute force, and what two methods does Hines mention that you can use to mitigate the effect of this cracking method? What problems are associated with the management of keys?
4. Continue to the third page of Hines's series. He introduces the concept of data integrity, which we explore in the next exercise. Which type of algorithm is used to detect violations of data integrity? How does the hashing algorithm differ from the encryption algorithm? What are the characteristics of the two common hashing algorithms?
5. On the same page, Hines introduces the third type of algorithm, asymmetric key cryptography, also known as public-key cryptography. What

are the four rules on which asymmetric key cryptography is based, and what are the characteristics of the two keys it uses?

6. The fourth page of the series summarizes the three cryptography algorithms and provides an article explaining how they are used together. Note how the algorithms are used together by Secure Multipurpose Internet Mail Extensions (S/MIME) and Secure Sockets Layer (SSL), both of which you explored in Chapter 2, "Communication Security."

7. For information on public-key and symmetric encryption algorithms, refer to http://www.infosyssec.org/infosyssec/algorithms.html. What are several common public-key and symmetric algorithms mentioned by this author? Write down a summary of the characteristics of each algorithm, and think about which purpose is best served by each one. Also compare and contrast the hashing functions that are described on this page.

8. Another symmetric encryption algorithm you should be familiar with is the Advanced Encryption Standard (AES). Navigate to http://en.wikipedia.org/wiki/Advanced_Encryption_Standard for a concise summary of AES. What is the name of the standard that was selected by the AES committee? What key lengths are used by AES, and how many successful attacks against this algorithm have occurred by 2004? Follow the links provided for additional information.

9. For a concise summary of all three types of cryptographic algorithms, refer to http://www.networkcert.net/security/Algorithms.htm. The tables on this page provide you with the basic information that you should be familiar with for the exam.

Ensure that you understand the differences between the various types of keys, public, private, and secret, and which types of algorithms use which types of keys. You should also be aware of the key lengths used by the more common algorithms.

What Did I Just Learn?

Now that you have looked at encryption algorithms, let's take a moment to review all the critical items you've experienced in this lab:

- The purpose of hashing algorithms is to produce a character string that can verify that a message has not been modified in transit. Note that hashes are also called message digests after the Message Digest (MD) family of hashing algorithms.

- Symmetric algorithms use a secret key to encrypt and decrypt messages. The same key is used for both encryption and decryption.
- Asymmetric or public-key algorithms use a key pair consisting of a public and private key to encrypt and decrypt messages. Remember that either key in a key pair can be used to encrypt a message, and the other key in the same key pair can then be used to decrypt the message.

4.2: Cryptography and Security Concepts

The use of cryptography addresses several key concepts, including confidentiality, integrity, authentication, and nonrepudiation. Digital signatures are integral to the integrity and nonrepudiation of data, as well as the authentication of the sender to the recipient of the data. The Security+ exam tests your knowledge of these concepts and their benefits to modern business.

Exercise 4.2.1: Understanding the Major Security Concepts

In this exercise, you research the means by which cryptography addresses several key security concepts:

1. Mohan Atreya provides a good introduction to cryptography and the concepts of authentication, confidentiality, data integrity, and nonrepudiation at http://www.rsasecurity.com/products/bsafe/overview/IntroToCrypto.pdf#xml=http://www.rsasecurity.com/programs/texis.exe/webinator/search/xml.txt?query=Atreya&pr=default_new&order=r&cq=&id=40b31a8c38. In particular, note Atreya's table of definitions for these terms and how each one is achieved. How do the algorithms that you studied in the last exercise work to achieve these benefits of cryptography? How does key length affect the balance between security and performance? Which type of algorithm is used for achieving data integrity, and which specific algorithm uses a 160-bit digest for this purpose?
2. Carlisle Adams and Steve Lloyd discuss authentication, integrity, and confidentiality of data in detail at http://www.microsoft.com/technet/security/topics/identity/corepki.mspx. Note how authentication can mean more than just the identification of a user to a server, as we have

discussed in earlier chapters of this book. It can include ensuring that data originates from a verified location and has not been sent by some imposter. Review the four categories of authentication types and the concept of multifactor authentication.

3. In Adams and Lloyd's discussion, pay particular attention to the mechanisms of authentication, integrity, and confidentiality, including the use of digital signatures.

4. For details on how a digital signature works, navigate to http://ils.unc.edu/~johnk/Digital_Signature.htm. Summarize the steps that take place at the sending and receiving ends when a digital signature is employed. Note how the signature verifies the integrity of the data (because the hashes would not match if the data has changed) as well as the authenticity of the sender (assuming that no one but the sender possesses his private key).

5. Refer to http://www.webopedia.com/TERM/n/nonrepudiation.html for a definition of nonrepudiation. Why is nonrepudiation important?

6. Return to the reference you visited in Step 4 and note how a digital signature provides nonrepudiation.

7. Another useful cryptography technique is that of a *digital envelope*. Navigate to http://www.rsasecurity.com/rsalabs/node.asp?id=2184, and note that this technique consists of a message that is encrypted using a secret (symmetric) key, which is in turn encrypted using the public key belonging to the intended recipient. When the recipient receives the message, she uses her private key to decrypt the secret key and then uses the secret key to decrypt the message. What advantage does this technique have over ordinary public-key cryptography? What are several additional advantages that are realized when sending multiple messages?

8. Mohan Atreya provides another concise introduction to digital signatures and digital envelopes at http://www.rsasecurity.com/products/bsafe/overview/Article5-SignEnv.pdf#xml=http://www.rsasecurity.com/programs/texis.exe/webinator/search/xml.txt?query=Atreya&pr=default_new&order=r&cq=&id=40b31a8c26. Note in particular that a digital signature does not secure the message text itself, but you can use a combination of the digital signature and digital envelope to provide confidentiality, authenticity, integrity, and nonrepudiation.

9. For a summary of public-key cryptography and its use in access control, go to http://www.syllabus.com/article.asp?id=7626. What

variation of XML can you use to control access to documents, and how does it work? This article also provides an introduction to certification authorities (CAs), which you study in Section 4.3 of this chapter.

Pay particular attention to which pairs of keys are used in which circumstances. Remember that a digital signature involves using the sender's private key to encrypt the hash of a message, which the recipient then decrypts using the sender's public key. The message itself is not encrypted. On the other hand, a digital envelope involves encrypting a message with a symmetric key, which is in turn encrypted with the recipient's public key. The recipient then decrypts the symmetric key with his private key and uses the symmetric key to decrypt the message.

Exercise 4.2.2: Using Digital Signatures

In this exercise, you install and deploy the trial version of a commercially available software application for digitally signing email messages. Perform this exercise on a computer running Windows 2000 Professional. The steps are the same if performing this exercise on a computer running Windows XP Professional:

1. Navigate to http://www.wondercrypt.com/wondercrypt.htm and note the features of the Wonder Software Technologies WonderCrypt program.
2. Click the Download link, click the Free Download link, and click Free Download–Envoy.
3. Extract the zipped files, double-click the Setup icon, and follow the instructions in the installation wizard.

To extract the zipped files, you need an extraction program installed, such as WinZip. A 21-day evaluation version of WinZip is available at http://www.winzip.com.

4. When the installation is finished, a folder opens on your computer containing a shortcut to the program plus a Help shortcut. Double-click the Help icon and read the overview screens. The information provided is a good overview of the use of Public Key Infrastructure (PKI) and asymmetric cryptography. Also select Quick Tutorial and follow the pages presented by this tutorial to learn about the features and use of WonderCrypt.
5. Double-click the WonderCrypt Envoy icon to start the program. Select New User Sign Up.
6. Ensure that Create New Identity is selected and then click OK.

7. As shown in Figure 4.1, type your name and email address. You may also type the additional information as indicated. Click Next and supply a username and password.

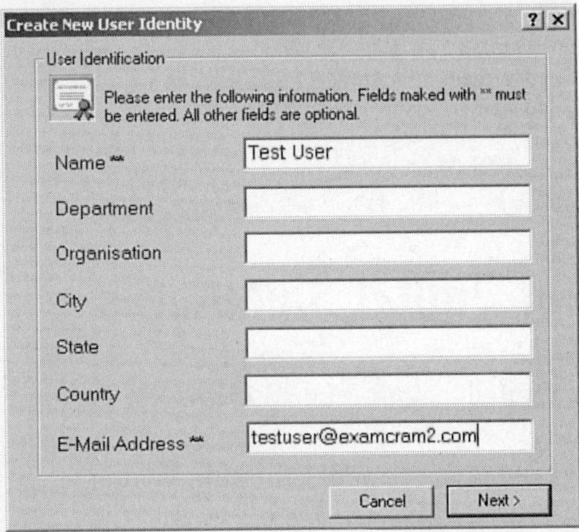

Figure 4.1 The Create New User Identity dialog box in WonderCrypt enables you to enter your identifying information that will be stored on your certificate and public/private-key pair.

8. Click Next again and click Yes to reconfirm the entries that you made. This step creates the new user identity.
9. To make a backup of your identity keys, click Yes on the User Identity Backup dialog box and select the folder in which you want to store the backup. You can store the backup on a floppy disk so that you can access your account from another computer on which this program is installed or protect from a disaster such as a hard disk failure.
10. To test the program, click Yes and specify a trusted friend or relative to whom you will email the public key and text files.
11. Sign in to WonderCrypt Envoy with the username and password you supplied when creating your identity, plus a session password of your choice. It need not be the same as the first password.
12. On the License Information dialog box that appears, click Continue to run the program in Limited Utility mode.
13. As shown in Figure 4.2, the WonderCrypt Envoy Wizard screen provides you with a choice of the actions the program enables you to perform.

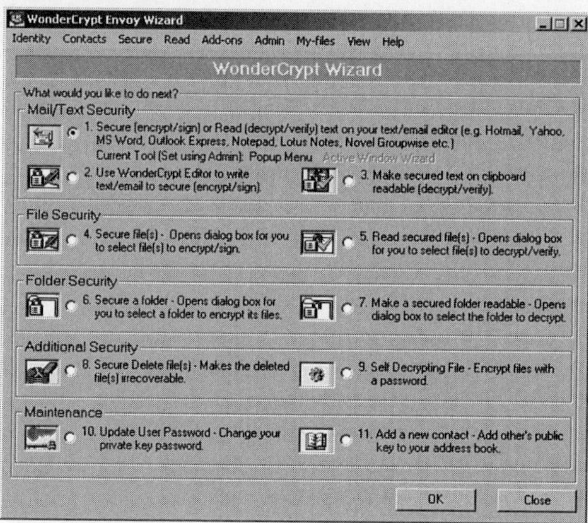

Figure 4.2 WonderCrypt enables you to perform a range of security-related activities.

14. To send a digitally signed or encrypted email message, select Option 2 and click OK. Select the appropriate option and then click OK.

Signing the message creates a digital signature but does not encrypt the message test. To encrypt the message test, you need to select the Sign and Encrypt option. This option creates a session key from your private key and the recipient's public key, which is used for encryption and decryption of the message.

15. Select the recipient from the Select Recipient(s) for Whom to Secure dialog box and then click OK.
16. Type the session password (not the user password) in the Session Password text box and then click OK.
17. Type the text of the message you want to send and click OK. The text is saved in the Clipboard.
18. Open your email program and paste the saved text into a new message. The message is saved as what appears to be a meaningless string of alphanumeric characters (see Figure 4.3). Then send this message to the user to whom you sent the files in Step 10.
19. The recipient of the message needs to log on and follow Steps 3 to 9 of this procedure to install WonderCrypt.
20. The recipient then needs to follow the instructions in the `HowToAdd.txt` file that is included in the email. This includes installing the certificate file, as shown in Figure 4.4.

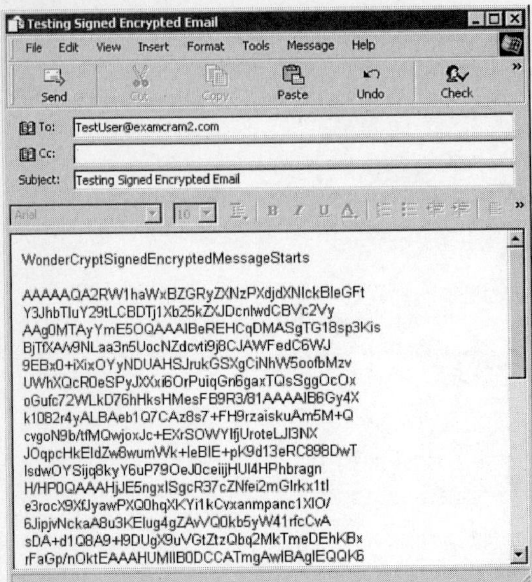

Figure 4.3 This message contains encrypted text plus an encrypted signature hash.

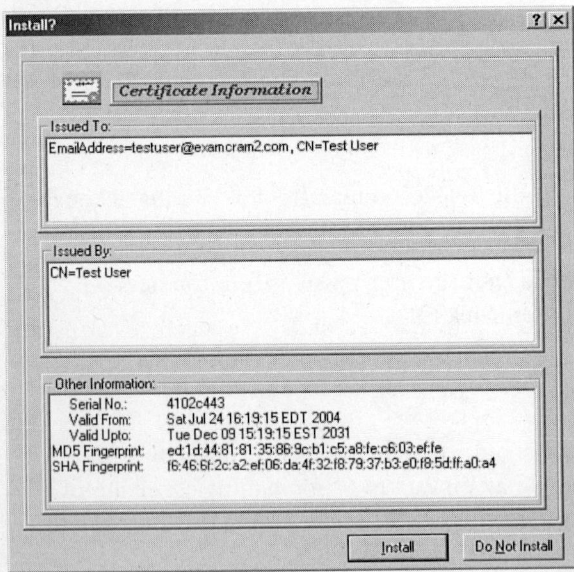

Figure 4.4 The recipient of your message needs to install the certificate that represents your public key.

21. To decrypt the message and verify the digital signature, the recipient needs to open the email message, select the Make Secured Text on Clipboard Readable (Decrypt/Verify) option, and then click OK.

22. Copy the encrypted message from the email program and paste it into the Paste from Clipboard dialog box. Then click Done.

23. The Signature Verification dialog box verifies the authenticity of the digital signature. Click OK.

24. The Secured Message dialog box opens with the decrypted message now visible. This dialog box also contains information about the signing certificate. See Figure 4.5.

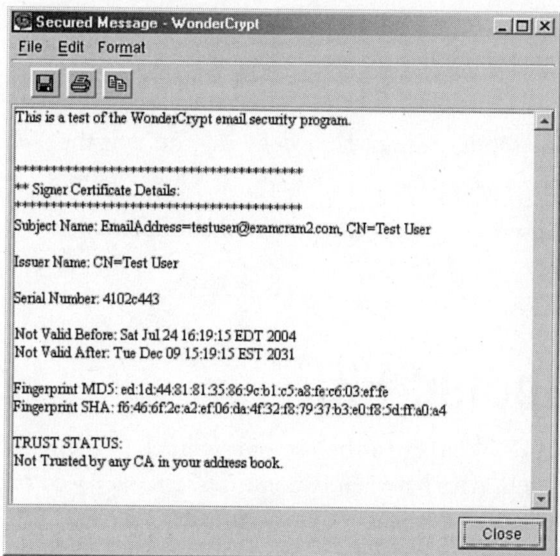

Figure 4.5 The sender's public key decrypts the message and enables the recipient to view it.

25. To simulate message modification in transit, repeat Step 22 but type some additional characters into the alphanumeric text before clicking Done. You receive an error message, as shown in Figure 4.6, informing you of the problem.

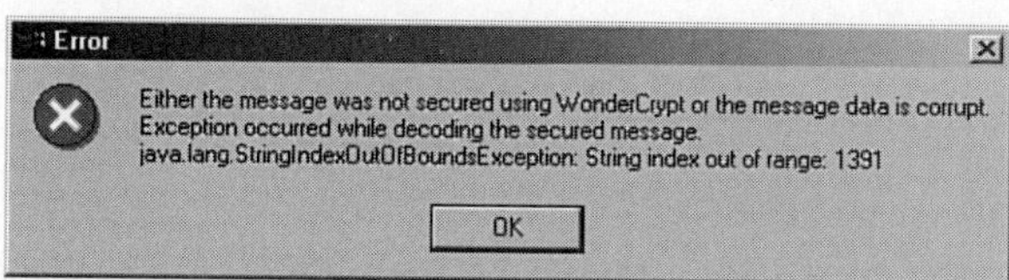

Figure 4.6 If a message is modified in transit, WonderCrypt produces this error message.

26. Close all messages and exit WonderCrypt.

What Did I Just Learn?

Now that you have looked at the use of cryptography to address various security concepts, let's take a moment to review all the critical items you've experienced in this lab:

- Confidentiality refers to the protection of a message from being viewed by unauthorized individuals.
- Integrity refers to the assurance that a message has not been modified in transit or in storage.
- Authentication verifies that the sender of a message is who she claims to be.
- Nonrepudiation means the sender cannot later deny that he sent the message in the first place.
- Digital signatures can be used to address the integrity, confidentiality, and nonrepudiation issues.

4.3: Understanding PKI

PKI includes a series of features relating to the use of asymmetric key pairs to enable the secure exchange of data between two entities. PKI is based on a system of certificates, certificate trusts, and certificate servers. The Security+ exam tests your knowledge of PKI and its components because it is the foundation of secure data exchange across insecure media such as the Internet.

Certificates issued by Microsoft Certificate Services and most public certification authorities are based on the International Telecommunications Union (ITU) X.509 version 3 (v3) standard.

Exercise 4.3.1: Installing a CA in Windows 2000 Server

The central feature of PKI is the system of certificates on which it is based. A certification authority (CA) is a server that is empowered to issue certificates. Microsoft provides a CA server that you can install on a computer running Windows 2000 Server. Normally, companies obtain certificates from an external agency such as VeriSign or Thawte, which are in the business of vouching for companies or individuals that need high-level protection.

Companies can use a certificate from such an agency to certify their own root CA, which in turn certifies subordinate CAs, other computers, and users as required. However, in low-security environments, the root CA, which is the most trusted CA in a hierarchy of certificate servers, can be self-signed.

In this exercise, you install a root CA. Perform this exercise on the same computer you used in Exercise 3.5.2, which is configured as a domain controller. Internet Information Services (IIS) is required so that you can display the Certificate Services Web pages that Windows 2000 Server Certificate Services provides; default installations of Windows 2000 Server include this component. You can also perform this exercise on a computer running Windows Server 2003, on which you have installed IIS:

1. Log on to a domain controller running Windows 2000 Server as an administrator.
2. Click Start, Settings, Control Panel, Add/Remove Programs.
3. Click Add/Remove Windows Components.
4. In the Windows Components Wizard, select Certificate Services.
5. Click Yes to accept the warning that the computer name and domain membership cannot be changed, and then click Next.
6. On the CA Type page, select Enterprise Root CA and then click Next.
7. On the CA Identifying Information page, type a common name for the CA and then click Next.
8. On the Data Storage Location page, accept the locations of the database and log files (or type alternate paths for these files), and then click Next.
9. Certificate Services warns you that IIS needs to be stopped to complete the installation. Click OK to accept this warning.
10. If prompted, insert the Windows 2000 Server CD-ROM when requested, and then click OK.
11. Click Finish when the installation completes, click Close, and then close Add/Remove Programs.

One purpose of digital certificates is to bind a public key to the entity that holds the corresponding private key.

Exercise 4.3.2: Issuing and Examining a Certificate

Having installed a certificate server, you are now able to request a certificate from a client computer that is connected to the certificate server and then examine the resulting certificate. Perform this exercise from a Windows 2000 Professional computer:

1. Log on to the Windows 2000 Professional computer as an administrator.
2. Open Internet Explorer and navigate to http://*server*/certsrv. (Substitute the name or IP address of the server for *server*.) The introductory Certificate Services Web page appears, as shown in Figure 4.7.

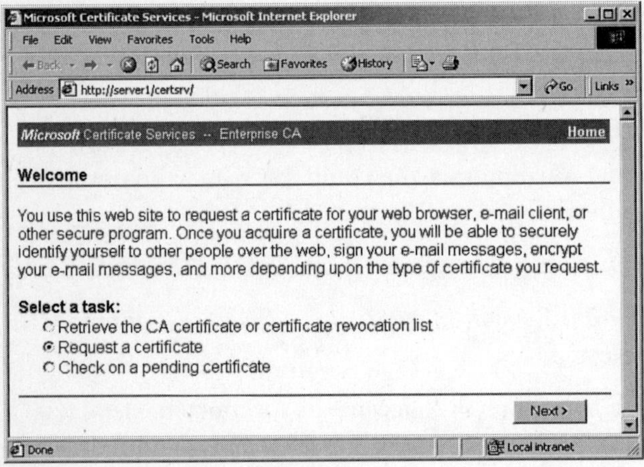

Figure 4.7 Certificate Services provides a series of Web pages that enable users to request certificates of various types from the CA.

3. Click Request a Certificate and then click Next.
4. On the Request a Certificate page, click User Certificate request and then click Next.
5. On the User Certificate–Identifying Information page, click Submit.
6. If you receive a warning informing you that you should allow only trusted Web sites to request a certificate, click Yes to complete the request.
7. A few seconds later, a Certificate Issued Web page appears. Click Install this certificate.

The certificate you just obtained is installed in a protected area of the Registry known as a *certificate store*. If you have obtained a certificate from an external agency such as VeriSign, it is possible to install this certificate in the certificate store, as well. The certificate provides a level of trust according to the purposes outlined on the certificate's General tab, which you view in the next exercise. A certificate obtained from VeriSign naturally carries a higher level of trust than one obtained from a private company CA that is self-signed; however, the latter still carries a level of trust for actions conducted within the organization, provided that the root certificate and its keys are kept secure from compromise.

Certificates are provided for various business purposes according to the template from which they are issued. Another example is the Web server certificate, which you looked at in Chapter 2. You can view the available purposes from the Properties dialog box for the template used to issue the certificate, visible in the right pane of the Certification Authority console when you select the Policy Settings node. We look at certificate templates in Exercise 4.5.1.

To view the certificate, you need to go back to the certificate server and proceed as follows:

1. Click Start, Programs, Administrative Tools, Certification Authority. This step opens the Certification Authority console.
2. If necessary, expand your server in the left pane to reveal a series of subfolders.
3. Select Issued Certificates. You will see one or more certificates in the right pane.
4. Double-click the appropriate certificate. As shown in Figure 4.8, the General tab displays information related to the purposes of the certificate and the entity that issued the certificate.
5. For additional details regarding the certificate, select the Details tab to obtain the information shown in Figure 4.9. Scroll this tab to view all available information.
6. When you are finished, click OK. Leave the Certification Authority console open for the next exercise.

CAs and the certificates they issue are but a small part of the overall concept of PKI. For information on other components of PKI, see the reference text by Adams and Lloyd in the "Need to Know More?" section at the end of this chapter.

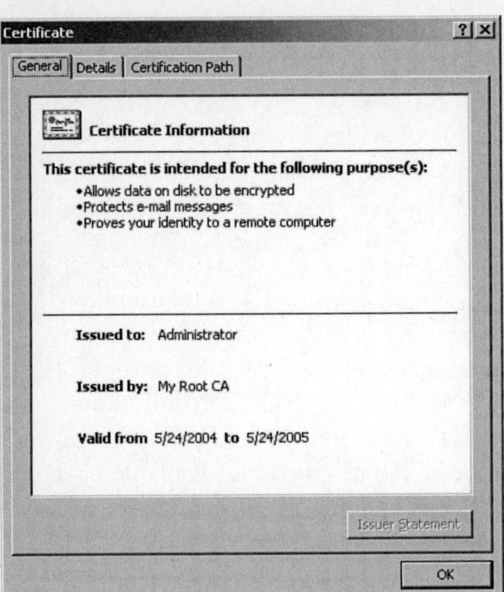

Figure 4.8 The General tab of a certificate displays general information about the certificate.

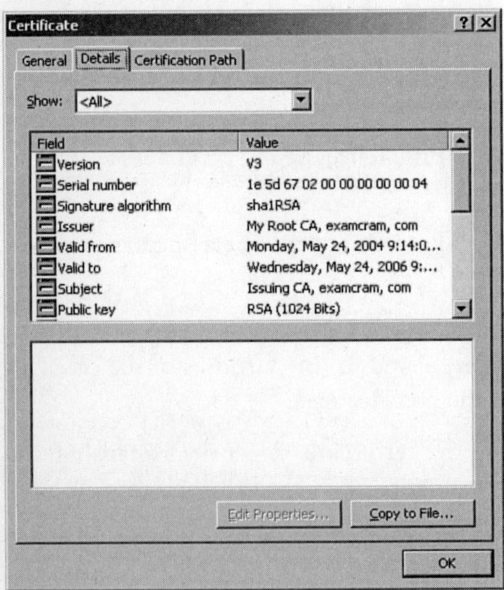

Figure 4.9 The Details tab of a certificate displays additional facts.

Exercise 4.3.3: Certificate Revocation in Windows 2000 Server

It might be necessary to revoke a certificate before its normal expiry date should the certificate or its keys become compromised in any manner. Other reasons for revoking a certificate also exist, such as termination of employment of an individual to whom a certificate has been issued. A revoked certificate is placed on a certificate revocation list (CRL) so that applications which depend on its validity can find out about the certificate's revocation. In this exercise, you revoke the certificate you just issued in the previous exercise:

1. On the right pane of the Certification Authority console, right-click the certificate you just examined and choose All Tasks, Revoke Certificate.
2. A Certificate Revocation message box confirms that you want to revoke the certificate and allows you to specify a reason for the revocation.
3. If you might need to restore the same certificate later, select Certificate Hold as the reason. Otherwise, select any other appropriate reason code, and click Yes.
4. Select Revoked Certificates in the left pane of the Certification Authority console. The revoked certificate is listed in the right pane.

Best practice dictates that you should inform the owner of a compromised certificate that the certificate is being revoked.

You should be aware that two types of CRLs exist: *full CRLs*, which include all certificates revoked up to the most recent CRL publication date, and *delta CRLs*, which include only those certificates published since the most recent full CRL publication. This concept, which is new to Windows Server 2003 and is not available in Windows 2000, means that the notification of each certificate revocation happens on a timelier basis without the use of excessive network bandwidth.

Exercise 4.3.4: CA Hierarchies and Trusts (Optional)

In the previous exercises of this section, you created a root CA and certificates. In the real world, anyone could install a certificate server and issue certificates. What is there to certify these CAs? This is the topic of CA hierarchies and trusts. In the simplest form, a hierarchy is the combination of a root CA with another server known as a *subordinate CA*. In this exercise, you create this hierarchy. To perform this exercise, you need a second computer running Windows 2000 Server:

1. Log on to the second computer running Windows 2000 Server as an administrator.
2. Repeat Steps 2 to 5 of Exercise 4.3.1 to begin the installation of Certificate Services.
3. On the CA Type page, select Stand-Alone Subordinate CA, and then click Next.
4. Repeat Steps 7 and 8 of Exercise 4.3.1.
5. On the CA Certificate Request page, type the name or IP address of the computer that holds the root CA role (in this case, the computer you configured in Exercise 4.3.1). The name of the parent CA should appear in the Parent CA text box. Then click Next.
6. Repeat Steps 9 to 11 of Exercise 4.3.1 to complete installation of the subordinate CA.
7. In the real world, you would take the root CA offline and store it in a safe place such as a bank vault. You would only bring it back online to issue certificates for additional subordinate CAs.

More than one level of subordinate CA can exist; for example, a three-tier hierarchy can include the root CA, one or more intermediate CAs, and a further series of issuing CAs that are subordinate to the intermediate CAs.

Companies that need to ensure the trustworthiness of their certificates purchase a root certificate from a commercial authority such as Thawte or VeriSign and use this certificate to install a subordinate CA.

What Did I Just Learn?

Now that you have looked at the concepts of PKI, let's take a moment to review all the critical items you've experienced in this lab:

- A certificate is a digital file that vouches for the authenticity of the entity that requested it.

- Microsoft provides Certificate Services, which can be installed on a Windows 2000 or 2003 server to issue certificates for various purposes.
- If you need to invalidate a certificate before its expiry date for any reason, such as its compromise, you can revoke it. Revoked certificates are published in CRLs.
- Trust models are hierarchies of CAs that are created to simplify the issuance of certificates and guard against the compromise of root CAs. By using a hierarchy of CAs, you can store the root CA offline in a protected vault so that it cannot be compromised.

4.4: Identifying and Differentiating Cryptographic Standards and Protocols

The Public Key Cryptography Standards (PKCS) are a series of standard protocols that define the means by which PKI is used for securing the exchange of data between individuals and organizations. In addition to these standards, the ITU has defined a series of X.509 standards that define the format of data contained within digital certificates.

Exercise 4.4.1: Understanding Cryptographic Standards and Protocols

In this exercise, you research the topics of cryptographic standards and protocols:

1. Connect to the Internet and navigate to Request for Comments (RFC) 2459 at http://www.ietf.org/rfc/rfc2459.txt. This document prepared by the Internet Society describes the protocols and standards for X.509 certificates. Write a summary of this document in your own words, addressing in particular the following items:
   - How do X.509 certificates provide confidence to users that the associated private key is owned by the proper entity?
   - What enhancements do v3 certificates provide over earlier certificate versions?
   - What are certification paths, and why are they important?

- Name an advantage and a limitation of the use of CRLs for publishing certificate revocation.
- Briefly discuss each function that should be supported by a series of management protocols.
- Describe the purpose of the three required certificate field sequences.
- What nine fields can be present in the TBSCertificate sequence? Which of these fields must be present? Briefly describe the purpose of each of these fields.
- Look through the list of available certificate extensions and summarize the basic purpose of each one. In particular, make sure you understand the CRL Distribution Points extension.
- What three fields are required to be present in a CRL? What is the purpose of each of these fields?
- Describe the purpose of the fields that can be present in the certificate list to be signed. Which of these fields must be present?
- Look through the list of available CRL extensions and CRL entry extensions and summarize the basic purpose of each one. In particular, make sure you understand the Delta CRL indicator and Reason Code extensions.
- How are certification paths validated?
- Review the cryptographic algorithms mentioned, and look for information of interest that you have not previously encountered when studying these algorithms earlier in this chapter.

2. Return to the Certification Authority console on the computer running Windows 2000 Server. Access the Details tab of a certificate and compare the entries in this tab with the TBSCertificate fields and extensions.

3. Also return to the procedure for certificate revocation and compare the available reason codes with those mentioned in the Reason Code CRL extension.

4. Mohan Atreya provides a summary of the PKCS standards at http://www.rsasecurity.com/products/bsafe/overview/IntroToPKCSstandards.pdf#xml=http://www.rsasecurity.com/programs/texis.exe/webinator/search/xml.txt?query=pkcs&pr=default_new&order=r&cq=&id=40b31a8d2. What benefits does the use of these standards provide?

Note what the various standards define. Also note how the various standards relate to the use of digital signatures, digital envelopes, digital certificates, and agreements for key exchange.

5. Another means of publishing revoked certificates is the Online Certificate Status Protocol (OCSP). Navigate to http://searchsecurity.techtarget.com/sDefinition/0,,sid14_gci784421,00.html for a concise definition of OCSP. How does OCSP improve on the limitations of CRLs? What three responses to certificate queries can OCSP return? For additional information about OCSP, refer to http://www.sans.org/rr/papers/20/748.pdf.

It is more important to know the reason for the PKCS standards as opposed to the actual contents of each standard.

What Did I Just Learn?

Now that you have looked at several types of access control, let's take a moment to review all the critical items you've experienced in this lab:

- RFC 2459 outlines the format of digital certificates and mandates the inclusion of certain items within the certificate, as well as the format and contents of the CRL. You can easily find these items in certificates issued by a Microsoft CA.
- The PKCS standards provide a basis for the function of public-key cryptography schemes.
- OCSP overcomes many of the limitations of CRLs. Windows 2000 does not contain support for OCSP, although you can use third-party providers. A certificate extension in Windows Server 2003 provides support for the OCSP responder location.

4.5: Understanding Key Management and Certificate Lifecycles

A *lifecycle* refers not to a brand of exercise bicycle but to the stages through which certificates and keys pass from the time they are first created to their ultimate disposal. The Security+ exam expects you to know about the various events that affect a key's lifespan and usage.

Exercise 4.5.1: Certificate Management in Windows 2000 Server

The Certification Authority console in Windows 2000 Server enables you to manage aspects of the lifecycles for the certificates that it issues. In this exercise, you are introduced to these management functions. Perform this exercise at either of the servers you configured as a CA earlier in this chapter:

1. Log on to the CA computer as an administrator.
2. Click Start, Programs, Administrative Tools, Certification Authority.
3. If necessary, expand the list under the server in the left pane.
4. Click Revoked Certificates. The right pane displays any certificates that have been revoked.
5. To view information about the CRL, right-click Revoked Certificates and choose Properties. As shown in Figure 4.10, the CRL Publishing Parameters tab of the Revoked Certificates Properties dialog box enables you to specify the CRL publication interval.

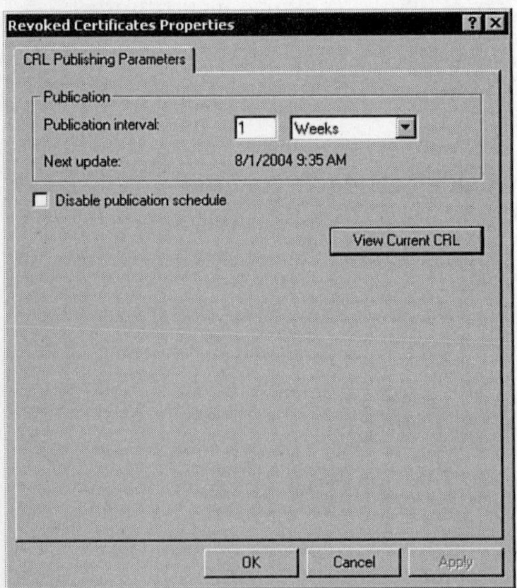

Figure 4.10 The CRL Publishing Parameters tab of the Revoked Certificates Properties dialog box enables you to configure the publication interval for the CA's CRLs.

6. Click the View Current CRL button. The General tab of the Certificate Revocation List dialog box provides information on the parameters of the CRL, as you observed in the X.509 parameters in the last exercise (see Figure 4.11). To view information on revoked certificates, select the Revocation List tab.

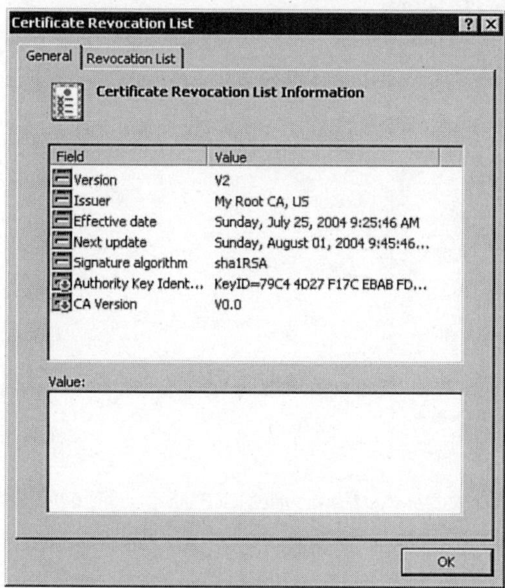

Figure 4.11 The Certificate Revocation List dialog box provides information about the CRL as well as the certificates that have been revoked.

7. Click OK twice to close the CRL dialog boxes.
8. Click Issued Certificates. The right pane displays the certificates issued by this CA. If you are working from the root CA, you should see a certificate for the subordinate CA you created in Exercise 4.3.4.
9. Click Pending Requests. This node provides a location to store any requests for certificates that must be approved by an administrator before becoming valid. If any item appears in the right pane, you can approve it by right-clicking it and choosing All Tasks, Approve.
10. Click Failed Requests. This node provides a location to store requests that have failed approval for any reason.
11. Click Policy Settings. The right pane displays a list of certificate templates that can be used for creating certificates designed for various purposes. Right-click a template and choose Properties to view the

properties associated with the template (as shown in Figure 4.12 for the computer certificate template).

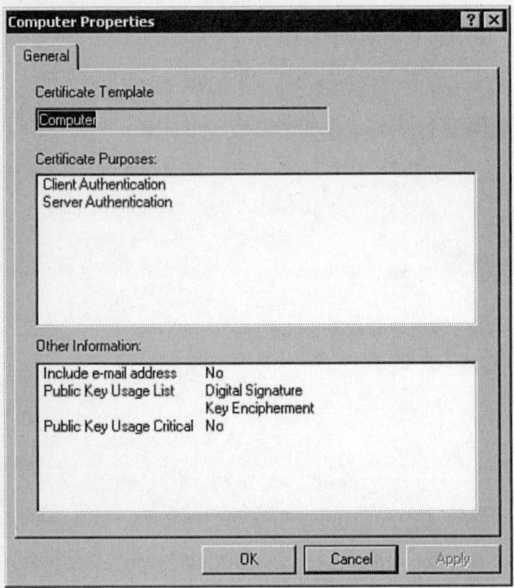

Figure 4.12 The Properties dialog box for a certificate template provides information on the purposes to which a certificate can be put.

12. You can add, remove, or modify certificate templates that are available for the CA to issue. Right-click Policy Settings and choose New, Certificate to Issue to view the list of possible templates.

13. Another important task is backing up the CA and the certificates it has issued. Right-click the CA server and choose All Tasks, Back Up CA. This step starts a wizard that takes you through the steps of creating a backup (see Figure 4.13).

Think about certificates and keys in much the same way that you think about documents such as credit cards and drivers licenses. They all have expiry dates and must be renewed prior to expiry. In addition, they can be suspended or revoked for reasons that are defined in law.

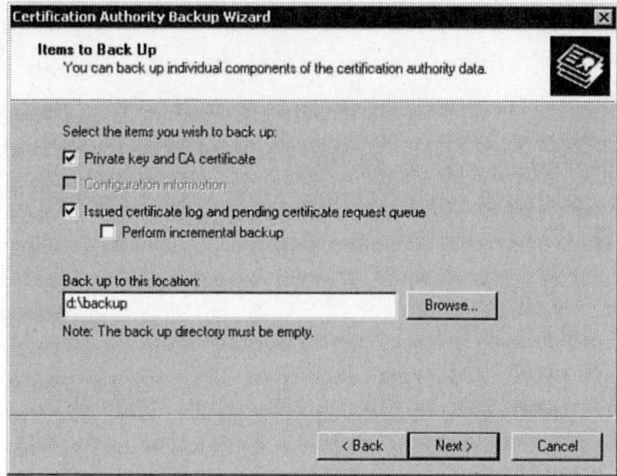

Figure 4.13 The Certification Authority Backup Wizard allows you to specify which items will be backed up as well as the location of the backup.

Exercise 4.5.2: Key Storage, Escrow, and Recovery

Digital certificates and asymmetric keys are an important component of PKI. Remember that your public key can be freely distributed to anyone, but you keep your private key guarded to yourself. Remember also that, of course, your public key is only useful as long as you have access to your private key. If you cannot encrypt documents with your private key, it really doesn't matter who has your public key. So what happens if you lose your private key?

If you hold the only copy of your private key and you lose it, you are out of luck. Your only choice at this point is to revoke your digital certificate and get another one. The hope is that you thought ahead and planned for such an occurrence.

This exercise directs you to research the basic problem of private key storage, escrow, and recovery. The topic is fairly straightforward but crucial in maintaining uninterrupted access to your private key:

1. Marcin Policht reviews software- and hardware-based key storage solution for Windows Server 2003 at http://www.serverwatch.com/tutorials/article.php/3311721. What is the new technology that you can use for private key storage? For more information on the two hardware modules discussed here, follow the links provided.

2. Continue to http://www.casamirador.com/sabbott/roleHW2.html for another view of technologies used in cryptographic key storage. What are the major advantages and disadvantages, in terms of cost, convenience, performance, and security, of both hardware and software key storage? What progress has been made toward making a token-based hardware security solution that is economical and portable enough for individuals to carry on their persons? How do the requirements for secure key storage on a server differ from those for individuals?

3. Continue to http://www.webopedia.com/TERM/K/key_escrow.html for a concise definition of key escrow. Why can key escrow become a security risk? What is the benefit of key escrow? Further information on key recovery, key escrow, and their risks appears at http://www.cdt.org/crypto/risks98/.

4. For another view on the controversies surrounding key escrow, go to http://encyclopedia.thefreedictionary.com/Key%20escrow. Under what conditions should a third party be permitted access to escrowed keys? In what ways do these conditions extend beyond a technical basis?

5. Write a recommendation for implementing key escrow in your organization. What are the reasons your organization would want to implement such a service? What are the risks? What steps should your organization take to protect escrowed keys?

6. After you address the issue of key escrow, document any additional steps users must take to be able to recover escrowed keys. What additional information will users need? How will users protect this information? Should your organization add or change any security policies to govern new identification credentials?

Users already have a private key, a public key, and a password used to revoke or suspend a digital certificate. If you use one set of keys for signing and another set for encryption, that number will be doubled. Now we are adding more information used to identify the owner of a private key for recovery purposes. Be careful to avoid adding too much overhead to users. When it gets too hard, users find workarounds.

7. Alan Young reviews many facets of PKI, including key management, renewal, revocation, and recovery, at http://www.cas.mcmaster.ca/~wmfarmer/SE-4C03-02/projects/student_work/youngcy.html. The first part of his paper presents an excellent review of topics you have already studied in this chapter. Note the contents of the X.509 certificates. In what way does the "m-of-n" key recovery scheme work for recovery of a private key? What is a registration authority (RA), and how is it involved in certificate management?

8. An example of a commercial key recovery system is that provided by RSA Security at http://www.whitehatinc.com/rsasecurity/keon/dskeonkrm.html. Review this document for the features provided by this system. How does the m-of-n scheme work? Describe in your own words how the key-recovery software works.

Exercise 4.5.3: Renewing and Destroying Digital Certificates

Each digital certificate has an expiration date. At some point, the certificate expires. The reason is threefold. First, it is generally a bad idea to authorize anything indefinitely. Forced expiration is a great way to periodically force maintenance. Second, the longer a key is valid, the greater the chance of its compromise; unused, unexpired keys could be forgotten about until someone uses them for a malicious purpose. Finally, expiration is a good point for billing. Remember, the CAs are in business for profit.

You need to understand how to renew a certificate. It is important that you know both how and when to renew your certificate. In addition, you need to know how to destroy a certificate if it becomes obsolete prior to the stated expiration date. A certificate becomes obsolete any time the owner entity no longer uses the certificate for its original purpose. For example, an organization might cease operations or an individual might no longer be affiliated with an organization in which he or she used a certificate. In any case, a certificate might need to be destroyed.

This exercise directs you to research the issues of certificate renewal and destruction:

1. If you currently use digital certificates, use a Web browser to look up the renewal procedures for your CA. If you do not currently use digital certificates, go to http://www.thawte.com/guides/pdf/StepByStepRenewal.pdf, which is a PDF document of Thwate's guidelines for certificate renewal. Read the appropriate sections to find out what you must do to renew a certificate.

2. Develop a checklist of steps you must follow to renew a digital certificate. Include any dates and deadlines. For example, are the steps different for an expired certificate, as opposed to one that has not yet expired? Also, how do you identify yourself to the CA?

3. For a certificate renewal procedure employed by an Australian university, visit http://www.its.monash.edu/security/certs/renew_cert.html.

Other organizations use similar procedures and might require the presentation of a public key as well as identification information to prove who you are.

Make a list of steps specific to your CA. If there are several options available for renewing a certificate, choose one for this exercise.

Now we focus on destroying a digital certificate.

4. The same university has published a procedure for certificate revocation and destruction at http://www.its.monash.edu.au/security/certs/revoke_cert.html. Under what conditions can a user revoke her certificate or not revoke it?

5. Now develop a checklist of steps you must follow to destroy a digital certificate. Can you destroy a digital certificate in a single step? What is the difference between revoking and destroying a digital certificate? How would any of these steps change your digital certificate implementation plan?

As with revoking digital certificates, you must be prepared to identify yourself as the digital certificate originator to the CA. How will you plan to secure the credentials (that is, your digital certificate password)?

What Did I Just Learn?

Now that you have looked at key management and certificate lifecycles, let's take a moment to review all the critical items you've experienced in this lab:

- You can perform many aspects of certificate management from the Windows 2000 Server Certification Authority console, including CRL management and backup of the CA.
- Key escrow is used to store copies of private keys in secured locations that are accessible only to authorized individuals. Users can recover lost keys from escrow by following a strictly mandated procedure.
- When a certificate is nearing or has passed its expiry date, you can renew it by following a defined procedure that is simpler than that of obtaining a new certificate.
- A mandated list of steps is also necessary should it be necessary to destroy a digital certificate.

Exam Prep Questions

Objective 4.1: Algorithms

1. What is an algorithm?
   - ❑ A. A series of steps used to guarantee a result
   - ❑ B. A group of mathematical additions
   - ❑ C. A process of using calculus
   - ❑ D. A solution to an equation

2. Which of the following algorithms uses symmetric keys?
   - ❑ A. RSA
   - ❑ B. Ring
   - ❑ C. Rijndael
   - ❑ D. Star

3. Which of the following are known weaknesses of symmetric cryptography? (Select all that apply.)
   - ❑ A. Speed
   - ❑ B. Limited security
   - ❑ C. Scalability
   - ❑ D. Key distribution

4. Which of the following algorithms use asymmetric keys? (Select all that apply.)
   - ❑ A. RSA
   - ❑ B. ECC
   - ❑ C. El Gamal
   - ❑ D. Twofish

5. Which of the following statements is true about asymmetric encryption?
   - ❑ A. Slower than symmetric encryption because of its client/server configuration requirements
   - ❑ B. Faster than symmetric encryption because it doesn't require client/server configuration
   - ❑ C. Slower than symmetric encryption because of its variable key length
   - ❑ D. Faster than symmetric encryption because of its variable key length

Objective 4.2: Concepts of Using Cryptography

1. Which of the following is the best term for this definition: a type of symmetric-key encryption algorithm that changes a fixed-size block of clear-text data into a block of ciphertext data of the same length?
   - ❑ A. Block plaintext
   - ❑ B. Block ciphertext
   - ❑ C. Block text
   - ❑ D. Block cipher
2. You have decided to implement a public-key cryptography system to ensure data integrity. Which of the following statements is valid for your system?
   - ❑ A. When you encrypt data using a public key, only the public key can decrypt that data.
   - ❑ B. When you encrypt data using a public key, only the private key can decrypt that data.
   - ❑ C. When you encrypt data using a public key, either public or private key can decrypt that data.
   - ❑ D. When you encrypt data using a public key, only the CA can decrypt that data.
3. Which of the following is used to create a unique digital signature?
   - ❑ A. Public key
   - ❑ B. Private key
   - ❑ C. Session key
   - ❑ D. Kerberos key
4. Which of the following refers to strong authentication?
   - ❑ A. Use of a public key to verify a digital signature for authenticity
   - ❑ B. Use of a private key to verify a digital signature for authenticity
   - ❑ C. Use of a PGP to verify a digital signature for authenticity
   - ❑ D. Use of a RADIUS to verify a digital signature for authenticity
5. Which of the following offers nonrepudiation and integrity?
   - ❑ A. Digital signatures
   - ❑ B. Message digest
   - ❑ C. Hashing algorithms
   - ❑ D. Symmetric algorithms

Objective 4.3: PKI

1. What does PKI stand for?
   - ❑ A. Private Krypto Intelligence
   - ❑ B. Public Krypto Intelligence
   - ❑ C. Private Key Infrastructure
   - ❑ D. Public Key Infrastructure
2. Which of the following best relates to a set of rules for the detailed use of certificates?
   - ❑ A. Certificate authority
   - ❑ B. Certificate rule set
   - ❑ C. Certificate policy
   - ❑ D. Certificate practice statement
3. Which of the following best explains how to implement the set of rules for the detailed use of certificates?
   - ❑ A. Certification authority
   - ❑ B. Certificate rule set
   - ❑ C. Certificate policy
   - ❑ D. Certificate practice statement
4. Which of the following is a reference list of certificates that have been identified for revocation prior to their original expiration date?
   - ❑ A. Certificate revocation list (CRL)
   - ❑ B. Expired certificate renewals (ECR)
   - ❑ C. Revocation security system (RSS)
   - ❑ D. Request revocation certificate list (RRCL)
5. Which of the following are *not* PKI trust models? (Select all that apply.)
   - ❑ A. Direct trust
   - ❑ B. Hierarchical trust
   - ❑ C. Key trust
   - ❑ D. Indirect trust

Objective 4.4: Standards and Protocols

1. Which of the following standards allows CAs to implement unique passwords that protect encrypted network transmissions?
   - ❑ A. X.509
   - ❑ B. PKCS #1
   - ❑ C. ISO17799
   - ❑ D. PKCS #11

2. Which of the following is a standard for information security management?
   - ❑ A. ISO17799
   - ❑ B. X.509
   - ❑ C. X.400
   - ❑ D. PKS #6

3. What does the acronym PKCS stand for?
   - ❑ A. Public Key Cryptography Security
   - ❑ B. Public Key Cryptography Sanctions
   - ❑ C. Public Key Cryptography Standards
   - ❑ D. Public Key Cryptography Software

4. Which of the following standards is concerned with the handling of email messages?
   - ❑ A. X.900
   - ❑ B. X.509
   - ❑ C. X.500
   - ❑ D. X.400

5. To check the validity of a digital certificate, which one of the following would be used?
   - ❑ A. Corporate security policy
   - ❑ B. Certificate policy
   - ❑ C. Certificate revocation list
   - ❑ D. Expired domain names

Objective 4.5: Key Management and Certificate Lifecycle

1. Which of the following relates to certificate lifecycle? (Select all that apply.)
   - ❑ A. Key expiration
   - ❑ B. Key revocation
   - ❑ C. Key renewal
   - ❑ D. Key usage

2. Which of the following allows for third-party agents to maintain knowledge of portions of a cryptographic key for later recovery?
   - ❑ A. Partitioning key
   - ❑ B. Escrow
   - ❑ C. Limited key access
   - ❑ D. Separation of keys

3. Which one of the following applies to the certificate expiration date?
   - ❑ A. After the Valid To date is reached, the certificate must be destroyed.
   - ❑ B. After the Valid To date is reached, the certificate must be renewed.
   - ❑ C. After the Valid To date is reached, the certificate must be returned or regenerated.
   - ❑ D. After the Valid To date is reached, the certificate must be destroyed or renewed.

4. If a company thinks that a user's private key has been compromised, what should it do?
   - ❑ A. Turn the CA server off and on.
   - ❑ B. Shut down the CA server.
   - ❑ C. Revoke the user's key before expiration.
   - ❑ D. Renew the user's key before expiration.

5. Which of the following applies to key renewal? (Select all that apply.)
   - ❑ A. Renewal is required when information changes.
   - ❑ B. Renewal is *not* required when information changes.
   - ❑ C. Renewal requires proof of identity.
   - ❑ D. Renewal does *not* require proof of identity.

Exam Prep Answers

Objective 4.1: Algorithms

1. Answer A is correct. An algorithm is a series of steps used to obtain a result.

2. Answer C is correct. Rijndael is a symmetric algorithm.

3. Answers B, C, and D are correct. Limited security, scalability, and key distribution are known weaknesses of symmetric cryptography. Speed is the only advantage.

4. Answers A, B, and C are correct. RSA, ECC, and El Gamal are algorithms that use asymmetric keys.

5. Answer A is correct. Asymmetric encryption is slower than symmetric encryption because of its client/server configuration requirements.

Objective 4.2: Concepts of Using Cryptography

1. Answer D is correct. Block cipher is a type of symmetric-key encryption algorithm that changes a fixed-size block of clear-text data into a block of ciphertext data of the same length.

2. Answer B is correct. When using a public-key cryptography system, after you encrypt data using a public key, only the private key can decrypt that data.

3. Answer B is correct. A private key is used to create a unique digital signature.

4. Answer A is correct. Strong authentication uses a public key to verify a digital signature for authenticity.

5. Answer A is correct. Digital signatures offer nonrepudiation and maintain integrity.

Objective 4.3: PKI

1. Answer D is correct. PKI stands for Public Key Infrastructure.

2. Answer C is correct. A certificate policy is a set of rules for the detailed use of certificates.

3. Answer D is correct. A certificate practice statement explains the implementation methods to a set of rules for the detailed use of certificates.

4. Answer A is correct. A certificate revocation list (CRL) is a reference list of certificates that have been identified for revocation prior to their original expiration date.

5. Answers C and D are correct. There are three PKI trust models: direct trust, hierarchical trust, and web of trust.

Objective 4.4: Standards and Protocols

1. Answer A is correct. X.509 allows CAs to implement unique passwords that protect encrypted network transmissions.

2. Answer A is correct. ISO17799 is a standard for information security management.

3. Answer C is correct. PKCS stands for Public Key Cryptography Standards, which deals with PKI methods to securely exchange data.

4. Answer D is correct. The X.400 standard is concerned with the handling of email messages.

5. Answer C is correct. A CRL provides a detailed list of certificates that are no longer valid.

Objective 4.5: Key Management and Certificate Lifecycle

1. Answers A, B, C, and D are correct. A certificate lifecycle deals with all the items listed and more.

2. Answer B is correct. Escrow allows for third-party agents to maintain knowledge of portions of a cryptographic key for later recovery.

3. Answer D is correct. After the Valid To date is reached, the certificate must be destroyed or renewed.

4. Answer C is correct. If a company thinks that a private key has been compromised, revoke the person's key before expiration.

5. Answers B and D are correct. Key renewal is *not* required when information changes and does *not* require proof of identity.

Need to Know More?

For further information on the basics of cryptography, see the following:

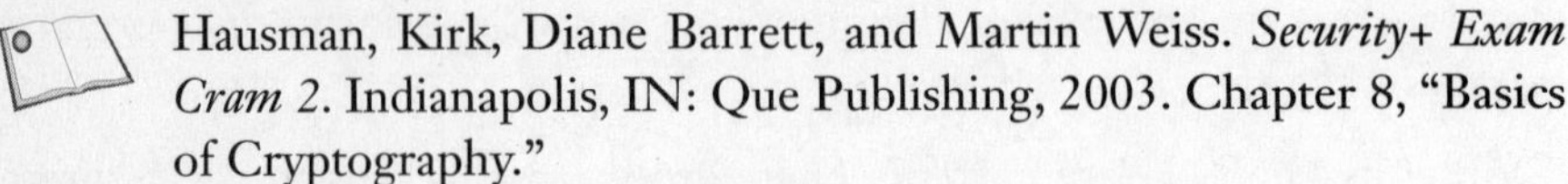

Hausman, Kirk, Diane Barrett, and Martin Weiss. *Security+ Exam Cram 2*. Indianapolis, IN: Que Publishing, 2003. Chapter 8, "Basics of Cryptography."

King, Todd and David Bittlingmeier. *Security+ Training Guide*. Indianapolis, IN: Que Publishing, 2003. Chapter 5, "Cryptography Algorithms," and Chapter 6, "PKI and Key Management."

For further information on security concepts, consult the following books:

Adams, Carlisle and Steve Lloyd. *Understanding Public-Key Infrastructure*. New York, NY: Macmillan Technical Publishing, 1999.

Pipkin, Donald. *Information Security: Protecting the Global Enterprise, First Edition*. Upper Saddle River, NJ: Prentice Hall, 2002.

For further information on PKI, see the following:

Adams, Carl and Steve Lloyd. *Understanding PKI: Concepts, Standards, and Deployment Considerations, Second Edition*. Boston, MA: Pearson Education, Inc., 2003.

For further information on Microsoft Certificate Services, consult the following books:

Adams, Carlisle and Steve Lloyd. *Understanding Public-Key Infrastructure*. New York, NY: Macmillan Technical Publishing, 1999.

Barrett, Diane, Bill Ferguson, and Don Poulton. *MCSA/MCSE 70-299 Exam Cram 2: Implementing and Administering Security in a Windows Server 2003 Network*. Indianapolis, IN: Que Publishing, 2004. Chapter 5, "Planning, Configuring, and Troubleshooting PKI."

For further information on certificate management in Windows 2000 Server and Windows Server 2003, consult these books:

Barrett, Diane, Bill Ferguson, and Don Poulton. *MCSA/MCSE 70-299 Exam Cram 2: Implementing and Administering Security in a Windows Server 2003 Network*. Indianapolis, IN: Que Publishing, 2004. Chapter 5, "Planning, Configuring, and Troubleshooting PKI."

Bragg, Roberta. *Exam Cram 2: Implementing and Administering Security in a Windows 2000 Network*. Indianapolis, IN: Que Publishing, 2003. Chapter 7, "Implementing and Managing PKI and EFS."

For further information on digital certificates, see this book:

Feghhi, Jalal and Peter Williams. *Digital Certificates: Applied Internet Security*. Boston, MA: Pearson Education, Inc., 1998.

Operational and Organizational Security

A company's security needs extend beyond its computers and its networks. In this day and age of terror threats and corporate espionage, a security technician must understand the need for physical security and business continuity as well as the requirements of preserving evidence, educating users, and documenting systems. CompTIA included the objective domain that is the focus of this chapter to ensure that security technicians understand these needs for organizational security.

The following is a list of the exam objectives you will be covering in this chapter:

- 5.1 Understand the application of the following concepts of physical security:
    - Access Control
        - Physical Barriers
        - Biometrics
    - Social Engineering
    - Environment
        - Wireless Cells
        - Location
        - Shielding
        - Fire Suppression

- 5.2 Understand the security implications of the following topics of disaster recovery:
  - Backups
    - Off Site Storage
  - Secure Recovery
    - Alternative Sites
  - Disaster Recovery Plan
- 5.3 Understand the security implications of the following topics of business continuity:
  - Utilities
  - High Availability/Fault Tolerance
  - Backups
- 5.4 Understand the concepts and uses of the following types of policies and procedures:
  - Security Policy
    - Acceptable Use
    - Due Care
    - Privacy
    - Separation of Duties
    - Need to Know
    - Password Management
    - SLAs (Service Level Agreements)
    - Disposal/Destruction
    - HR (Human Resources) Policy
      - Termination (Adding and revoking passwords and privileges, etc.)
      - Hiring (Adding and revoking passwords and privileges, etc.)
      - Code of Ethics
  - Incident Response Policy

- 5.5 Explain the following concepts of privilege management:
  - User/Group/Role Management
  - Single Sign-on
  - Centralized vs. Decentralized
  - Auditing (Privilege, Usage, Escalation)
  - MAC/DAC/RBAC (Mandatory Access Control/Discretionary Access Control/Role Based Access Control)
- 5.6 Understand the concepts of the following topics of forensics:
  - Chain of Custody
  - Preservation of Evidence
  - Collection of Evidence
- 5.7 Understand and be able to explain the following concepts of risk identification:
  - Asset Identification
  - Risk Assessment
  - Identification
  - Vulnerabilities
- 5.8 Understand the security relevance of the education and training of end users, executives, and human resources:
  - Communication
  - User Awareness
  - Education
  - Online Resources
- 5.9 Understand and explain the following documentation concepts:
  - Standards and Guidelines
  - Systems Architecture
  - Change Documentation
  - Logs and Inventories
  - Classification
    - Notification

- Retention/Storage
- Destruction

5.1: Applying Principles of Physical Security

All the access controls, network monitors, security logs, and so on do not mean a thing if an intruder can walk into the server room, unplug a server, and carry it out to her car. Therefore, you must understand the purpose for various methods of physical security and how to apply them.

Exercise 5.1.1: Understanding Physical Security

In this exercise, you research methods of physical security from the Internet:

1. Connect to the Internet and navigate to http://techrepublic.com.com/5100-6329-5054057.html for a series of three articles on physical and operational security. Summarize the points made by the authors, obtaining answers to the following questions:
   - How can curious employees present a security risk?
   - What are some of the problems presented by conventional lock-and-key security methods, and how can card-access systems overcome these problems?
   - How can you secure servers when space constraints prevent you from locating them in locked rooms?
   - What should you do to secure backups? We discuss backups further in Section 5.2.
   - Summarize the ways you can employ video monitoring effectively to enforce physical security.
2. Continue to http://www.microsoft.com/technet/community/columns/5min/5min-203.mspx for a concise summary of physical security related to Windows-based computers but applicable to any computer. Where do some small companies locate their servers, and what environmental risks can occur? What means are available for

securing a desktop computer, both physically and software-based? What steps should you take to physically secure networking components?

3. Continue to http://www.cert.org/security-improvement/practices/p074.html for another view of physical security. What are three reasons why physical security is important? What are two ways in which you can provide physical security, and what can you accomplish by undertaking each of these ways?

4. Security of corporate data is the business of companies such as NetDocuments. Go to http://www.netdocuments.com/Solutions/ServiceInformation/Security/ and review NetDocuments' highly stringent security procedures, which include a strong level of physical security as well as other types of security that we covered in previous chapters. Although much of these security measures are beyond the requirements of many companies, they serve to inform you of measures that can be taken to provide absolute data and system security.

5. Michael James produced a practical assignment for the SANS Global Information Assurance Certification (GIAC) security certifications at http://www.giac.org/practical/GSEC/Michael_James_GSEC.pdf, which reviews a common-sense approach to physical security. After starting with a quoted powerful definition of physical security and adding his own, James provides a comprehensive review of most aspects of physical security including the use of biometrics. Summarize his major points and follow the links he has provided to obtain additional information related to this exam objective.

If the URLs provided in this or other exercises no longer exist, simply use your favorite search engine to locate other sites that contain information pertinent to the topics at hand.

Note that physical security can overlap with other types of security. For example, the same biometric controls (fingerprints, retinal scans, and so on) that can be used to authenticate users to computers and domains can also be used to authenticate access to buildings and offices.

Exercise 5.1.2: Exploring Environmental Factors in Physical Security

Another aspect of physical security is environmental factors such as temperature, humidity, and the presence of electrostatic discharge (ESD) or electromagnetic interference (EMI), as well as risks associated with fire, flood, or other disasters. In this exercise, you research these factors from the Internet:

1. Navigate to http://amas.syr.edu/physicalsecurity.htm for a security procedure from Syracuse University that includes both the physical factors you studied in the last exercise as well as environmental ones. What types of detectors do the authors advocate for server rooms? How should servers be protected from loss of electrical power, both in the short term and the long term? Note the need for access controls to locations such as wiring closets.
2. Continue to http://www.labcompliance.com/info/2003/1010-data-centers.htm and study the recommendations for data center physical and environmental security. What location within a building do the authors recommend for the data center and why? What environmental variables should be monitored? Summarize the recommended means of physical control for access to computers. We return to this reference later in the chapter with regard to training and documentation concerns.
3. For another perspective on physical security in the data center, go to http://www.ffiec.gov/ffiecinfobase/booklets/information_secruity/04b_physical%20_security.htm. What threats to the physical environment do these authors mention? Why is shielding important, and what type of shielding do they recommend for walls and windows?
4. Seth Friedman includes a practical assignment for the SANS GIAC Security Essentials Certification (GSEC) at http://www.sans.org/rr/papers/43/270.pdf. This paper discusses the construction of a Web hosting facility from the perspective of physical security. Summarize Friedman's recommendations for an ideal facility, including physical barriers, biometrics, location, personnel security, shielding, and fire suppression. Note the recommendations for additional security components, such as man traps, fire extinguishers, redundant power supplies, and so on. This paper also touches on some of the Security+ objectives you studied in other chapters of this book.
5. For further information on shielding a facility, go to http://www.intpro.co.uk/room.htm. Why is it important to deploy an architectural shielding system such as the one described by these vendors?

6. Fire suppression around computer networks involves sophisticated technology. Go to http://www.pmengineer.com/CDA/ArticleInformation/features/BNP__Features__Item/0,2732,24054,00.html for a report on a clean fire suppressant called FM 200. What are the characteristics of this substance that makes it a desirable solution for protecting computers and networks from fire?

What Did I Just Learn?

Now that you have looked at issues related to physical security, let's take a moment to review all the critical items you've experienced in this lab:

- It is essential that mission-critical servers be housed in a locked room that is equipped with monitors that record environmental conditions such as temperature and humidity.
- Breaches of security can come from curious employees as well as outside individuals or contractors such as cleaning staff or repairmen.
- Some companies exist for the purpose of securing other companies' data by means of multiple physical safeguards.
- You also need to secure your networks from environmental hazards such as ESD and EMI and ensure that fire detection and suppression systems are in place.

When formulating your plans for fire protection in your server room, don't forget to include procedures for the emergency shutdown of servers, routers, and other equipment.

5.2: Preparing for Disaster Recovery

The events of September 11, 2001, emphasized the need for a comprehensive disaster recovery policy and especially the need for offsite data backups. The Security+ exam tests your knowledge of disaster recovery procedures, including data backup and secure storage and recovery procedures.

Exercise 5.2.1: Backing Up and Restoring Data in Windows 2000

All modern Windows operating systems include procedures for backing up and restoring the operating system, applications, and data. In this exercise, you back up the contents of your computer to removable storage media. Perform this exercise from a computer running Windows 2000 Server or Windows 2000 Professional:

1. Log on to the Windows 2000 computer as an administrator.
2. Click Start, Programs, Accessories, System Tools, Backup. The Backup or Restore Wizard starts with a welcome screen.
3. Click Backup Wizard, and on the Welcome to the Windows 2000 Backup and Recovery Tools screen, click Next.
4. The What to Back Up screen (see Figure 5.1) provides several choices of what to back up. To back up the contents of the computer, select the Back Up Everything on My Computer option and then click Next.

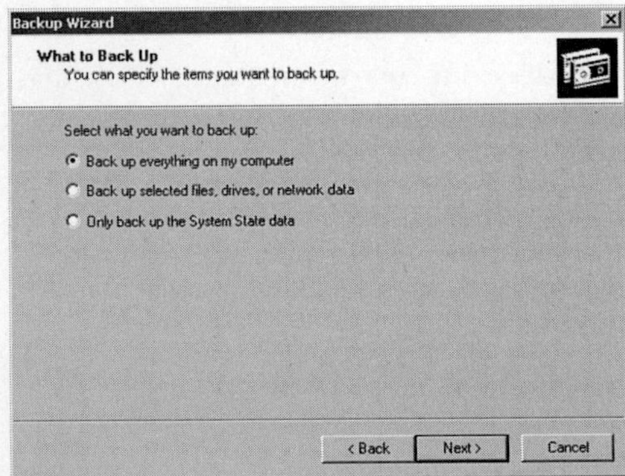

Figure 5.1 The What to Back Up screen in Windows 2000 Server provides three choices of items that will be backed up.

5. On the Where to Store the Backup screen, choose a place to save the backup. If you're saving a backup file to a hard disk, select the location and type a filename. You can then burn the backup file to external media, such as a CD-ROM, if you choose. Note that you will also need a floppy disk, which will be used to store system recovery data. Click Next.
6. Click Finish to complete the wizard and perform the backup.

The options on the What to Back Up screen and Backup Type, Destination, and Name screens in Windows XP Professional and Windows Server 2003 are slightly different but accomplish essentially the same result as those on the What to Back Up and Where to Store the Backup screens of the Windows 2000 Backup Wizard.

To select specific items for backup and to access additional backup options, you should select the Back Up Selected Files, Drives, or Network Data option shown in Figure 5.1. Then proceed as follows:

1. Click Next to display the Items to Back Up screen.
2. Expand the My Computer entry in the left pane to display the available drives as well as the System State object. This object includes everything that would enable you to restore your computer's system settings, such as the Registry, the Component Services Class (COM+) Registration database, and system startup files. See Figure 5.2.

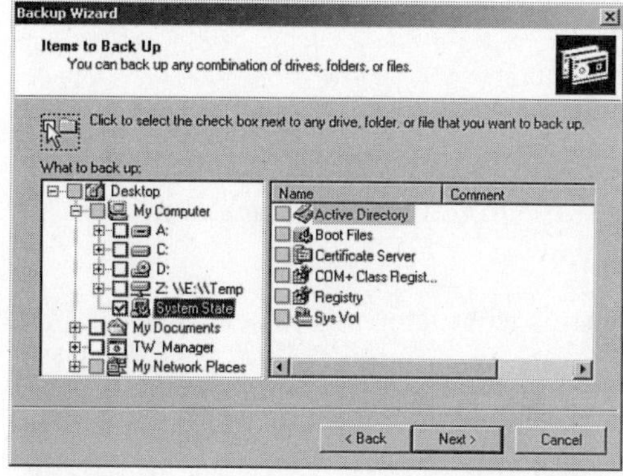

Figure 5.2 You can back up the Windows 2000 Server system state.

On a server computer, versus a client computer, additional items are backed up when you back up the system state. On a domain controller, this includes the Active Directory database and **SYSVOL** folder.

3. Click Next. In the Where to Store the Backup screen, choose a location for saving the backup.
4. Click Next to display the completion screen. To access additional backup options, click Advanced.

5. Specify a backup type from the options on the Type of Backup screen. The following options are available:

   - *Normal*—Backs up all selected files and marks the files as backed up.
   - *Copy*—Backs up all selected files but does not mark them as backed up.
   - *Incremental*—Backs up only those files that have changed since the last backup and marks the files as backed up.
   - *Differential*—Backs up only those files that have changed since the last backup but does not mark them as backed up.
   - *Daily*—Backs up only those files that were created or modified on the day the backup was performed.

You should know the differences between the various backup types, when they are used, and how they affect your restore procedure.

6. On the How to Back Up screen, select the Verify Data After Backup option if you want the backup program to verify the backed-up files. Click Next.
7. The Media Options screen controls what happens if backups are already present on the chosen media. You can either append the backup to the existing ones or replace them. Click Next.
8. The Backup Label screen allows you to choose a label for your backup media. Make the appropriate choice and click Next.
9. The When to Back Up screen enables you to specify the time when you want the backup to occur. Selecting the Later option on this screen opens the Set Account Information dialog box. Confirm the username and enter the password, and then enter the password again to confirm.
10. You are returned to the When to Back Up screen. Enter a job name, and then click the Set Schedule button. The Schedule Job dialog box opens, which enables you to specify the date and time the backup will take place and allows you to schedule repeated backups of the same data. Make the appropriate choice (see Figure 5.3), specify the scheduling options as required, click OK, and then click Next.

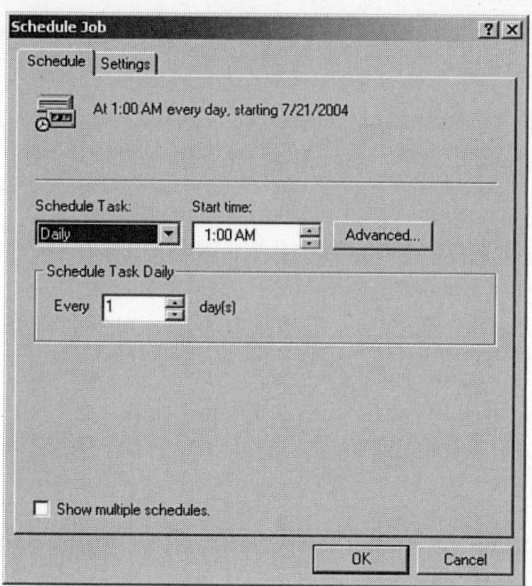

Figure 5.3 Here you can schedule a backup to occur nightly at 1:00 a.m.

11. You are returned to the completion screen. Click Finish to start the backup or schedule it, according to the options selected in the previous step.

For additional information on backup and restore options, see *MCSE/MCSA Training Guide (70-215): Windows 2000 Server*, referenced in the "Need to Know More?" section.

You must ensure that you test the recovery procedures from your backups regularly, or else a significant risk of data loss still exists. The test should involve restoring the backups to a different location such as an alternate server.

Exercise 5.2.2: Preparing a Disaster Recovery Plan

You almost never have a warning of impending disaster, so it is necessary for companies to have a plan in place to deal with unexpected emergencies. In this exercise, you research the creation of a disaster recovery plan (DRP) on the Internet, including secure data recovery and the use of alternate sites:

1. Geoffrey Wold presents a comprehensive three-part review of the disaster recovery planning process at http://www.drj.com/new2dr/w2_002.htm, http://www.drj.com/new2dr/w2_003.htm, and

http://www.drj.com/new2dr/w2_004.htm. From these articles, find answers to the following questions:

- What are the primary and five additional objectives of disaster recovery planning? Summarize the 10 steps that he describes.
- Note the need for clearly writing the plan using a standard format. What background information and instructions should be included? What type of language should be used while writing the plan?
- What basis should you use for creating the plan, and what are some of the assumptions that you should follow? From the list of potential teams, select those that you would include in a disaster plan for your organization, and discuss them with someone who would be involved in disaster recovery.
- What types of questions should you ask of the various departments while gathering information required for formulation of the plan?
- Summarize the more important data-gathering techniques you should use in preparing your plan.
- In conclusion, what are the benefits your company should achieve from the comprehensive disaster recovery plan?

2. Mark Schertler presents a guide to business continuity and disaster recovery planning at http://www.serverworldmagazine.com/monthly/2001/12/continuity.shtml. From this article, find answers to the following questions:

- What is the difference between disaster recovery planning and business continuity planning? The latter topic is covered in Objective 5.3 of the Security+ exam.
- Outline and summarize Schertler's five-step plan for keeping business-critical functions operating during and after a disaster.
- How do service level agreements (SLAs) enter into the recovery planning process? This topic is covered in Objective 5.4 of the Security+ exam.
- Schertler presents a comprehensive list of tasks you can do even in a small organization that help you recover from disaster. Apply them to your own case and ask yourself, how prepared is your company for disaster and what could you do to improve the level of preparedness? These items include topics covered in various Security+ exam objectives discussed in this chapter.

- How do you prioritize the types of services that your company's computers and networks provide? Also note the need for redundancy of highly critical services.

3. Another topic that should be included in a disaster recovery plan is the need for an alternate site. Go to http://www.rebuz.com/retech02/0402/disaster_recovery_plan.htm and compare the need for, functionality, and costs associated with hot, warm, and cool (or cold) sites.

Know the differences between hot, warm, and cold sites and the level of functionality associated with each type of alternate site.

When formulating the disaster recovery plan, you should include only those systems identified during the formal risk analysis procedure. Consequently, the disaster recovery plan should include a risk assessment. We study this procedure later in this chapter.

What Did I Just Learn?

Now that you have looked at factors associated with disaster recovery, let's take a moment to review all the critical items you've experienced in this lab:

- Windows 2000/XP/2003 provides a backup program that allows you to back up all critical data on your computers according to several configurable options.
- You can schedule your backups to occur during times when network and server activity is low. You can perform different kinds of backups, including normal, incremental, differential, copy, and daily.
- You cannot predict when disaster will strike. A disaster recovery plan enables your company to return to normal business operations on a timely basis.
- Alternate sites help enable a company to minimize downtime in the event of a disaster. Hot sites are the most expensive type of alternate site, containing all the required hardware, software, and infrastructure for a company to immediately transfer its business with minimal downtime. Warm sites and cold sites offer reduced functionality levels at lower cost and a longer downtime in the event of disaster.

5.3: Business Continuity Planning

Keeping a business going after a disaster involves more than just disaster recovery as discussed in the previous section. Aspects of business continuity planning (BCP) also include planning for continued network connectivity, alternate facilities, clustering of servers, and fault tolerance on existing servers.

Exercise 5.3.1: Fault Tolerance in Windows 2000 Server

Windows 2000 Server and Windows Server 2003 offer two fault-tolerant disk configurations, which provide a limited extent of protection for your data against disk failure. These configurations are as follows:

- *RAID 1*—Also known as disk mirroring, Redundant Array of Inexpensive Disks (RAID) 1 creates an exact copy of your data on a second physical hard disk. Data is copied in real time to each disk so that if one disk fails, the second disk is available and contains all your data. You can use RAID 1 to protect your operating system, application, and data files.
- *RAID 5*—Also known as disk striping with parity, RAID 5 writes data across all members of an array of 3 to 32 hard disks in 64KB blocks and writes parity information to each disk in turn. The parity information enables RAID 5 to reconstruct data if any one disk in the array fails. RAID 5 cannot be used to protect the operating system but can protect all application and data files.

In this exercise, you create a mirrored volume (RAID 1). Perform this exercise on a computer running Windows 2000 Server that is configured with two physical hard disks (not two partitions on one disk). The steps are similar in Windows Server 2003:

1. Log on to the Windows 2000 Server computer as an administrator.
2. On the desktop, right-click My Computer, and choose Manage. The Computer Management console opens.
3. Select Disk Management. The right pane displays information on the disks present in the computer.
4. To create a mirrored volume, if you have not already done so, you must first convert your disks to dynamic storage. Right-click any one disk and choose Upgrade to Dynamic Disk.

5. In the Upgrade to Dynamic Disk dialog box that opens (see Figure 5.4), select both Disk 0 and Disk 1, and then click OK.

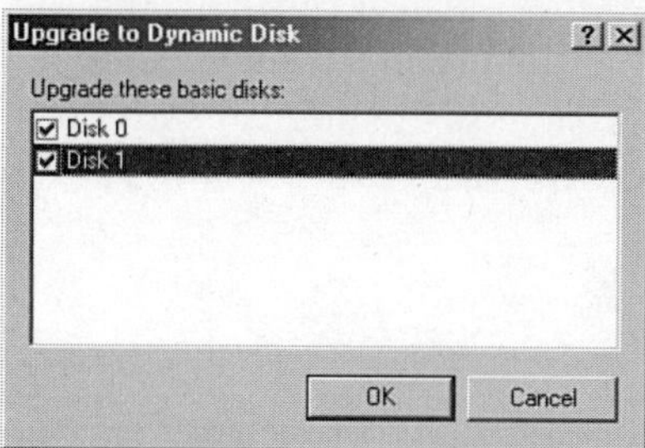

Figure 5.4 To convert your disks to dynamic storage, select both disks from the Upgrade to Dynamic Disk dialog box.

6. The Disks to Convert dialog box displays information about the disks that will be made dynamic. To proceed, click Convert, and then click Yes to confirm that you want to convert.
7. If you are converting the disk containing the operating system file, you receive a Confirm message box that informs you that the computer will restart. Click OK.
8. When the computer restarts, log back on as an administrator and restart Disk Management.
9. If you receive a second message asking whether you want to restart your computer, click No. Only a single restart is needed.
10. Return to Disk Management in the Computer Management console, right-click the volume (partition) that you want to mirror, and choose Add Mirror (see Figure 5.5).

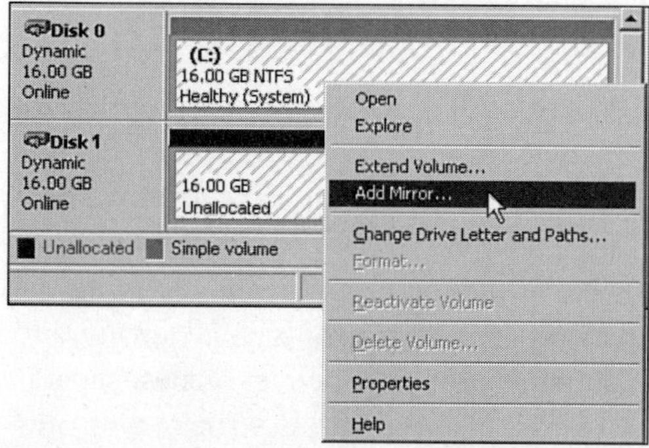

Figure 5.5 Add a mirror to an existing volume.

11. In the Add Mirror dialog box, select the disk (in this case, Disk 1) to use for mirroring, and then click Add Mirror.

12. When the process finishes, Disk Management displays a volume on the selected disk with the same drive letter as the original volume. This volume is formatted with the same file system as the original and contains copies of all files and folders. Note that this process might take several minutes for a large volume.

13. Close Disk Management.

Remember that a business continuity plan contains several components, including fault tolerance and disaster recovery procedures. It also contains plans for recovering and resuming business as well as upgrading alternate facilities. In addition, the business continuity plan should include some level of integration and validation.

What Did I Just Learn?

Now that you have looked at business continuity planning, let's take a moment to review all the critical items you've experienced in this lab:

- Business continuity planning includes disaster recovery planning, planning for recovering and resuming business, using alternate facilities, and planning for server clustering and data fault tolerance.
- Windows 2000 Server and Windows Server 2003 offer RAID solutions that provide fault tolerance. The Enterprise and Datacenter versions also offer multinode server clustering.

5.4: Creating and Enforcing Security Policies and Procedures

Detailed security policies and procedures outline what types of activities are permitted or forbidden on a company's network and with other devices owned by the company, including servers, desktop computers, laptops, personal digital assistants (PDAs), cellular telephones, and so on. The policies also state security standards and objectives for such activities as accessing the server room or other restricted areas on company property, acquiring and accessing data, acceptable use of company property, privacy issues, separation of duties, management of passwords, disposal and destruction of outdated information and resources, incident response, and so on. Human resources policies that relate to procedures to be followed during hiring and termination of employees are also included.

Exercise 5.4.1: Understanding Security Policies

In this exercise, you investigate several types of security policies and the consequences of not having policies in place:

1. Connect to the Internet and navigate to http://www.sans.org/resources/policies/. The SANS Security Policy Project Web page provides the resources for developing security policies for all types of organizations. Write a summary of the opening sections in your own words and then select the links to the following sample policies related to Security+ subobjectives, as well as others related to your company's business. Note the sections and formatting of the policies and the material contained within each one:

   - *Acceptable use policy*—Defines how the network and computers are to be used in conducting the company's business and lists those activities that are specifically prohibited.
   - *Antivirus process*—Expands on the acceptable use policy with regard to preventing virus infections.
   - *Audit vulnerability scanning policy*—Defines procedures to be followed during security auditing of networks by an external company hired for that purpose.
   - *Email use policy*—Defines acceptable use and privacy standards for email communication.
   - *Email retention policy*—Defines conditions and procedures for retention or disposal of email messages, related to the disposal and destruction subobjective.
   - *Information sensitivity policy*—Covers access to information, its distribution within and outside the company, and its disposal and destruction.
   - *Internal lab security policy*—Defines security policies applied to computer labs used for testing (not production) purposes.
   - *Internet DMZ security policy*—Defines the security requirements for the portion of the company's network located in the demilitarized zone (DMZ).

- *Password policy*—Defines standards to be followed in creating, changing, and protecting passwords for user and system accounts as well as passphrases for public and private key authentication.
- *Server security policy*—Defines the procedures to be used in configuring, securing, and monitoring servers.
- *Wireless communication policy*—Defines security standards to be followed for wireless communications, including authentication and data encryption.

Another good source for sample security policies is http://www.mcqsoft.com/secure/sample.htm.

2. A one-page excerpt from Certified Information Systems Security Professional (CISSP) certification notes that is also applicable to Security+ studies appears at http://www.n-cg.net/netcharts/sec_management3.pdf. In studying this excerpt, locate the definitions for the following terms: due care, separation of duties, standards, and guidelines. Also note the schemes of classification and their relation to the use and destruction of data.
3. For definitions of several terms included in this objective, see http://curl.planetmirror.com/pub/lynn/secure.htm. Locate and describe the following terms: acceptable use, need to know, and separation of duties. You might also want to locate definitions of terms studied in other sections and chapters of this book.
4. For some real-world incidents of problems that resulted from not having the appropriate policies in place, go to http://www.nwfusion.com/news/2001/1009itsec.html and review the problems and security tips mentioned. Think about possible incidents at your company that could have been averted with the proper security policy in place.

Many of the security policies have a legal basis that is defined in the laws of the state, province, or country in which the company is located. Companies operating in more than one jurisdiction might need to take into consideration multiple differing laws.

Exercise 5.4.2: Defining an HR Policy

New employees need to understand what is expected of them so that they do not perform activities that risk the network security. Disgruntled employees who quit or are fired might attempt to attack the network to gain a sense of revenge or obtain information that is useful to a competitor. In this exercise, you look at what components should be included in an HR policy:

1. Connect to the Internet and navigate to http://transit-safety.volpe.dot.gov/security/SecurityInitiatives/Top20/3%20--%20Employee%20Selection/11%20--%20Criteria%20for%20Investigations/Human%20Resources%20Best%20Practices.ppt. What should you do before you hire an employee? In particular, when you are hiring systems administrators or security administrators, note that you should perform a strong background check. Why do the components of a background check need to be outlined in detail within the HR policy? What level of access should a new employee receive on the first day of employment and why? What penalties will be applied for violating the policy terms? If you need to fire an employee, note the need for an effective termination policy. What components should this policy have? How should the policy differ for employees who resign? What is the proper basis for policies that involve contractors?

2. A draft document that outlines principles and procedures of creating a security policy, including hiring and termination, appears at http://www.usg.edu/acit/docs/security_guide.pdf. Read the introductory remarks and then proceed to Chapter 5, "Personnel Security." What steps should you take in screening prospective employees? What items need to be specified to define an employee's responsibilities and needs for data access? Note the guidelines that follow, which repeat many of the policy provisions that you studied in the previous exercise. This document also contains several training guidelines, which we study in a later exercise in this chapter.

3. For an article that provides security policy guidelines for organizations that are subject to Health Insurance Portability and Accountability Act (HIPAA) regulations, navigate to http://www.hipaadvisory.com/action/Security/secsum.pdf. This article addresses several items of importance in the termination of employment. Summarize four items that you need to look after when an employee leaves, as well as five specific issues that you need to consider (see Section 2.4.11).

4. Systems and network administrators generally have greater access to network and server resources than other employees of nearly all companies. For a code of ethics that administrators should adhere to, navigate to http://www.unt.edu/ccadmin/security/standards/saethics.htm.

Summarize several practices that should be considered unethical and provide reasons for your decisions. Also summarize the ethical practices that management should follow with regard to granting privileged access to computers and networks.

5. For another code of ethics related to systems administrators, navigate to http://www.sage-au.org.au/ethics.html. Compare and contrast the nine principles of ethical conduct on this page with those specified by the previous reference. Note that a code of ethics relates to the values of day-to-day ethical behavior as well as acceptable uses of computers and networks.

Be sure you understand the difference between a code of ethics as studied here and the acceptable use policy that you studied earlier in this chapter. The code of ethics includes provisions of day-to-day ethical behavior as well as acceptable use guidelines that you find in the earlier policy.

Exercise 5.4.3: Creating an Incident Response Policy

What should you do when some kind of security breach occurs? No matter how detailed your security policies and provisions are, a breach will occur sooner or later, and it is important to take a proactive approach so you are prepared. In this exercise, you research the considerations you should note when creating an incident response policy:

1. Return to http://www.usg.edu/acit/docs/security_guide.pdf, which we visited in the previous exercise. Scroll to the "Reporting and Handling Security Incidents" section of Chapter 5. What steps do you need to follow when reporting a security breach? Note the four components of a user report, and write a sample incident report for some breach that you experienced in the past or one that has been in the news recently. What additional procedures should be followed after the breach has occurred?

2. A step-by-step plan for responding to an incident appears at http://www.washington.edu/computing/security/cycle.html. Note the need for being prepared in advance. Summarize in your own words the steps you should follow in detecting, containing, eradicating, recovering, and following up to an incident.

3. Refer to http://www.cs.uidaho.edu/security.html for a comprehensive five-section security policy that touches on many of the objectives studied in this chapter. In particular, note the seven-step plan for

incident response near the end of this policy. Think of how you could have applied this plan to an incident with which you have been involved in the past or another incident that has been in the news or that you find from an Internet search. This reference also mentions a five-step procedure for evidence collection that relates to computer forensics, which you study later in this chapter.

What Did I Just Learn?

Now that you have looked at security policies and procedures, let's take a moment to review all the critical items you've experienced in this lab:

- Written security policies provide a basis for the standards and objectives for an organization and define the employees' responsibilities and obligations toward keeping the company secure. Sample security policies are available on the Internet that you can customize for your company's needs and uses.
- Human resources policies work together with written security policies to define steps that should be taken during the hiring or termination of employees.
- Incident response policies serve as a framework to identify the information that should be collected when an incident occurs so that the problem can be properly dealt with and its source located. Such policies provide a proactive approach to dealing with incidents.

5.5: Understanding Privilege Management

The term *privilege management* refers to managing the extent of control that individuals are entitled to exert over specified network and system resources. All modern network operating systems provide the means to control who is permitted to perform certain tasks, called *user rights*, on the network. Two means exist by which you can control user rights:

- You can assign rights to specific users at various computers or across the entire network.
- You can add the users to groups that are granted the appropriate rights by default.

The use of groups has many advantages, including the ability to assign the same set of rights to several individuals as well as reduce the chance of error in assigning rights.

Exercise 5.5.1: Using Groups in Windows 2000 Server

In this exercise, you look at the use of groups in Windows 2000 Server. Perform this exercise at a server that is configured as a domain controller. Steps for performing this exercise on a Windows Server 2003 domain controller are similar:

1. Log on to the domain controller as an administrator.
2. Click Start, Programs, Administrative Tools, Active Directory Users and Computers. If necessary, expand the domain to reveal the containers therein.
3. In the left pane, select the Builtin container. As shown in Figure 5.6, the right pane displays a list of built-in groups that are created by default in an Active Directory domain. Note the description for each group that tells you what the groups are able to do.

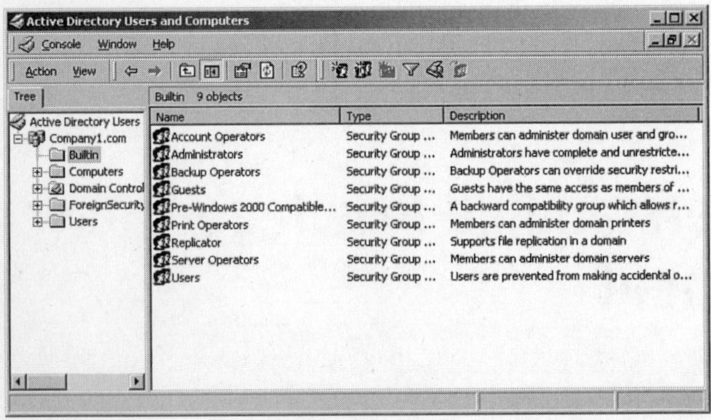

Figure 5.6 Active Directory Users and Computers enables you to administer all aspects of users and groups in Windows 2000 Server domains.

4. In the left pane, right-click the Users container and choose New, User. Type **User2** in the First Name and User Logon Name fields and then click Next.

5. Type **Abcdef2** in the Password and Confirm Password text boxes, confirm that the User Must Change Password at Next Logon option is not selected, click Next, and then click Finish.

Remember that the names and passwords you are creating in this exercise are somewhat simplistic and that you would be creating more complex passwords and requiring users to change them in the real world.

6. Repeat Steps 4 and 5 to create another new user named `User3` with a password of `Abcdef3`.

7. In the left pane, select the Builtin container again. Right-click the Account Operators group and choose Properties.

8. Select the Members tab and then click Add. In the Select Users, Contacts, Computers, or Groups dialog box that opens, type **User2** and then click OK. (See Figure 5.7.)

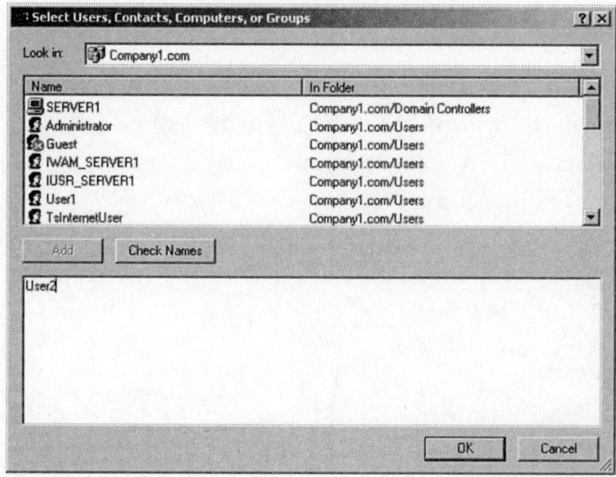

Figure 5.7 Add a user to a group in Windows 2000 Server Active Directory.

9. Note that User2 appears in the list of members of the Account Operators group. Click OK.

10. Right-click the Server Operators group and choose Properties.

11. Repeat Steps 8 and 9 to add User3 to this group.

12. Log off and log on as User2 with the password you created in Step 5.

13. Repeat Steps 2 to 4 to create another new user named `User4` with a password of `Abcdef4`. The Account Operators membership of User2

enables this user to perform this task. Close the Active Directory Users and Computers console.

14. Click Start, Settings, Control Panel, Date/Time. What happens? You are informed that you do not have the proper privilege level to change the system time. This occurs because system time controls security aspects such as Kerberos authentication. Consequently, account operators are not granted the right to perform this task by default. Close Control Panel.
15. Log off and log on as User3 with the password you created in Step 6.
16. Attempt to create another new user by following the procedure in Steps 2 to 4. When you right-click the Users container, you do not receive the New, User option because members of the Server Operators group do not have the right to create users. Close the Active Directory Users and Computers console.
17. Repeat Step 14 to set the time one hour ahead. What happens? You are successful because server operators are granted this right by default.
18. Return the time to its correct setting.
19. Log off and attempt to log on as User4. What happens? You receive a message informing you that you do not have the right to log on interactively (see Figure 5.8). For security purposes, ordinary users are not entitled to log on to domain controllers.

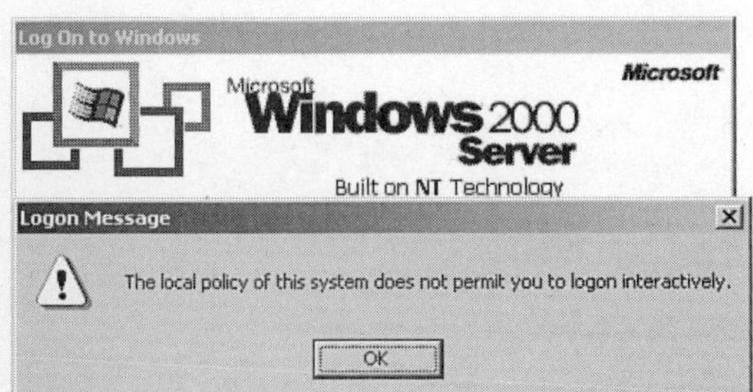

Figure 5.8 Ordinary users do not receive the privilege to log on to a domain controller in Active Directory.

Remember that the network is most secure only when users are granted the minimum amount of privileges needed to perform their jobs. You can use groups to assign permissions to resources, as you studied with individual users in Chapter 1, "General Security Concepts."

What Did I Just Learn?

Now that you have looked at several types of access control, let's take a moment to review all the critical items you've experienced in this lab:

- User rights refer to the privileges to perform system tasks on computers and networks, such as creating user accounts.
- Modern operating systems such as Windows contain default groups that are assigned a basic series of rights by default.
- You can use groups to simplify the granting of rights as well as assigning permissions to resources on the network.

5.6: Using Chain of Custody, Preserving Evidence, and Collecting Evidence

After a security breach occurs, the science of computer forensics comes into play. When a crime is committed, evidence must be collected and preserved in a manner consistent with its being admissible to a court of law. This process involves a complete chain of custody—in other words, the ability to account for the evidence continuously from the time the breach is discovered until it is presented to a court.

Exercise 5.6.1: Understanding the Principles of Collecting and Preserving Evidence

To be admissible in a court of law, evidence must be properly collected and preserved. This rule is no different in the case of computer crime; moreover, a computer contains data stored in volatile locations such as RAM, which would be lost if the computer is shut down immediately upon discovery of an intrusion. In this exercise, you research the principles of chain of custody and the collection and preservation of evidence:

1. Connect to the Internet and navigate to http://www.forensics-intl.com/def4.html for a definition of computer forensics. What four activities are included in processing computer evidence during a forensics investigation? Note especially the phrase in bold text that describes the

means by which evidence is processed to ensure accuracy and completeness. Why is it important to use multiple software tools when processing computer evidence? Follow the links provided to obtain more information related to computer forensics.

2. Continue to http://www.washington.edu/computing/security/responding.html. This article continues from one that we referenced for incident response earlier in this chapter. What should you do first when you realize your computer has been compromised? What steps should you take to preserve evidence and limit the extent of damage? Why is "need to know" important under this situation? Note the need for secure backups of data on the compromised computer. What additional backup steps should you take? How should you communicate your initial findings? Note the need to reconfigure your computer afterward for a high level of security to prevent another breach.

3. The Computer Emergency Response Team (CERT) hosts a series of Web pages that provide valuable information on computer forensics procedures. Most are linked from the article you studied in the last step. In particular, navigate to "Steps for Recovering from a Unix or NT System Compromise" at http://www.cert.org/tech_tips/win-UNIX-system_compromise.html. Prepare a detailed summary of all the steps involved. In particular, document all the steps required for performing a thorough examination of the compromised system. This page also provides links to additional CERT documents for improving system security; however, the Windows document addresses Windows NT 4.0 and is out-of-date for Windows 2000/XP/2003 systems. (In particular, you can use Group Policy to accomplish many of the changes for which they suggest Registry edits.)

4. CERT also provides a page at http://www.cert.org/security-improvement/practices/p048.html that discusses chain-of-custody procedures. Summarize the steps you should take to preserve the chain of custody. Why are these steps important? What three items are important in ensuring an unbroken chain of custody?

5. Franklin Witter presents an informative paper for the SANS GSEC certification at http://www.giac.org/practical/gsec/Franklin_Witter_GSEC.pdf. Compare his steps for preserving a chain of custody with those presented in the previous reference. Why are log files important, and what should you do to ensure the legal admissibility of log files? What is the first, and most important, rule that must be followed when collecting evidence? When copying data from a compromised computer, what type of copy should be used and why? What

information should be recorded in the evidence notebook? Follow the links provided by Witter for more information on the computer forensics procedures.

You can enable the display of a legal statement similar to that suggested by Witter on computers in a Windows 2000/2003 Active Directory domain by enabling the "Interactive logon: Message text for users attempting to log on" policy in Group Policy.

6. Several commercially available applications can assist you in the computer forensics field. Navigate to http://techrepublic.com.com/5100-6270-1053241.html for an article on the EnCase tool from Guidance Software. Note how this program was able to recover a simple Word document that had been deleted from a floppy disk.
7. Another computer forensics program of interest is SafeBack. Navigate to http://www.forensics-intl.com/safeback.html for an introduction to this tool and a summary of its capabilities. Note in particular its primary uses, features, and benefits.
8. One area of a Windows-based computer that you must preserve for investigation is the pagefile. Navigate to http://www.forensics-intl.com/def7.html for information on this file. Most computer forensics programs provide the capability to save data from the pagefile for later examination. You will notice this capability in the ProDiscover program that you examine in the next exercise.

Remember that data on a hard disk is not physically erased until another program overwrites it. This point is true even for temporary files such as the pagefile, and it is even true when you reformat a hard disk. Programs are available that can recover data from almost all these situations.

Although you do not need to be quite as meticulous when investigating a violation of company policy, it still pays to be as thorough as possible. This rule is especially true if you plan to terminate an employee who might file suit for wrongful dismissal or institute a union grievance procedure.

In legal cases, you should hire a forensic expert to handle the collection, bagging, and tagging of all evidence. Inexperienced individuals will likely contaminate such evidence rapidly, resulting in its being inadmissible in court. Contact the local authorities if your company wants to prosecute. Before the proper investigators arrive, your involvement should be limited to disconnecting the network cable from the computer involved and securing the room from members of the organization who are not directly involved in the case.

Exercise 5.6.2: Securing a Computer to Protect Evidence

In the previous exercise, you learned the importance of preserving data related to computer intrusions. This exercise demonstrates a simple step that you can take to secure a computer running Windows 2000 Server. You then download and evaluate ProDiscover, a software package that performs forensic analysis on computers. You can perform similar steps on a computer running Windows 2000 Professional or Windows XP Professional:

1. Log on to the computer running Windows 2000 Server as an administrator.

2. To view network connections to the computer, click Start, Run; type **`cmd`** in the Open text box; and click OK. In the command prompt window, type **`netstat`** and press Enter. The output displays active connections to your computer, which might include connections established by an intruder. See Figure 5.9 for an example. If you want to see IP addresses rather than names in the `netstat` output, type **`netstat -n`**. When you are finished, type **`exit`** at the command prompt to close the window.

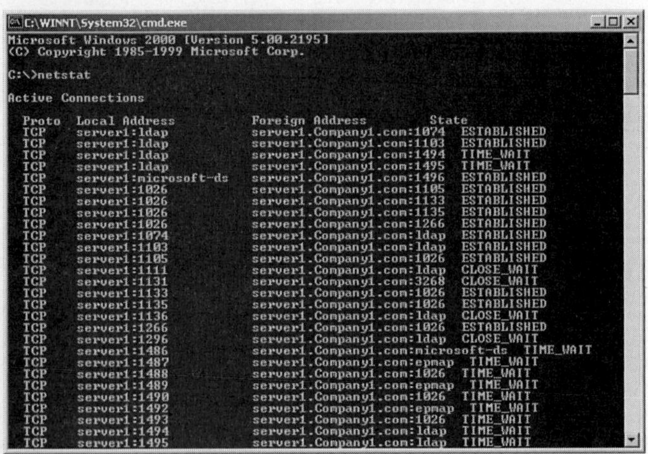

Figure 5.9 The output of the **netstat** command displays all active connections from remote computers.

3. You will evaluate the ProDiscover application from Technology Pathways. Navigate to http://www.techpathways.com/ProDiscoverIR.htm and to http://www.techpathways.com/uploads/suspecthostir.pdf for articles on this program. Summarize the features

of the program and note how hackers can access information from Windows NT/2000/XP/2003 kernel mode operations. How do kernel mode rootkits operate, and what problem can arise with two common ways used to detect the presence of a rootkit? Review the steps presented for live analysis of a disk on a remote computer to see examples of the capabilities of this program.

4. Click the Product Demo link near the bottom of the HTML file. You will need to fill out and submit some information about yourself.
5. After submitting the requested information, you receive a link. Click this link and save the program to the appropriate location on your hard drive.
6. Extract the downloaded zip file to a folder on your hard drive.

You will need WinZip or another similar extraction program to extract the zip file in Windows 2000. Windows XP and Windows Server 2003 include their own extraction program and do not require WinZip.

7. Navigate to that folder, double-click the installation file, and follow the instructions provided by the installation wizard. An icon is placed on your desktop.
8. Before running ProDiscover, create a test file in your `My Documents` folder using Notepad or WordPad. Type some identifying information in the file and save it. Delete the file and remove it from the Recycle Bin.
9. Double-click the ProDiscover Windows icon and click Try in the dialog box that opens.

If a dialog box opens requesting that you install the **PARemove.sys** driver, click OK, click Cancel in the resulting window, and close ProDiscover. Navigate to the **ProDiscover\Driver** directory (for example, **ProgramFiles\Technology Pathways\ProDiscoverWin\Driver**), double-click the **Readme.txt** file, and follow the instructions to load the driver. When finished, repeat Step 9 to start ProDiscover Windows.

ProDiscover installs a **ProDiscoverManual.pdf** file in the installation folder. This file provides detailed information with regard to running the program. Refer to it or the help files provided for additional details.

10. ProDiscover opens the Launch Dialog dialog box. Type a project number, project filename, and optional description in the text boxes provided, and then click Open.

11. To add a disk to the project, expand the Add entry in the left pane and select the Disk entry. The Add Disk to Project dialog box opens.

12. Select a disk (in our example, we chose the local hard disk labeled PhysicalDrive0), type an identifying name in the text box labeled Please Enter Unique Name for Physical Disk (see Figure 5.10), and click Add.

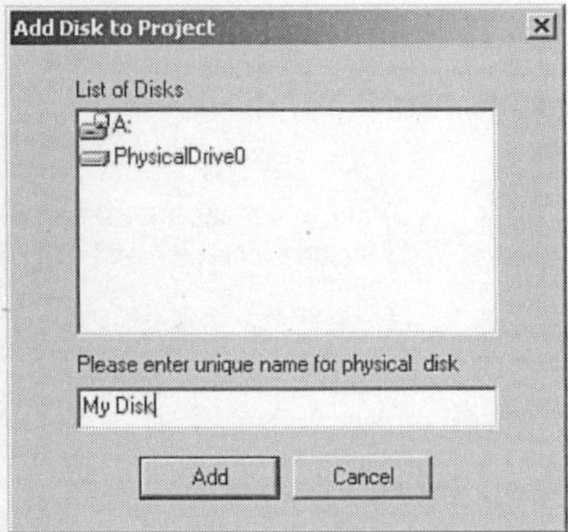

Figure 5.10 Select a disk for examining.

13. If you select the local hard disk, an Add Disk dialog box informs you that working directly on an evidence disk is not recommended and that you should work from an image file. For purposes of this test, click OK to continue working on the local disk.

14. To view files on the added disk, expand Disks under Content View in the left pane. Expand PhysicalDrive0 to find the C: drive and its folders. To view deleted files, expand the C: drive node and select the Deleted Files node at the bottom of the folder list. The top part of the right pane displays a list of the files found by ProDiscover. You should be able to find the file you created and deleted. If necessary, scroll to locate it.

15. To view information about a file, highlight it. As shown in Figure 5.11, you can see the contents of the deleted file.

16. To view the pagefile, select the root of C: in the left pane and scroll the contents to locate `pagefile.sys`. Highlight this file to display information in the bottom-right pane. In this case, you receive command buttons that help you navigate through the large number of pages

contained in the file. Use these buttons to scroll until you locate legible information, as shown in Figure 5.12.

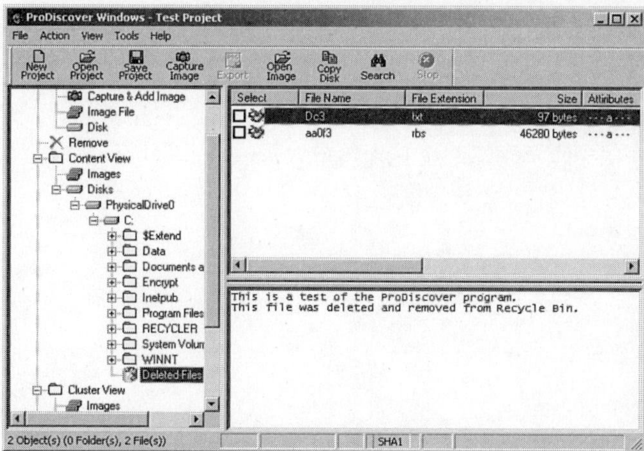

Figure 5.11 ProDiscover Windows allows you to view the contents of a deleted file.

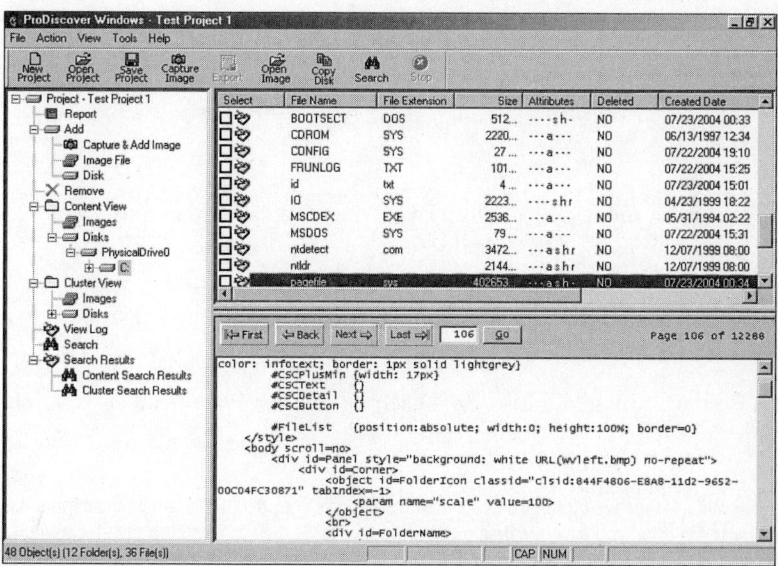

Figure 5.12 You can view information on the Windows pagefile using ProDiscover.

17. If this were a suspicious file, you could capture a bitstream image of the drive you are working with. To do so, select Capture Image from the toolbar. In the Capture Image text box that opens, select the appropriate drive. Type a folder name in the Destination dialog box,

add information in the ProDiscover Image section that identifies the image capture, and then click OK. See Figure 5.13.

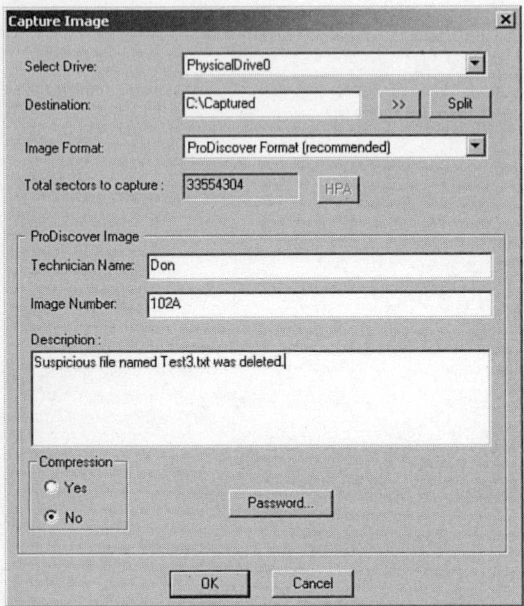

Figure 5.13 The Capture Image dialog box enables you to save a bitstream image of a drive for later study and analysis.

18. If you receive a message informing you that the capture cannot be done due to the lack of free disk space, select a different destination. If another destination is unavailable, create and delete a file on a floppy disk and repeat the appropriate steps of this procedure to create an image of the floppy disk.
19. When you are finished, close ProDiscover and save the project as a project file.

When you save bitstream copies (or other copies) of data for forensic examination, ensure that you save the data on forensically sterile media. Any other data located on the disk or CD that is used to save the data can render the evidence inadmissible in a legal court.

It is possible to create a memory dump on a computer running Windows 2000 Server by following the procedure described here. Note that you should gather all other evidence, including the contents of the pagefile, before attempting this procedure and save this information to a location elsewhere on the network. You can also perform these steps on a computer running Windows 2000 Professional, Windows XP Professional, or Windows Server 2003:

1. Click Start, Run; type **`regedit`**; and then press Enter.
2. In the Registry Editor, navigate to `HKEY_LOCAL_MACHINE\SYSTEM\CurrentControlSet\Services\i8042prt\Parameters`.

Be very careful when using the Registry Editor. Any changes you make are applied immediately. You should back up the Registry before making changes. Improper modification of the Registry could result in loss of functionality and the need to reinstall the operating system.

3. Right-click Parameters and choose New, DWORD Value.
4. Type **`CrashOnCtrlScroll`** as the name of the value.
5. Double-click this value and set the value data to `1`.
6. Close the Registry Editor.
7. Right-click My Computer and choose Properties.
8. Select the Advanced tab, and then click Startup and Recovery.
9. In the Startup and Recovery dialog box, expand the drop-down list under Write Debugging Information and choose Complete Memory Dump, as shown in Figure 5.14.

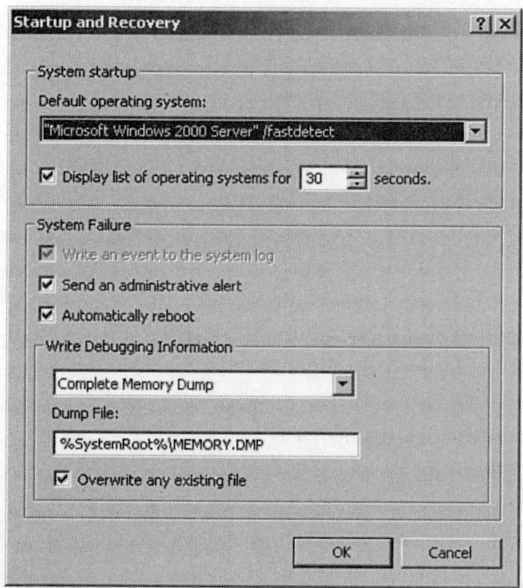

Figure 5.14 You can configure Windows 2000 to display a complete memory dump.

10. Click OK twice and accept the prompt to restart your computer.
11. When the computer restarts, log back on as an administrator.
12. Hold down the right Ctrl key and press the Scroll Lock twice. The computer displays a Blue Screen of Death (BSoD) containing a message stating that the end user manually generated the crash dump. When the dump is created, it will restart.
13. When the computer restarts, log back on as an administrator. You can now follow the appropriate steps of the previous procedure to run ProDiscover Windows and save the contents of the `%systemroot%\Memory.dmp` file.

A Windows XP computer reboots immediately on Step 12 without displaying a BSoD. The system displays a dialog box informing you that the system has recovered from a serious error. Click the link provided to see the data written by the computer, and then click the second link to view the files contained in the error report. You can use ProDiscover Windows to save the contents of the files produced.

What Did I Just Learn?

Now that you have looked at computer forensics, let's take a moment to review all the critical items you've experienced in this lab:

- The chain of custody refers to the documentation of all transfers of evidence between individuals from the first time of suspecting that an incursion has taken place until the evidence is used in court. This chain must remain unbroken or the evidence can be ruled inadmissible.
- You need to document all aspects of the computers and networks at the time you are acquiring evidence that might be used later in prosecuting intruders or building a case against employees who have violated security policies.
- CERT provides many good references that detail the meticulous requirements in collecting and preserving evidence to be used in prosecution of intruders.
- Several companies have produced applications that are geared toward computer forensics situations.
- ProDiscover is one computer forensics application that allows you to recover deleted files as well as save data from the Windows pagefile.

5.7: Understanding Risk Identification

A *threat* is any potential danger to your information system of the data it contains. A *vulnerability* is any weakness that could allow a threat to be realized. A *risk* is the probability of an undesirable effect resulting from a threat being realized. Effective risk management requires that risks be identified and addressed in order of importance. There are several methods of assessing risk. The most common two are quantitative and qualitative risk assessment.

Quantitative risk assessment assigns dollar amounts to each risk. After you create a comprehensive list of risks and calculate the accompanying risk costs, ranking is pretty simple: All you have to do is sort the risks by the impact cost.

Qualitative risk assessment is less precise. Instead of assigning dollar values to each risk, you evaluate the relative impact of each risk. Qualitative risk analysis lets you consider the many intangible impacts of risks.

Exercise 5.7.1: Identifying and Quantifying Risks

This exercise directs you to create a simple quantitative risk assessment table for a fictitious organization. You work through the basic steps of calculating the annualized loss for each identified risk:

1. Before calculating a risk assessment, navigate to http://www.cse-cst.gc.ca/en/documents/knowledge_centre/publications/manuals/ITSG-04e.pdf, which is a threat and risk assessment guide for IT systems. Review and summarize the purposes and procedures given in this guide. Take a look at the threat agents listed in Annex G, the types of threat events in Annex H, and the sample list of vulnerabilities in Annex I. Use these lists to assist you in completing the next step.

2. Start the process by creating a list of all potential risks that could interrupt or substantially impact your organization's primary business function. Although many risks are common among organizations similar to yours, your list will be specific to your organization.

Creating a risk list requires substantial effort. You must carefully consider all risks from many categories that could impact your organization. For some additional information on risk management, do a little research using a search engine on the topic of risk management. When collecting quantitative data for your risk assessment, another source of information you might want to investigate is insurance companies.

3. After you create a list of risks, you need to assess the impact of each one. Start by calculating the risk exposure. For each risk, assign the percentage of the asset value that will be lost if the threat is realized. For example, a disk crash might result in a 50% loss.

4. Calculate the dollar loss each time a threat is realized. (See Figure 5.15.) If your file server is valued at $50,000 and a disk crash results in a 50% loss, the single loss expectancy (SLE) is $25,000.

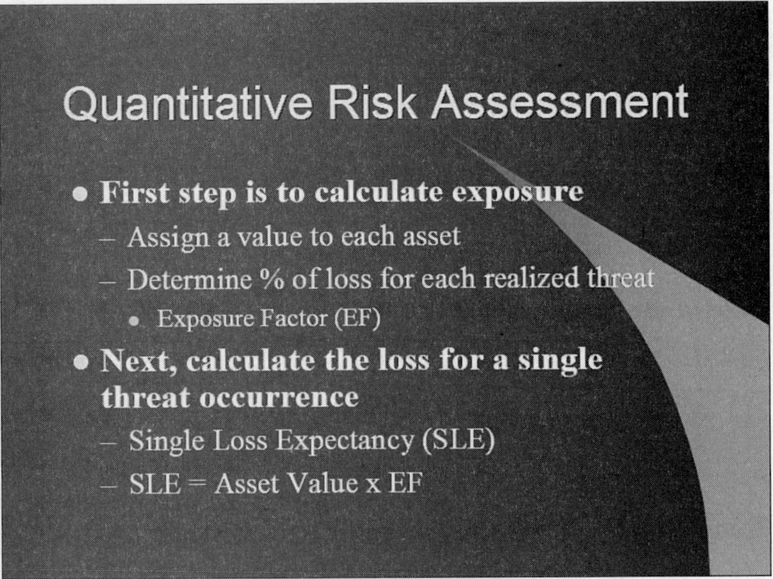

Quantitative Risk Assessment
• First step is to calculate exposure
– Assign a value to each asset
– Determine % of loss for each realized threat
• Exposure Factor (EF)
• Next, calculate the loss for a single threat occurrence
– Single Loss Expectancy (SLE)
– SLE = Asset Value x EF

Figure 5.15 Calculate the SLE.

5. Once you know the loss for a single occurrence, you need to annualize the loss, which is calculating the probability of a loss in a single year. For example, if you expect a disk crash once every 5 years, the annual rate of occurrence (ARO) would be 20%.

6. The last calculation step is to derive the annual dollar loss of each risk (see Figure 5.16). This value is the SLE (Step 4) times the ARO (Step 5).

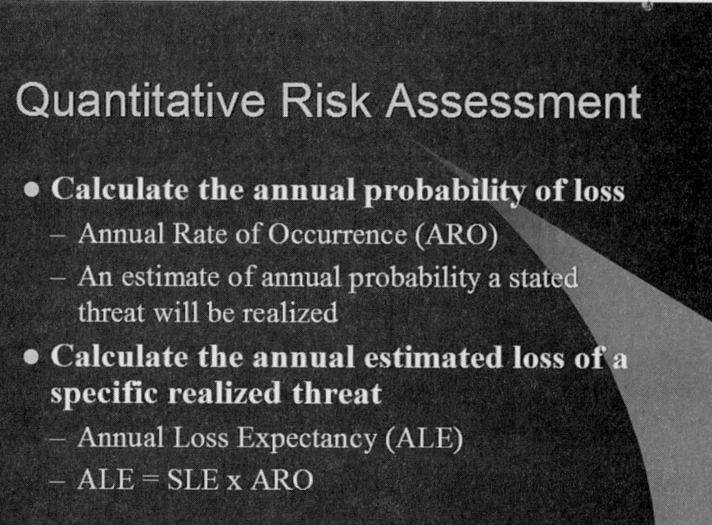

Figure 5.16 Calculate the ARO and annualized loss expectancy (ALE).

7. Compile ALE values for all risks, and sort the resulting table by the ALE. The table in Figure 5.17 shows the risks that will result in the largest economic impact to our fictitious organization.

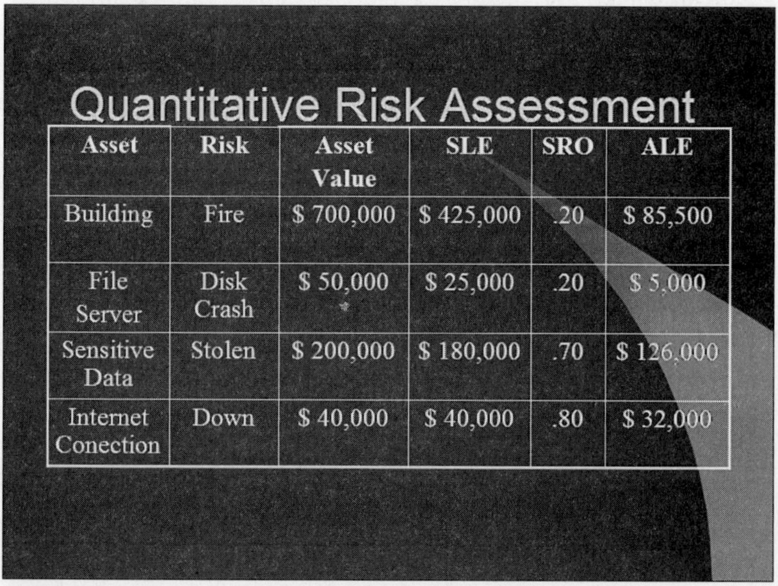

Quantitative Risk Assessment

Asset	Risk	Asset Value	SLE	SRO	ALE
Building	Fire	$ 700,000	$ 425,000	.20	$ 85,500
File Server	Disk Crash	$ 50,000	$ 25,000	.20	$ 5,000
Sensitive Data	Stolen	$ 200,000	$ 180,000	.70	$ 126,000
Internet Conection	Down	$ 40,000	$ 40,000	.80	$ 32,000

Figure 5.17 This table shows a complete quantitative risk analysis.

Creating the ranked risk impact table is only one step in the overall risk management process. Although a particular risk might appear to have a large impact, you need to compare the impact to the cost of remediating the risk. If it costs more to remediate the risk than the expected loss, you might need to consider other options.

The main reason for a company to perform a risk analysis related to computer security is to quantify the impact of potential threats relative to the cost of business losses. This is the reason behind conducting an analysis similar to that described in this exercise.

Exercise 5.7.2: Understanding Threats and Vulnerabilities

We introduced the concept of threats and vulnerabilities in the introduction to this exam topic. Threats can originate from many different sources. It is important to understand the many threats that can provide an opportunity for loss within your organization. The process of safeguarding a system involves identifying all vulnerabilities in a system and implementing as many controls as possible to prevent threats from being realized.

This exercise directs you to research general threats and vulnerabilities that impact your organization. Although many threats and vulnerabilities are common among organizations, this exercise only scratches the surface. Developing a complete list of threats and vulnerabilities requires substantial effort:

1. Using a Web browser, connect to http://www.sans.org/top20/. This is the SANS 20 Most Critical Internet Security Vulnerabilities page. Click each Top Vulnerabilities link (the list of 20 is divided into 10 for Windows systems and 10 for Unix systems) and read through the descriptions of the issues.

2. For an up-to-date list of recent threats and vulnerabilities, go to http://www.us-cert.gov/. This home page of the U.S. Computer Emergency Readiness Team contains direct links to recent vulnerabilities. You should revisit this site from time to time to keep abreast of the latest occurrences.

3. Navigate to http://www.wasc.noaa.gov/wrso/security_guide/intro-15.htm for an overview of computer vulnerabilities that includes topics covered in a large number of Security+ objectives. Use the links on this page to review and reinforce your knowledge of the common threats and vulnerabilities, and return to this page again before sitting for your exam.

4. From your research, develop a list of threats from the different categories (weather, acts of God, man-made, and so on) that could have an impact on your organization.

5. In your list of threats, itemize as many vulnerabilities as you can that would allow each threat to be realized. Feel free to brainstorm with your classmates. The more complete your list is, the more prepared you will be to address vulnerabilities of all types.

When developing threat and vulnerability lists, don't forget to consult trade organizations. They can be a great source for common threats and vulnerabilities that other organizations similar to yours have encountered, saving you a considerable amount of research time.

What Did I Just Learn?

Now that you have looked at risk identification and vulnerabilities, let's take a moment to review all the critical items you've experienced in this lab:

- A risk is any possibility of incurring a loss from some vulnerability or other circumstance.
- Quantitative risk assignment attempts to assign dollar amounts to each risk, and qualitative risk assessment merely evaluates the relative impact of each risk.
- Vulnerabilities are weaknesses that can allow threats from any of numerous different sources to be realized.

5.8: Training End Users, Executives, and Human Resources

The best security policies in the world are useless if end users, managers, and others are unaware of their existence. The Security+ exam tests your awareness of the need to educate individuals on proper security policies and procedures.

Exercise 5.8.1: Understanding the Need for Proper Education of Individuals

Several Web pages that we already have visited for other objectives in this chapter also present information related to proper user education. In this exercise, you revisit these pages and others that stress this need:

1. Connect to the Internet and navigate to http://www.labcompliance.com/info/2003/1010-data-centers.htm, which we visited earlier in this chapter. Note the importance of training workers and retaining their training records and certificate information.

2. Continue to http://searchsecurity.techtarget.com/originalContent/0,289142,sid14_gci867941,00.html, which emphasizes the need for educating users about security policies. A new employee receives many pieces of information on the first day and needs to sign several forms, so she might "gloss over" the piece of paper that outlines the security policy. Why should you only provide relevant information to different groups of employees? What additional step should you take after making all employees aware of the security policies?

3. For another viewpoint related to training, go to http://www.usg.edu/acit/docs/security_guide.pdf, from which we reviewed security policies related to HR and incident response earlier in this chapter. Note the need for input from the HR and legal departments. Describe the three guidelines on page 5-5 of this document in your own words, including the importance of each one in the overall education program.

4. Section 2.4.12 of http://www.hipaadvisory.com/action/Security/secsum.pdf describes the need for training professionals who access health care data. Note how the areas of training include topics that we have discussed with regard to overall computer and network security. What are several vulnerabilities often found in user training programs?

5. Drew Phelps emphasizes the need for user training and proper communication at http://boston.bizjournals.com/boston/stories/2004/01/05/focus4.html. What are some of the items that the education process should accomplish? What is the specific goal of the corporate security awareness program?

6. John Wack outlines the procedure for creating a computer security incident response capability (CSIRC) at http://csrc.nist.gov/publications/nistpubs/800-3/800-3.pdf. The CSIRC addresses numerous facets of a computer security program, including the need for user

awareness training. What are several reasons why a user awareness training program improves computer and network security?

7. A panel of experts provides their opinions on thwarting social engineering attacks at http://www.itsecurity.com/asktecs/may2203.htm. Note the need for user awareness that is stressed by several contributors. What components should the awareness program include?

8. Online resources are a valuable asset for educating users to security issues. Figure 5.18 shows an example of online education used by the U.S. Army for training end users in computer security. The link displayed leads to a seven-lesson security awareness course.

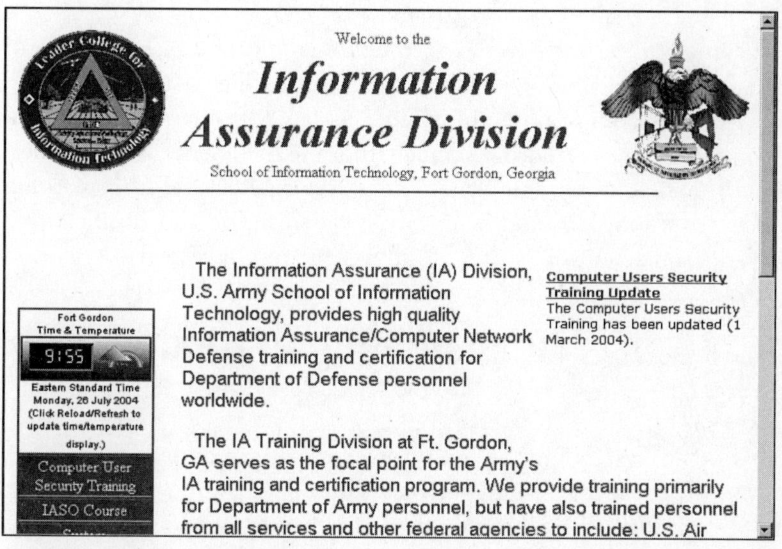

Welcome to the
Information Assurance Division
School of Information Technology, Fort Gordon, Georgia
The Information Assurance (IA) Division, U.S. Army School of Information Technology, provides high quality Information Assurance/Computer Network Defense training and certification for Department of Defense personnel worldwide.
Computer Users Security Training Update
The Computer Users Security Training has been updated (1 March 2004).
Fort Gordon Time & Temperature
9:55
Eastern Standard Time Monday, 26 July 2004 (Click Reload/Refresh to update time/temperature display.)
The IA Training Division at Ft. Gordon, GA serves as the focal point for the Army's IA training and certification program. We provide training primarily for Department of Army personnel, but have also trained personnel from all services and other federal agencies to include: U.S. Air
Computer User Security Training
IASO Course

Figure 5.18 The U.S. Army is among the growing list of organizations that have utilized online training for computer security education.

Users with a moderate degree of computer knowledge can be dangerous. They might have installed software or made modifications on a home computer and think they can do the same at work. For this reason, it is often said that the weakest link in an organization's security is typically the users. It is important to educate these users about the consequences of doing similar actions at work and their potential impact on network security.

What Did I Just Learn?

Now that you have looked at user education awareness, let's take a moment to review all the critical items you've experienced in this lab:

➤ A good security policy does no good if you have not educated users on its provisions and the reason for their existence.

- User awareness training needs to be ongoing and updated as information on new threats appears. In particular, new employees are often inundated with information on the first day and might overlook computer security information.
- Online resources provide an easy way to disseminate computer security training to end users.

5.9: Understanding Documentation Concepts

Security documentation involves one of the most important tasks of a security administrator's job. The written information provides details of procedures carried out, patches applied, systems updated, policies created and applied, computers recovered, and much more. Documentation includes standards and guidelines; computer and network architectural information; change documentation; logs and inventories; classification and notification; and information on retention, storage, and destruction of records.

Exercise 5.9.1: Documenting a Windows Computer

Documentation of systems architecture provides information on the base configuration of its hardware and software components. You can save this information or print it for future reference should problems occur. The steps to be performed are different according to the operating system installed on the computer. Perform either Exercise 5.9.1.1 or 5.9.1.2 according to the operating system on your computer.

Exercise 5.9.1.1: Documenting a Windows 2000 Server Computer

In this exercise, you create an inventory of components contained on a Windows 2000 Server computer. You can perform the same steps on a computer running Windows 2000 Professional:

1. Log on to the Windows 2000 computer as an administrator.
2. Right-click My Computer and choose Manage.
3. In the left pane of the Computer Management dialog box, expand the System Information entry and click System Summary. The right pane

displays summary information about your computer, which might be similar to that shown in Figure 5.19.

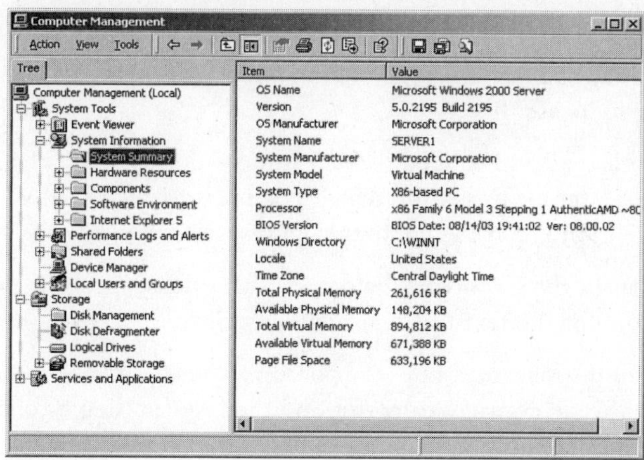

Figure 5.19 The System Summary feature in Computer Management in Windows 2000 provides general information about components on the computer.

4. Right-click System Summary and choose Save as Text File. In the Save As dialog box, specify a location and filename for the text file, and then click Save.
5. To obtain summary information about other hardware and software components, right-click the appropriate category, choose Save as Text File, and proceed as in Step 4. You only need to select a subcategory if you want to display data directly in the System Information dialog box.
6. You can view the resulting information using Notepad. You can then print it or save it to removable media as required.

Exercise 5.9.1.2: Documenting a Windows XP or Windows Server 2003 Computer (Optional)

In this exercise, you create an inventory of components on a Windows XP Professional or Windows Server 2003 computer. This exercise exists because the steps for Windows XP and Windows Server 2003 are appreciably different from those for Windows 2000:

1. Log on to the computer as an administrator.
2. Click Start, Help and Support.

3. On a Windows XP computer, under Pick a Task, select Use Tools to View Your Computer Information and Diagnose Problems. On a Windows Server 2003 computer, select Tools under Support Tasks.
4. Under Tools, select Advanced System Information. On a Windows Server 2003 computer, you need to expand the Help and Support Center Tools entry to locate this tool.
5. In the right pane, select View Detailed System Information (`Msinfo32.exe`). The System Information dialog box opens, which contains general information about the computer hardware.
6. Choose File, Export. In the Export As dialog box that opens, specify a location and filename for the text file, and then click Save.
7. To obtain summary information about other hardware and software components, select the appropriate category, and then repeat Step 6 to save the information obtained.
8. You can view the resulting information using Notepad. You can then print it or save it to removable media as required.

The **Msinfo32** command enables you to create documentation information from the command line on a Windows XP or 2003 computer. You can use this tool to script data collection on the network from a large number of computers. For more information, see the Windows Help and Support Center.

Exercise 5.9.2: Documenting an Active Directory Domain

An Active Directory domain in Windows 2000 or Windows Server 2003 contains various containers such as organizational units (OUs) and groups, as well as objects such as users and computers. Microsoft built its Active Directory service using the principles of Lightweight Directory Access Protocol (LDAP), thereby allowing programs that deal with LDAP to interact with directory files. In this exercise, you display details of a domain using the `Ldifde.exe` command-line tool. Perform this exercise on the same domain controller you used for Exercise 5.5.1. The steps in Windows Server 2003 are similar:

1. Log on to the Windows domain controller as an administrator.
2. Click Start, Run; type **cmd** in the Open text box; and click OK. A command prompt window opens.

3. Type **`ldifde -f domain.ldf`**. This command outputs LDAP information on all objects in the domain to the `Domain.ldf` file, which is located in the default path from which the command prompt was launched. When finished, type **`exit`** to close the command prompt window.

Ldifde contains many options that enable you to export portions of the directory database as well as perform batch operations on the directory. For more information, see http://www.microsoft.com/windows2000/techinfo/planning/activedirectory/bulksteps.asp. Only very experienced users should perform these batch operations.

4. Open My Computer, navigate to the proper folder (such as the root of the C: drive), and double-click `Domain.ldf` (not `Ldif.log`, which is also created by the `ldifde` command).
5. The document might not automatically open in Notepad. If you receive the Open With dialog box, select Notepad, clear the check box labeled Always Use the Selected Program to Open This Kind of File, and then click OK.
6. The `Domain.ldf` file opens in Notepad. As shown in Figure 5.20, the entries in this file are not intuitive; however, they do constitute a means of documenting all objects contained within the domain.

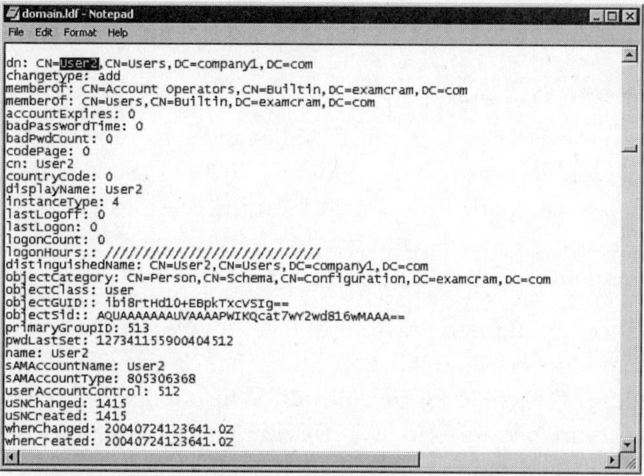

domain.ldf - Notepad
File Edit Format Help
dn: CN=User2,CN=Users,DC=company1,DC=com
changetype: add
memberOf: CN=Account Operators,CN=Builtin,DC=examcram,DC=com
memberOf: CN=Users,CN=Builtin,DC=examcram,DC=com
accountExpires: 0
badPasswordTime: 0
badPwdCount: 0
codePage: 0
cn: User2
countryCode: 0
displayName: User2
instanceType: 4
lastLogoff: 0
lastLogon: 0
logonCount: 0
logonHours:: ////////////////////////////
distinguishedName: CN=User2,CN=Users,DC=company1,DC=com
objectCategory: CN=Person,CN=Schema,CN=Configuration,DC=examcram,DC=com
objectClass: user
objectGUID:: ibi8rtHd10+EBpkTxcVSIg==
objectSid:: AQUAAAAAAAUVAAAAPWIKQcat7wY2wd816wMAAA==
primaryGroupID: 513
pwdLastSet: 127341155900404512
name: User2
sAMAccountName: User2
sAMAccountType: 805306368
userAccountControl: 512
uSNChanged: 1415
uSNCreated: 1415
whenChanged: 20040724123641.0Z
whenCreated: 20040724123641.0Z

Figure 5.20 Output of the **ldifde** routine includes information about all objects in an Active Directory domain, including users' membership in groups.

7. To prove this point, click Edit, Find and type **`User2`**. You created this user in Exercise 5.5.1 and made the user a member of the Account Operators group. You can find this user's membership in the Account

Operators group (see Figure 5.20), as well as details about the user account itself, by executing repeated finds.

8. Repeat Step 8 to find references to User3, User4, and one or more computer accounts.

9. When you are finished, close all dialog boxes.

Other Active Directory support tools also let you export information on portions of the directory database. These include **Ldp.exe**, which is an LDAP editor, and ADSI Edit, which is a low-level directory editor.

These Active Directory editing tools all have the potential to do irreparable harm to Active Directory if used improperly. Only experienced users should use their editing capabilities, and you should have a recent backup of Active Directory before using them. Consult the Windows Help and Support Center for additional information.

Although using **ldifde** provides documentation of all the objects in Active Directory, do not overlook the fact that you need a current backup of Active Directory to ensure business continuity should a disaster occur.

Exercise 5.9.3: Understanding the Need for Logs and Inventories

Throughout this manual, we have mentioned audits and logs of security-related data that computer systems such as Windows 2000/XP/Server 2003 create. Documentation of computers and networks in the previous exercises represents a type of inventory. In this exercise, you look at the role of logs and inventories in computer and network security:

1. Connect to the Internet and navigate to http://www.wesecure.com/computer-security-white-paper.htm for a white paper on computer security that addresses the need for inventories. Why are organizations that do not have accurate inventories of their equipment vulnerable? What components should audit logs contain? In addition, this paper addresses other components of organizational security discussed in this chapter. Review their suggestions for physical security, network security policy, and incident response.

2. Continue to http://www.cqu.edu.au/documents/compsec/guidelines/cqu_sec80.html, scrolling to Section 8.2 for logging requirements and

to Section 8.6 for the requirements of a university computer inventory. What steps should be taken to maintain the safety of logs? What data should be included on hardware and software inventory records? What practice should be employed to safeguard inventory records against disaster?

3. For information on event logging as related to security on Microsoft computers, go to http://www.microsoft.com/technet/security/tips/deteclog.mspx. Find as many reasons you can that auditing and logging is important in detecting intrusions. Why should you not log everything that can be logged? What Microsoft server application can assist you in maintaining inventories?

Exercise 5.9.4: Understanding Classification Schemes

Systems of classification dictate how information and documentation may be shared and disseminated. For example, you might have one set of documents for public disclosure, a second set that is available to company employees but not to be distributed outside the company, and a third set that is confidential to managers only. In this exercise, you research classification schemes on the Internet:

1. Connect to the Internet and navigate to http://www.itsecurity.com/dictionary/secclass.htm for a definition of security classification. Note the private and government classification schemes as well as their differences according to access control levels that we studied in Chapter 1.
2. Continue to http://www.cccure.org/Documents/SSCP/studyguides/ISSA_-_SSCP_-_Chpt_2.pdf and scroll down to pages 36–41. How do the levels of top secret, secret, confidential, and unclassified differ from each other? What are four benefits of classifying data using these levels? What are three additional issues that you should consider?
3. For another view of these classification levels, go to http://www.rose-hulman.edu/class/csse/csse490/csse490-security/Lectures/Security-040318-confidentiality-policies.ppt. Describe the apparent paradox that can arise from subdividing the classification levels.
4. For another security classification scheme, navigate to http://dis.umc.edu/UMCcompSecPol.html for an information classification system used by the University of Mississippi Medical Center. Describe the four classification levels in your own words, emphasizing the difference between these levels.

5. For a sample data security policy that includes a classification scheme, go to http://www.sun.com/blueprints/tools/samp_sec_pol.pdf. Note that this policy is structured along the lines of security policies discussed earlier in this chapter. Why is it necessary to classify data? Describe the five categories that the authors recommend and compare them with other classification schemes that you have studied.

6. For information on the need for change notification, go to http://www.entrecs.com/documentView.asp?docID=106 for a white paper on outsourcing IT services, including computer security. Scroll to Appendix A and note the need for notification of password changes. Documentation, communication, and change notification go hand-in-hand with regard to infrastructure and network services.

7. Although the notification of users regarding service disruption due to security problems is important, change notification can sometimes go too far. Refer to http://www.scd.ucar.edu/nets/docs/reports/stratplan/strategy.html, scrolling down to Section 7.1, and enumerate several reasons for doing a value judgment on the scope for notifying users of changes or problems. What could happen if you send out too many notices of changes?

Exercise 5.9.5: Understanding Security Practices in Data Retention, Storage, and Destruction

Data, whether on paper or magnetic media, needs to be managed securely, both in storage and retention, and in its ultimate destruction. In Chapter 1, we mentioned the problem of "dumpster diving" in which intruders obtain information by searching through discarded material. In this exercise, you research practices related to data retention, storage, and disposal:

1. Return to http://www.sun.com/blueprints/tools/samp_sec_pol.pdf, which you visited in the last exercise on data classification. These authors also discuss data storage, retention, and disposal. What practices are recommended for secure data storage? How should the proper disposal of data be conducted?

2. Navigate to http://www.kastenchase.com/index.aspx?id=10. Summarize the reasons why security in data storage and retention is important. How can the practice of encryption actually help when the time comes to destroy data?

3. Continue to http://www.usda.gov/directives/files/dr/DR3440-002.htm, scrolling to paragraph 13, for the U.S. Department of Agriculture policies on data destruction. What means of destruction for sensitive security information (SSI) are mandated, and how do they vary with the level of sensitivity?

4. In the United States, the Sarbanes-Oxley Act of 2002 mandates data retention periods for financial data by public companies. Navigate to http://techrepublic.com.com/5100-6313-5034345.html and review the impact of this act on the storage and retention of records, including email messages. For how many years can an individual be jailed for obstructing investigations under the Act? What do retention policies need to specify, and can they discriminate among different types of documents? What types of storage media can be used?

5. For a legal view of data retention and destruction in the United Kingdom and Europe, go to http://www.intechnology.co.uk/downloads/WhitePapers/Making%20Sense%20of%20Data%20Law.pdf. Summarize the challenges facing organizations and the requirements that data handlers must adhere to.

6. For information on data destruction and the possibility of residual data remaining on erased media, refer to http://www.rohanclan.com/library/tg025-2.cfm. What are several risks that should be considered when erasing or overwriting data? What procedures should be followed for the overwriting, degaussing, and physical destruction of magnetic media?

Documentation is the key to proving that some type of action actually did take place or that certain assets actually existed at some time after a disaster has occurred. Paper documentation is valuable at all times and should be safeguarded as much as electronic records.

What Did I Just Learn?

Now that you have looked at the needs for various types of documentation, let's take a moment to review all the critical items you've experienced in this lab:

- Documenting systems and networks involves creating a list of all hardware and software present, procedures applied, updates performed, patches installed, and other procedures done on the network.
- You can export systems summaries from Windows computers that provide a valuable source of documentation of the software and hardware present on each computer.

- Active Directory provides a few tools that you can use to produce documentation of the objects present in the directory database.
- Classification schemes dictate the permitted level of sharing and dissemination of data.
- Legal policies in the United States, Europe, and elsewhere specify required data retention periods for various types of information created by companies.

Exam Prep Questions

Objective 5.1: Physical Security

1. Which of the following provide some degree of physical security for your network? (Select all that apply.)
   - ❑ A. Use intrusion detection systems.
   - ❑ B. Develop and adhere to security procedures.
   - ❑ C. Install antitheft devices.
   - ❑ D. Review facilities engineering to protect against fire or water damage.
2. Which of the following are examples of physical security controls? (Select all that apply.)
   - ❑ A. A double-locked server room
   - ❑ B. Night watchmen
   - ❑ C. Storing backups of critical files
   - ❑ D. Training an emergency response team
3. What is the purpose of implementing physical security? (Select all that apply.)
   - ❑ A. Prevent theft
   - ❑ B. Prevent unauthorized disclosure of data
   - ❑ C. Prevent physical damage
   - ❑ D. Prevent system integrity
4. Which of the following are physical access controls? (Select all that apply.)
   - ❑ A. Locks
   - ❑ B. Passwords
   - ❑ C. Iris scans
   - ❑ D. Security guards
5. Which of the following physical barriers are reasonable alternatives to a separate or centralized server room? (Select all that apply.)
   - ❑ A. Use a server cluster.
   - ❑ B. Use a locked cabinet.
   - ❑ C. Use an offsite storage facility.
   - ❑ D. Use a secure rack.

6. You want to implement biometrics as an access control for your network. Which of the following orders of biometric methods is listed as most accurate to least accurate methods?
   - ❑ A. Fingerprint, voice verification, iris scan
   - ❑ B. Iris scan, voice verification, fingerprint
   - ❑ C. Voice verification, iris scan, fingerprint
   - ❑ D. Iris scan, fingerprint, voice verification
7. Social engineering takes advantage of which organizational weakness?
   - ❑ A. Network design or topology
   - ❑ B. Network hardware or software
   - ❑ C. Human work schedules
   - ❑ D. Human behavior
8. Your office is moving to a new location downtown. You want to recommend the safest area for the main network department to locate computers and other major networking equipment. The building height is eight floors. What do you recommend?
   - ❑ A. Locate your department on the ground floor.
   - ❑ B. Locate your department on the first floor near the exit.
   - ❑ C. Locate your department on the third or fourth floor.
   - ❑ D. Locate your department on the top floor.
9. Which of the following are effective fire suppression systems?
   - ❑ A. Halon systems
   - ❑ B. CO_2 systems
   - ❑ C. Soda acid systems
   - ❑ D. H_2O systems

Objective 5.2: Disaster Recovery

1. Which of the following should you select when you want to copy only files that were modified since the last full backup?
   - ❑ A. Incremental
   - ❑ B. Selected
   - ❑ C. Differential
   - ❑ D. Partial
2. Which of the following equipment would you likely see at a cold site? (Select all that apply.)
   - ❑ A. Electricity
   - ❑ B. Air conditioning
   - ❑ C. Flooring
   - ❑ D. Networked computers

3. Which of the following are considered alternative sites for secure recovery in case of a disaster? (Select all that apply.)
   - ❑ A. Hot site
   - ❑ B. Warm site
   - ❑ C. Secondary site
   - ❑ D. Primary site

4. You are establishing a disaster recovery plan. Which of the following must be included?
   - ❑ A. A security plan
   - ❑ B. A risk assessment plan
   - ❑ C. A standing operating procedure
   - ❑ D. A fire plan

5. Which person should make short-term recovery decisions just after a disaster?
   - ❑ A. The nearest person to the accident or incident
   - ❑ B. A person who has been earmarked as the disaster recovery manager
   - ❑ C. The network administrator
   - ❑ D. A person working directly for the chief operations officer for disaster recovery

Objective 5.3: Business Continuity

1. Which of the following should be seen within a solid business continuity plan? (Select all that apply.)
   - ❑ A. A business impact analysis
   - ❑ B. A risk analysis
   - ❑ C. Integration and validation
   - ❑ D. Maintenance and training

2. Which of the following networking activities best maintains data in a high state of availability?
   - ❑ A. Firewall software implementation
   - ❑ B. Security auditing
   - ❑ C. IDS monitoring
   - ❑ D. RAID implementation

3. Which of the following terms is the meaning of RAID?
   - ❑ A. Redundant Array of Intelligent Disks
   - ❑ B. Remote Administration of Internal Doctors
   - ❑ C. Redundant Array of Inexpensive Disks
   - ❑ D. Ready Aids to Internetworking Devices

4. When planning for business continuity, which backup method offers the most complete restoration?
   - ❑ A. Incremental backup
   - ❑ B. Differential backup
   - ❑ C. Complete backup
   - ❑ D. Full backup
5. When planning for business continuity, which backup method has the fastest restore time?
   - ❑ A. Incremental backup
   - ❑ B. Differential backup
   - ❑ C. Shortcut backup
   - ❑ D. Full backup

Objective 5.4: Policy and Procedures

1. Which of the following explains the requirements needed to protect an organization's network data and computer systems?
   - ❑ A. The IT weekly security bulletin
   - ❑ B. The organization's security newsletter
   - ❑ C. The business continuity plan
   - ❑ D. The company's security policy
2. Which of the following policies clarify users' roles and limitations when using network equipment, hardware, and software, as well as email and Internet access?
   - ❑ A. The organization's security newsletter
   - ❑ B. The acceptable use policy
   - ❑ C. The disaster recovery plan
   - ❑ D. The company's security policy
3. You are reviewing your organization's security policy and procedures guidebook and come across the term *due care*. Which of the following best explains this term?
   - ❑ A. Actions taken to reduce the probability of damage or injury
   - ❑ B. Preventative measures taken to reduce the probability of liabilities
   - ❑ C. Actions taken to secure loose cabling and prevent theft
   - ❑ D. Preventative measures taken to reduce the cost of sick time taken
4. You are establishing company IT policies and procedures. Which of the following should you consider important to include when planning for email, downloading unauthorized software, and your Web site data?

- ❑ A. Due care policy
- ❑ B. Privacy policy
- ❑ C. Need to know policy
- ❑ D. Separation of duties policy

5. Your company plans to implement a security policy that uses separation of duties as a main theme. What characterizes this separation of duties concept? (Select all that apply.)
   - ❑ A. Tasks are divided among different employees.
   - ❑ B. Each employee works on a section of the overall task.
   - ❑ C. No one employee is able to complete the task alone.
   - ❑ D. Only the supervisor has complete control of all tasks.

6. One of your employees has been given only the minimum information required about the network system to complete his assigned task. Which security policy relates to this concept?
   - ❑ A. Acceptable use
   - ❑ B. Due care
   - ❑ C. Privacy
   - ❑ D. Need to know

7. Which of the following terms relates to the effective destruction of data on magnetic media, such as floppy disks or backup tapes?
   - ❑ A. Tape disposal
   - ❑ B. Magnetizing
   - ❑ C. Degaussing
   - ❑ D. Erasing

8. Which of the following general policies provides employees with ethical guidelines and clarifies expected behavior?
   - ❑ A. Acceptable use policy
   - ❑ B. Ethical use policy
   - ❑ C. Behavioral guidelines policy
   - ❑ D. Code of ethics

9. Which of the following organizational policies provides employees the guidelines, or the who, what, where, when (and maybe why), in cases of a physical disaster, network disaster, or security attack?
   - ❑ A. Emergency disaster plan
   - ❑ B. Disaster recovery plan
   - ❑ C. Incident response policy
   - ❑ D. Emergency response policy

Objective 5.5: Privilege Management

1. Which of the following privilege management concepts gives individuals only those permissions to perform their assigned tasks?
   - ❑ A. Separation of duties
   - ❑ B. Mandatory access
   - ❑ C. Least privilege
   - ❑ D. Management by objectives

2. Network administrators will find managing network security much easier if they adhere to which of the following concepts?
   - ❑ A. Assign user permissions by individual job functions.
   - ❑ B. Assign user permissions based on group roles or assigned jobs.
   - ❑ C. Assign roles to individuals and give them individual permissions.
   - ❑ D. Assign roles to groups and assign separate permissions to each user.

3. You have a growing networking department, and you are wondering whether you should select a centralized or decentralized method of storing your servers. Which of the following offers the advantage of fault tolerance?
   - ❑ A. Centralized servers and decentral IT staff.
   - ❑ B. Decentralized servers and central IT staff.
   - ❑ C. Centralized servers in a secure server room.
   - ❑ D. Decentralized servers to support remote departments.

4. Although computer performance might be an issue, auditing is an important security feature that must be carefully planned. Which of the following should you monitor and examine as part of an internal networking audit? (Select all that apply.)
   - ❑ A. Network resources for appropriate privilege assignments
   - ❑ B. Success or failure of user logons
   - ❑ C. Use of accounts at irregular hours
   - ❑ D. Escalation of user privileges

5. As part of a network security audit team, you are pretending to be a cracker and perform a penetration system test. What tasks are you trying to accomplish? (Select all that apply.)
   - ❑ A. You are testing for system weaknesses.
   - ❑ B. You are trying to break through access control lists.
   - ❑ C. You are trying to unscramble encrypted data.
   - ❑ D. You are trying to identify and use passwords.

6. You are a member of a forensic team that is investigating a possible cyber attack. Which of the following terms refers to the gathering of network information, such as authorized and unauthorized user access to the network, folders, or files?

- ❑ A. Penetration
- ❑ B. Audit trail
- ❑ C. Forensic search
- ❑ D. Auditing

Objective 5.6: Forensics (Awareness, Conceptual Knowledge, and Understanding—Knowing What Your Role Is)

1. Instead of modifying data on a machine that has been under a cyber attack, you remember to make a duplicate to protect data integrity. How can you verify that you have an exact data duplicate?
   - ❑ A. Copy the folders and set permissions to Read Only after the copy is complete.
   - ❑ B. Use Ghost software to duplicate the hard drive.
   - ❑ C. Configure RAID 1 to duplicate the hard drive.
   - ❑ D. Run a cyclic redundancy check with a checksum.
2. You are the first responder from the IT team at the scene of a potential cyber crime. Which of the following are *not* appropriate actions to take? (Select all that apply.)
   - ❑ A. Keep the servers and workstations running, even if this allows a cracker continued access.
   - ❑ B. Turn off all servers and workstations to prevent a cracker from causing further damage.
   - ❑ C. Allow network users to return to their workstations.
   - ❑ D. Allow forensics personnel access to the room.
3. Which of the following guidelines minimizes loss of data during collection of evidence?
   - ❑ A. Protect the weakest link.
   - ❑ B. Remove the weakest link.
   - ❑ C. Respond to an incident within one hour.
   - ❑ D. Follow the chain-of-custody guidelines.

4. After a computer crime is committed, evidence must be preserved. Which of the following actions will help your forensic team in the preservation of evidence? (Select all that apply.)
   - ❑ A. Seal evidence in tamper-resistant containers.
   - ❑ B. Turn off the power supply to that section of the building to stop changes in network activity.
   - ❑ C. If possible, take snapshots of displayed monitors.
   - ❑ D. At a minimum, write down any messages that are displayed on the monitors.
5. After a computer crime is committed, evidence must be collected, tagged, bagged, and inventoried. Who is responsible for this action?
   - ❑ A. Forensic technician
   - ❑ B. IT technician
   - ❑ C. First responder
   - ❑ D. Anyone who works in the office

Objective 5.7: Risk Identification

1. Which of the following is a business function that determines which threats pose a danger to an organization so that proactive measures can be implemented?
   - ❑ A. Risk assessment
   - ❑ B. Risk identification
   - ❑ C. Vulnerability assessment
   - ❑ D. Vulnerability identification
2. Which of the following risk analysis formulas is a useful tool that is based upon these three concepts: single loss expectancy, annualized rate of occurrence, and annual loss expectancy?
   - ❑ A. SLE + ARO = ALE
   - ❑ B. SLE × ARO = ALE
   - ❑ C. ALE – ARO = SLE
   - ❑ D. ALE – ARO = SLE
3. You are conducting a risk assessment for your network department to determine the ARO. Where could you go for assistance with your project? (Select all that apply.)
   - ❑ A. Financial and historical records
   - ❑ B. Another network administrator from a similar company
   - ❑ C. Your insurance company records
   - ❑ D. Police department records

4. You are new to the company and are surprised when you read the results of a threat identification and risk analysis. Which of the following would be the source of greatest threat?
   - ❑ A. Crackers are primarily found working at the ISP.
   - ❑ B. Crackers are primarily security students.
   - ❑ C. Crackers are employees from competitive companies.
   - ❑ D. Crackers are primarily disgruntled employees.

5. Which of the following security terms best explains vulnerability?
   - ❑ A. A network weakness that leaves the computer systems exposed to a threat
   - ❑ B. A computer weakness that leaves the network systems exposed to a loss
   - ❑ C. An organizational weakness that leaves the employees exposed to a virus
   - ❑ D. An employee weakness that leaves the organization exposed to a risk

Objective 5.8: Education—Training of End Users, Executives, and HR

1. Most organizations ensure that the networking IT department receives certification training, new equipment, and software training. What other efforts should be made to ensure security? (Select all that apply.)
   - ❑ A. Training on security policy and procedures for HR staff
   - ❑ B. Executive training on security policies
   - ❑ C. Social-engineering training for end users
   - ❑ D. Software installation and configuration training for the CEO

2. What is the benefit of providing scheduled user awareness training on social engineering?
   - ❑ A. Increases user interest in your organization
   - ❑ B. Increases user interaction with others socially
   - ❑ C. Provides the best offense for creating social engineering responses
   - ❑ D. Provides the best defense against socially engineered attacks

3. What is the primary method of ensuring that end users are aware of security requirements and possess the skills to take appropriate action?
   - ❑ A. Classroom lecture
   - ❑ B. Education through hands-on training
   - ❑ C. Group meetings
   - ❑ D. Open discussions

4. Which of the following is one of the best sources of network security information for the largest group of end users?
   - ❑ A. Online resources
   - ❑ B. Documentation
   - ❑ C. Posted policies
   - ❑ D. IT staff visits
5. Which is a good choice for achieving security awareness among your users in your organization? (Select all that apply.)
   - ❑ A. Periodic presentations
   - ❑ B. Monthly emails
   - ❑ C. Yearly seminars
   - ❑ D. Training during employee orientation

Objective 5.9: Documentation

1. Which of the following is a critical component of forensics that assists in the conviction of a networked cyber terrorist?
   - ❑ A. Verbal discussion
   - ❑ B. Written documentation
   - ❑ C. Third-party hearsay
   - ❑ D. Macroscopic fingerprints
2. You have all kinds of personnel and clients that might have access to your company network, including end users, programmers, and vendors. Which of the following terms relates to a quality of excellence that you expect from these individuals?
   - ❑ A. Guidelines
   - ❑ B. Standards
   - ❑ C. Policies
   - ❑ D. Procedures
3. Which of the following terms applies to maintaining a certain level of performance, which can be used to evaluate network equipment as well as personnel?
   - ❑ A. Standards
   - ❑ B. Policies
   - ❑ C. Procedures
   - ❑ D. Guidelines
4. Which of the following should be established as a baseline and held in confidence within the IT department?

- ❑ A. Hardware requirements
- ❑ B. Software requirements
- ❑ C. Email accounts
- ❑ D. Systems architecture

5. What should you use to maintain a record of software and hardware within your network?
   - ❑ A. Logs
   - ❑ B. Tabulations
   - ❑ C. Inventories
   - ❑ D. Manufacturer lists

6. Which of the following tasks are critical to the understanding of various classifications? (Select all that apply.)
   - ❑ A. Obtain management support and clarification.
   - ❑ B. Provide classification classes to all end users.
   - ❑ C. Audit and review folders for proper classification and make corrections.
   - ❑ D. Adjust user permissions, denying them the ability to classify folders.

7. Whom do you call when a cracker has hacked into your network and started poking around? Where should the answer to this question be?
   - ❑ A. Updated in your alert response book
   - ❑ B. Written in your notification documents
   - ❑ C. Posted on the IT wall
   - ❑ D. Posted in the users' cafeteria

8. You should establish a policy that clearly specifies the length of time that folders, files, and other data should be stored before destroying them. Which of the following documents pertains to this policy?
   - ❑ A. Logging policy
   - ❑ B. Auditing policy
   - ❑ C. Retention policy
   - ❑ D. Destruction policy

Exam Prep Answers

Objective 5.1: Physical Security

1. Answers A, B, C, and D are correct. All items listed provide some degree of physical security to your network.

2. Answers A, B, and C are correct. Examples of physical security controls include, but are not limited to, a double-locked server room, night watchmen, and storing backups of critical files.

3. Answers A, B, and C are correct. The purpose of implementing physical security is to prevent theft, prevent unauthorized disclosure of data, prevent physical damage, and maintain system integrity.

4. Answers A, C, and D are correct. Locks, iris scans, and security guards are examples of physical access controls.

5. Answers B and D are correct. Reasonable alternatives to a separate or centralized server room include use of a locked cabinet or secure rack.

6. Answer D is correct. The following order of biometric methods lists the most accurate to least accurate methods: iris scan, fingerprint, and voice verification.

7. Answer D is correct. Social engineering takes advantage of weakness in human behavior.

8. Answer C is correct. Locate your department on the third or fourth floor.

9. Answer B is correct. CO_2 systems are effective fire suppression systems.

Objective 5.2: Disaster Recovery

1. Answer C is correct. Choose differential when you want to copy only files that were modified since the last full backup.

2. Answers A, B, and C are correct. Electricity, air conditioning, and flooring are what you would likely see at a cold site.

3. Answers A and B are correct. Alternative secure recovery sites include hot sites, warm sites, and cold sites.

4. Answer B is correct. You must include a risk assessment plan when establishing a disaster recovery plan.

5. Answer B is correct. A person who has been earmarked and trained as the disaster recovery manager should make short-term recovery decisions just after a disaster.

Objective 5.3: Business Continuity

1. Answers A, B, C, and D are correct. All the items listed should be in a solid business continuity plan.

2. Answer D is correct. Implementation of RAID maintains data in a high state of availability.

3. Answer C is correct. RAID stands for Redundant Array of Inexpensive Disks.

4. Answer D is correct. A full backup offers the most complete restoration.

5. Answer B is correct. A differential backup has the fastest restore time.

Objective 5.4: Policy and Procedures

1. Answer D is correct. The company's security policy explains the overall requirements needed to protect an organization's network data and computer systems.

2. Answer B is correct. The acceptable use policy clarifies user's roles and limitations when using network equipment—hardware and software—as well as email and Internet access.

3. Answer A is correct. Due care refers to actions taken to reduce the probability of damage or injury.

4. Answer B is correct. You should consider your company privacy policy when planning for email, software downloads, and Web site data.

5. Answers A, B, and C are correct. When establishing a security policy of separation of duties, the intent would be to prevent employees from completing the overall task alone.

6. Answer D is correct. Need to know is the security policy that limits the employee's knowledge of the network system but still gives him or her enough information to perform the assigned tasks.

7. Answer C is correct. Degaussing is the process of effective destruction of data on magnetic media.

8. Answer D is correct. A code of ethics provides employees with ethical guidelines and clarifies expected behavior.

9. Answer C is correct. An incident response policy provides employees the guidelines in cases of a physical disaster, network disaster, or security attack.

Objective 5.5: Privilege Management

1. Answer C is correct. Least privilege is a privilege management concept that gives individuals only the permissions to perform assigned tasks.

2. Answer B is correct. Assign user permissions based on group roles or assigned jobs.

3. Answer D is correct. If your goal is to ensure fault tolerance, then decentralize your servers to support remote departments.

4. Answers A, B, C, and D are correct. You should monitor and examine all these items as part of an internal networking audit.

5. Answers A, B, C, and D are correct. During a penetration system audit, you try to accomplish all these tasks.

6. Answer B is correct. An audit trail refers to gathering network information, such as authorized and unauthorized user access to the network, folders, or files.

Objective 5.6: Forensics (Awareness, Conceptual Knowledge, and Understanding—Knowing What Your Role Is)

1. Answer D is correct. Run a cyclic redundancy check with a checksum.

2. Answers B and C are correct. You should keep the servers and workstations running, even if this allows a cracker continued access, until computer forensics personnel can access the room.

3. Answer D is correct. Following the chain-of-custody guidelines minimizes data loss during the collection of evidence.

4. Answers A, C, and D are correct. You should seal evidence in tamper-resistant containers, if possible; take snapshots of displayed monitors; and at

a minimum, write down any messages that are displayed on the monitors to preserve evidence.

5. Answer A is correct. A forensic technician is responsible for collecting evidence.

Objective 5.7: Risk Identification

1. Answer B is correct. Risk identification is a business function that determines which threats pose a danger to an organization so that proactive measures can be implemented.

2. Answer B is correct. Single loss expectancy (SLE) times (×) annualized rate of occurrence (ARO) produces (=) annual loss expectancy (ALE).

3. Answers A, B, C, and D are correct. All the items listed may be sources to help you in your project.

4. Answer D is correct. Crackers are primarily disgruntled employees.

5. Answer A is correct. The security term *vulnerability* refers to a network weakness that leaves the computer systems exposed to a threat.

Objective 5.8: Education—Training of End Users, Executives, and HR

1. Answers A, B, and C are correct. Include your HR staff, executives, and other end users on all aspects of the organization's security policy, including social engineering.

2. Answer D is correct. You might offer the best defense against socially engineered attacks by conducting user awareness training on social engineering topics.

3. Answer B is correct. Education through hands-on training is the primary method of ensuring that end users are aware of security requirements and possess the skills to take appropriate action.

4. Answer A is correct. Online resources provide one of the best sources of network security information for the largest group of end users.

5. Answers A, C, and D are correct. The use of emails is passive; therefore, answer B is not the best choice. Security training during employee orientation, periodic presentations, and yearly seminars are better choices because they are active methods of raising security awareness.

Objective 5.9: Documentation

1. Answer B is correct. Written documentation is a critical component of forensics that assists in the conviction of a networked cyber terrorist.

2. Answer B is correct. The term *standard* relates to a quality of excellence that you expect from others.

3. Answer A is correct. Standard applies to maintaining a certain level of performance, which can be used to evaluate network equipment as well as personnel.

4. Answer D is correct. Systems architecture should be established as a baseline and held in confidence within the IT department.

5. Answer C is correct. You should use inventories to maintain a record of software and hardware within your network.

6. Answers A, B, and C are correct. Obtain management support and clarification; provide classification classes to all end users; and audit and review folders for proper classification and make corrections are steps that are critical to the understanding of various classifications. In essence, it should be part of user education.

7. Answer B is correct. Your notification documents will vary based on your organizational needs, but they should answer the question, "Whom should I call?"

8. Answer C is correct. A retention policy clearly specifies the length of time that folders, files, and other data should be stored before destroying them.

Need to Know More?

For further information on operational and organizational security, see the following books:

Hausman, Kirk, Diane Barrett, and Martin Weiss. *Security+ Exam Cram 2*. Indianapolis, IN: Que Publishing, 2003. Chapter 10, "Organizational Security," and Chapter 11, "Privilege Management, Forensics, Risk Identification, Education, and Documentation."

King, Todd and David Bittlingmeier. *Security+ Training Guide*. Indianapolis, IN: Que Publishing, 2003. Chapter 7, "Organizational Security."

For further information on physical security and disaster recovery, see the following:

Levitt, Alan. *Disaster Planning and Recovery: A Guide for Facility Professionals*. New York: John Wiley & Sons, 1997.

For further information on backing up and restoring data in Windows 2000 Server, see the following:

Malone, Dennis. *MCSE/MCSA Training Guide (70-215): Windows 2000 Server, 2nd Edition*. Indianapolis, IN: Que Publishing, 2003. Chapter 4, "Managing, Monitoring, and Optimizing System Performance, Reliability, and Availability."

For further information on incident response, see the following:

Mandia, Kevin and Chris Prosise. *Incident Response: Investigating Computer Crime*. New York: McGraw Hill, 2001.

For further information on computer forensics, see this book:

Vacca, John. *Computer Forensics: Computer Crime Scene Investigation*. Hingham, MA: Charles River Media, 2002.

For further information on risk identification and threat assessment, read the following:

Pipkin, Donald. *Information Security: Protecting the Global Enterprise, First Edition*. Upper Saddle River, NJ: Prentice Hall, 2002.

For further information on threats and vulnerabilities, see the following:

McNamara, Joel. *Secrets of Computer Espionage: Tactics and Countermeasures*. Indianapolis, IN: John Wiley & Sons, 2003.

For further information on risk management, see these books:

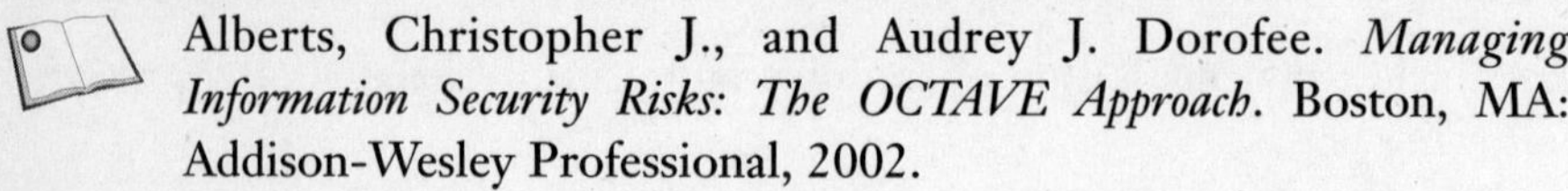
Alberts, Christopher J., and Audrey J. Dorofee. *Managing Information Security Risks: The OCTAVE Approach*. Boston, MA: Addison-Wesley Professional, 2002.

Pipkin, Donald. *Information Security: Protecting the Global Enterprise, First Edition*. Upper Saddle River, NJ: Prentice Hall, 2002.